IMAGES
of America

CHINO

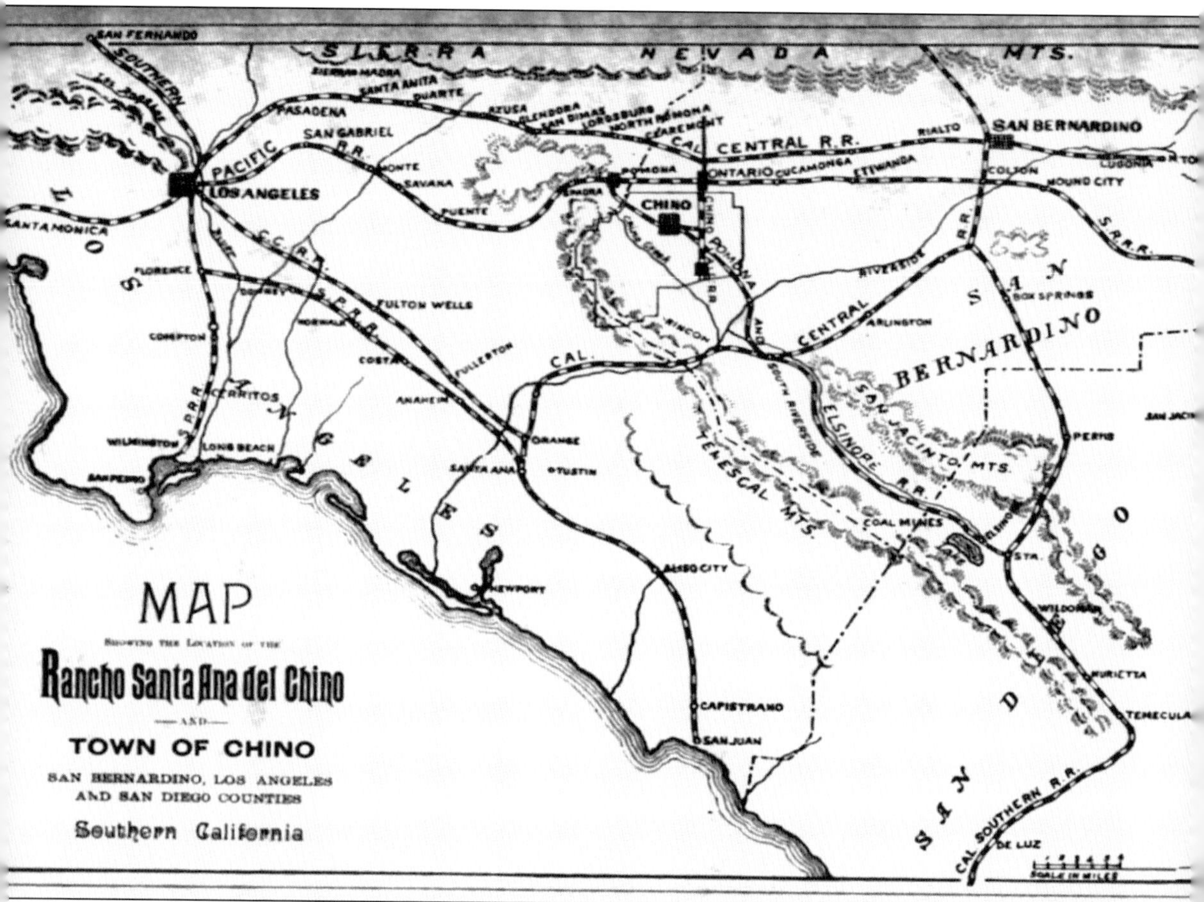

RANCHO SANTA ANA DEL CHINO. In 1841, Don Antonio Maria Lugo, a prominent Californio from Pueblo Los Angeles, was awarded 18 square leagues of land (79,000 acres) from Governor Alvarado. Don Lugo established the sprawling Rancho Santa Ana del Chino on half of the land grant, and the other half was split between his three sons. (CN.)

ON THE COVER: The fire department proudly drives its engine past city hall in this early parade. According to the *Chino Champion*, the Chino Land and Water Company gifted a deed for a city park to be built on block No. 1 between Central and Ninth Streets, south of D Street. They donated $2,000 toward its development. Plans for Chino's city hall and a fire station were also implemented. (CN.)

IMAGES
of America

CHINO

Thomas de Martino, Jeff Sanders,
and Nancy I. Sanders

ARCADIA
PUBLISHING

ISBN 978-0-7385-8142-2

Published by Arcadia Publishing
Charleston, South Carolina

Printed in the United States of America

Library of Congress Control Number: 2010928276

For all general information, please contact Arcadia Publishing:
Telephone 843-853-2070
Fax 843-853-0044
E-mail sales@arcadiapublishing.com
For customer service and orders:
Toll-Free 1-888-313-2665

Visit us on the Internet at www.arcadiapublishing.com

CONTENTS

ACKNOWLEDGMENTS

For much of our research, we gathered information from the *Champion*'s historical files with the help of publisher emeritus Allen P. McCombs, as well as the *Chino Champion*'s column, "100 Years of Chino." For this invaluable assistance, we are greatly thankful.

A very special thanks goes to Gregory Vanderbilt and his parents, Allen and Melinda Brown Vanderbilt, for sharing numerous family photographs. Greg's grandfather, Gerald Brown (1913–2010), realized he lived to see Chino change from the era of horses and teams to the age of computers. Gerald Brown took the time to have his memories of Chino written down, which Greg shared for this project. Consequently, Gerald Brown's memoirs formed the framework for the information found in this text.

Champion Newspapers (CN) provided the majority of photographs in this book.

Remaining images used in this book come courtesy of the following sources: the family of Gerald Brown (GB); Vann Alton Daniels (VAD); *Up from Second Street*, an autobiography by Sen. Ruben S. Ayala (RSA); Georgia Bennett Rudin and the Fred Walters family (FW); the Pine family (PF); the Berterretche family (BF); David and Irene George (DG); M. K. Smith Chevrolet (MKS); the California Institution for Men (CIM); Casa Colina Centers for Rehabilitation (CCC); and the United Methodist Church (UMC).

A special thank you to our friend Terry Mathews from the California Institution for Men (and Buddy) and Val Koukal who helped organize the photographs. Also thanks needs to go to Lt. Mark E. Hargrove, Fred Aronow, Pastor Alice M. Elmquist, and the dedicated historians at the Planes of Fame museum—Karen Maloney Hinton, Andrea Eldridge, and Grant Millikan.

Thank you for the gracious help of pioneer families, including Bud Ayala, Maurice Ayala, and Sen. Ruben S. Ayala; Vann Alton Daniels; Georgia Bennet Rudin; Bernadette Berterretche Helton; David and Irene George; Bill and Dennis Pine; and Bob Smith.

We want to thank our capable editor, Debbie Seracini, for spurring us on, and Scott Davis for guidance with images.

Efforts were made to present correct information and honor copyright laws. If there is a question about copyright or if there is information to improve the accuracy of the content, please contact the authors at jeffandnancys@gmail.com.

Not all pioneer families, businesses, or historic sites could be included. This is just a glimpse into the lives and hearts of people who shaped our city's history. We invite you to explore Chino's rich heritage, using this book as a point of reference on your journey.

INTRODUCTION

Before the Spaniards arrived in Southern California, Native Americans settled along the banks of Chino Creek. Tribes such as the Gabrieleno/Tongva of San Gabriel passed through the surrounding hillsides each year to gather acorns, walnuts, and other seeds that were found among the region's shady groves of trees.

In 1771, the San Gabriel Mission was founded, whose holdings included present-day Chino and extended all the way to the Santa Ana River and the mission's *assistencia* (auxiliary chapel) at San Bernardino. Cattle from the mission grazed upon the rich grass in the Chino Valley. Years later, with the secularization of the missions in 1834, Don Antonio Maria Lugo applied for a regularized land grant in the San Bernardino Valley.

At the time, the usual size of a grant was 11 square leagues (48,000 acres). However, when Governor Alvarado conferred the grant in 1839 to Lugo and his three sons, Jose Maria, Vicente, and Jose del Carmen, he enlarged the amount of this property, under the stipulation that the sons colonize the San Bernardino area. Don Lugo, with the land he was granted, established the Rancho Santa Ana del Chino.

In 1831, a Pennsylvanian named Isaac Williams came to California as a member of Kit Carson's fur trappers. Ten years later, he married Antonio Lugo's daughter Maria and purchased the rancho from his father-in-law for $10,000. Within a few years, Williams had increased his landholdings from 39,000 to 48,000 acres, and by 1848, it was recorded that he had 10,000 head of cattle and 500 horses on his ranch grazing. By 1850, Williams's livestock holdings had tripled, and his spread was one of the largest privately owned properties in Southern California.

The Williams Ranch was also the scene of one of the few conflicts that Southern California experienced in the Mexican-American War of 1846. On September 27 of that year, a group of approximately 50 Californios, led by Jose del Carmen Lugo, besieged 21 Americans, commanded by Benjamin Wilson. Wilson was on his way to Los Angeles with his compatriots to arrest Lugo for the support that Jose del Carmen had given to a recent revolt at the pueblo. The revolt had ousted a U.S. Marine occupying force that was under the command of Capt. Archibald Gillespie, and the officer had called upon Wilson for assistance.

Lugo heard of Wilson's intent and intercepted Wilson's forces at the Williams Ranch. The Americans repulsed a Californian charge but ran out of ammunition. When Lugo and his men set the rancho's roof on fire, the Americans surrendered and were transported to Los Angeles for a brief confinement. Although it was little more than a skirmish, the "battle of Chino" took its place in history as a symbol of Californian resistance to the imperialist schemes of the United States.

With the discovery of gold, the Chino Ranch became a stopover for forty-niners on their way from Warner Hot Springs to Los Angeles, and Isaac Williams became known as a genial host to footsore travelers. When Williams died in 1856, his son-in-law Robert Carlisle acquired the property and leased it to the Butterfield Stage Company. At Carlisle's death in 1865, his widow, Francesa Williams Carlisle, sold the land to cattleman Joseph Bridger, who resold it in 1881 to Richard

Gird, the father of modern-day Chino. Gird had made his fortune in mining near Tombstone, Arizona, a town he helped to establish. Within a few years, Gird had increased his holdings to 50,000 acres, transformed his lowly ranch house into an impressive edifice, and created the largest farm in the area. A horse fancier, Gird kept 12 stud horses and 300 mares on the property, along with several thousand head of cattle and several hundred dairy cows.

Gird moved forward into the arena of entrepreneur by subdividing 23,000 acres of his holdings into 10-acre plots located around the square-mile township designated as Chino. When the plots went on sale in August 1887, a large portion were quickly snapped up by speculators who had been alerted to the possibility of a railroad line running from Pomona directly through Chino, down to Elsinore, and terminating in San Diego. Town construction now began in earnest, with Gird leading the way.

A camp for the construction of the railroad spur connecting Chino with the Pomona-Elsinore link to the Southern Pacific Railroad was set up on Central Avenue. Gird spent $200,000 for a water-development plant in Claremont, which would service both the camp and the township. In addition, Gird oversaw the basic design and layout of the expanding city and ordered five million bricks from a nearby supplier to begin converting the vision into a reality.

With an influx of Scandinavian immigrants to the area, town construction boomed. Episcopalian, Baptist, and Unitarian churches were established in Chino, along with local businesses, including a branch of Wells Fargo and Company. The city's first schoolhouse opened its doors in September 1888. The previous April, the Chino Valley Railroad line had begun service with one engine and one passenger car. A water reservoir to supply both the town and the train depot was completed in 1889.

In the same year, Gird began toying with the idea of opening the Sugar Beet Refining Factory and approached the Oxnard brothers to help finance the project. After testing the soil for productivity, the Oxnards entered into an agreement with Gird to build a $500,000 factory in return for shares in the business, 2,500 acres cultivated for beet production, water rights to the acreage, and advantageous rates for hauling beets on the Chino Valley Railroad line.

When construction of the factory began in 1891, workers poured into the area, increasing the town population to 10 times its original number nearly overnight. Approximately, half the working populace tended the 4,000 acres of beets, while the other half worked in the new factory. Gird purchased prefabricated dwellings from nearby Ontario and moved them to Chino to house his labor force.

Despite an auspicious start, sugar beet refining was never wildly profitable, although it did help to put the city of Chino on the map. With the closing of the Sugar Beet Refinery Factory, walnuts became the largest agricultural industry in Chino. In the meantime, the diary industry moved to Chino, making the city a top dairy producer by 1940. In 1975, Chino set a record as the fastest growing city in Southern California. Individuals and families arrived by the droves to this agricultural and garden community, boosting the population to an estimated count of 27,650, an increase of over 7,000 residents since the 1970 census.

In 2010, the city of Chino celebrated its centennial anniversary of incorporation. Mayor Dennis R. Yates and the 100-plus member Centennial Advisory Committee held key events throughout the year, including a "Happy Birthday Chino—100 Years of Progress" event in February and Chino's July 4th Freedom Festival held at Ayala Park on the corner of Central and Edison Avenues. *Champion Newspapers* joined the celebrations by publishing the weekly feature, "100 Years of Chino." Publisher emeritus Allen P. McCombs shared many nostalgic memories in the *Chino Champion* throughout the year by reminiscing in his column, "Rolltop Roundup."

One

The Early Years

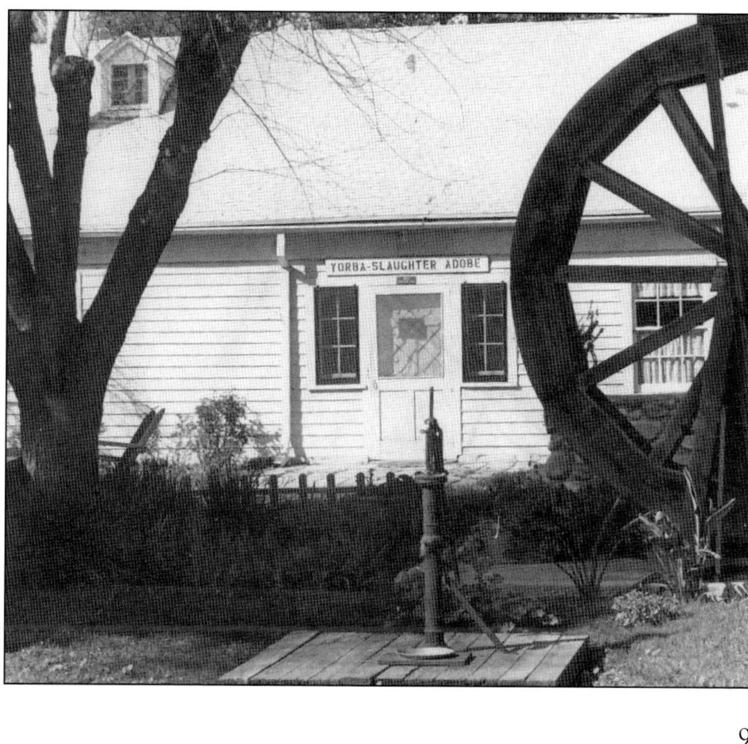

Yorba-Slaughter Adobe. In 1852–1853, local Native American workers built this adobe for Bernardo Yorba's son Raymondo, the wealthiest and most influential landowner in the Prado Basin. It replaced an earlier structure on the same site, which had been destroyed by fire the previous year. The Butterfield Stage rode by the base of the hill where the adobe was located. (CN.)

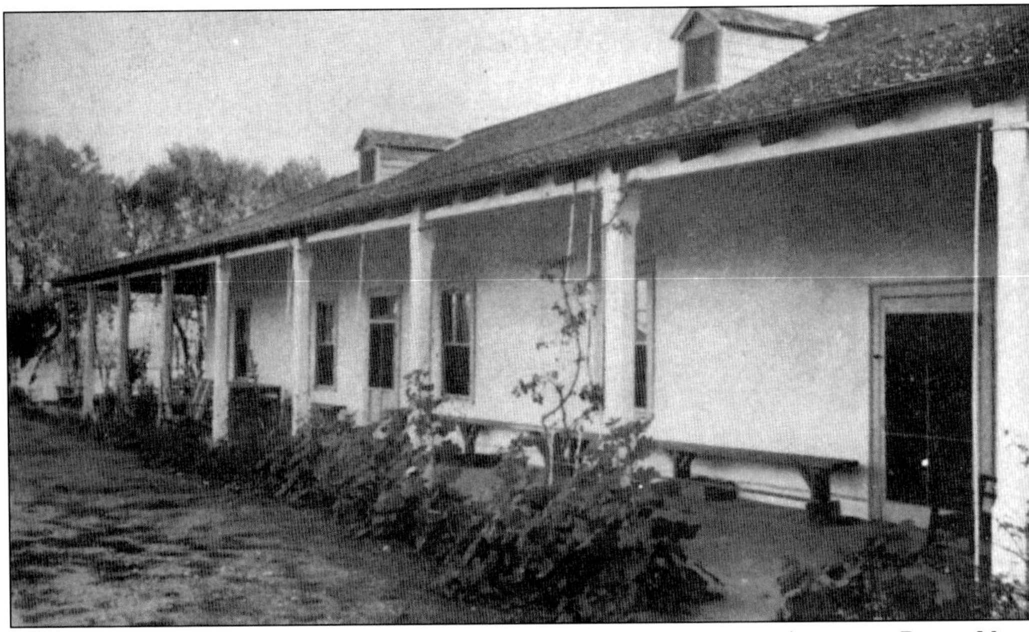

Buena Vista Rancho. At the time the Yorba Adobe was built, it was known as Buena Vista. Its thick walls kept the family cool during the high temperatures experienced in this region of Southern California. With three bedrooms in a sleeping loft above the main floor, a few of the four original rooms opened to the outside. Wide porches on all four sides of the adobe offered a welcome shade and cool breeze. (CN.)

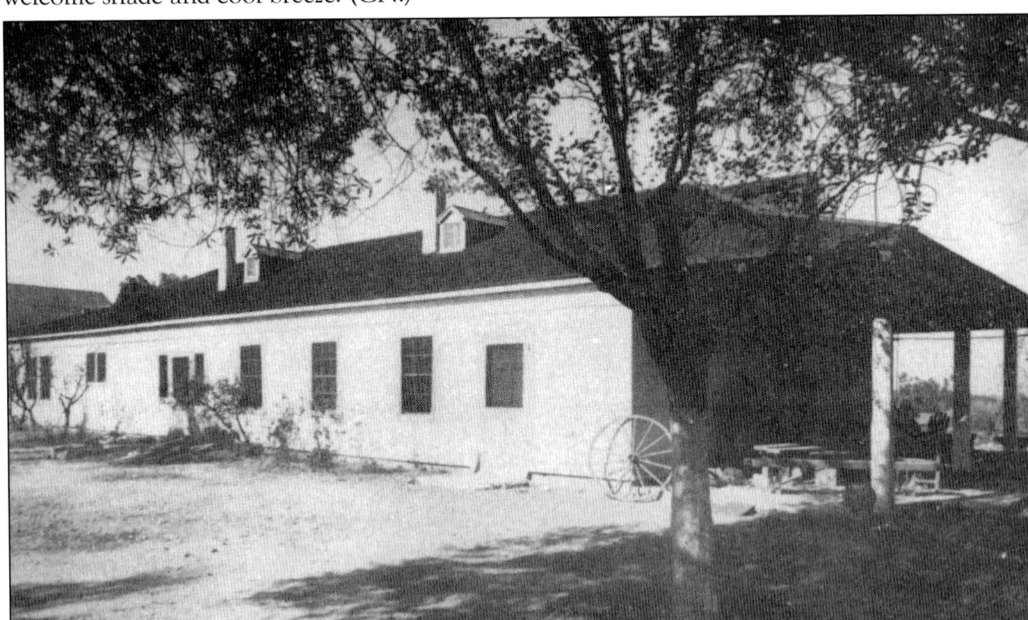

Home of Julia Slaughter Fuqua. In 1868, Fenton M. Slaughter purchased the Buena Vista Rancho, and the adobe became the hub of a small community that he built up around it known as Rincon. His daughter Julia Slaughter Fuqua began restoring the adobe in 1928. Still standing and open to visitors as a historic site, the Yorba-Slaughter Adobe is one of the oldest buildings in San Bernardino County. (CN.)

RICHARD GIRD, A TRUE PIONEER. Known as the father of modern-day Chino, landowner Richard Gird gave vision to the city. A gentleman rancher, Gird subdivided his immense holdings into 10-acre plots located around a square-mile township that was designated as Chino. The plots went on sale in August 1887, and construction of the town was underway. (CN.)

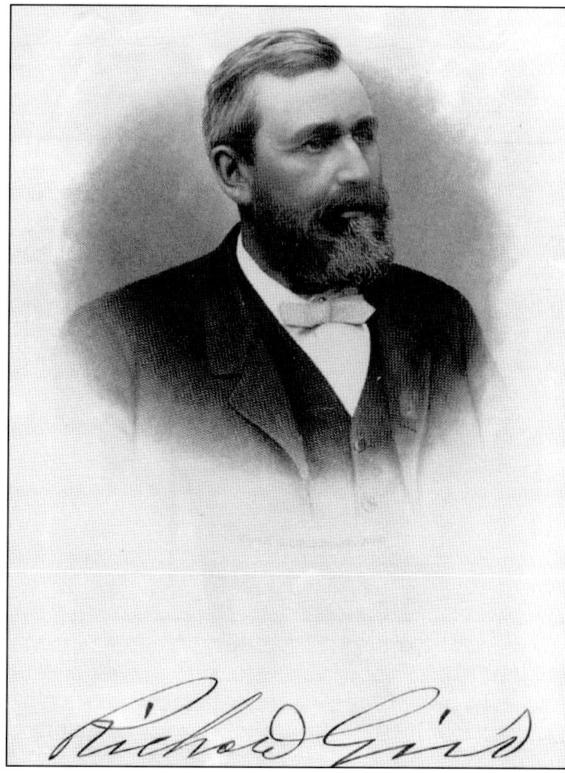

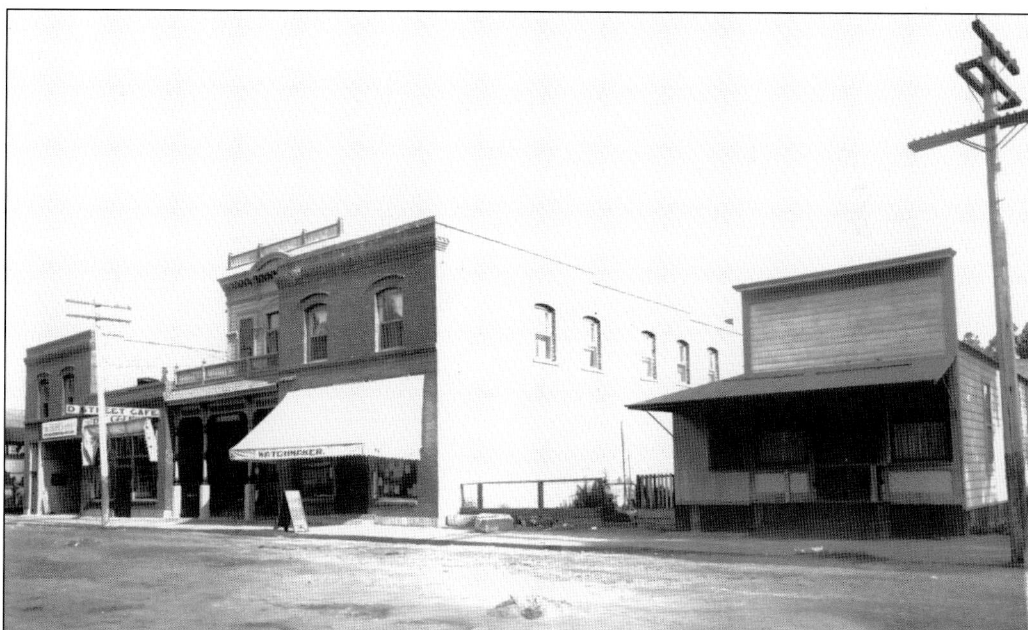

RICHARD GIRD BANK, GLASS NEGATIVE, C. 1906. From establishing schools to selecting the location of fire hydrants to constructing a bank to handle the community's financial needs, Richard Gird was a true visionary. In 1887, he founded the first bank in town on Seventh Street. Later, it was sold and moved around the corner on D Street. (CN.)

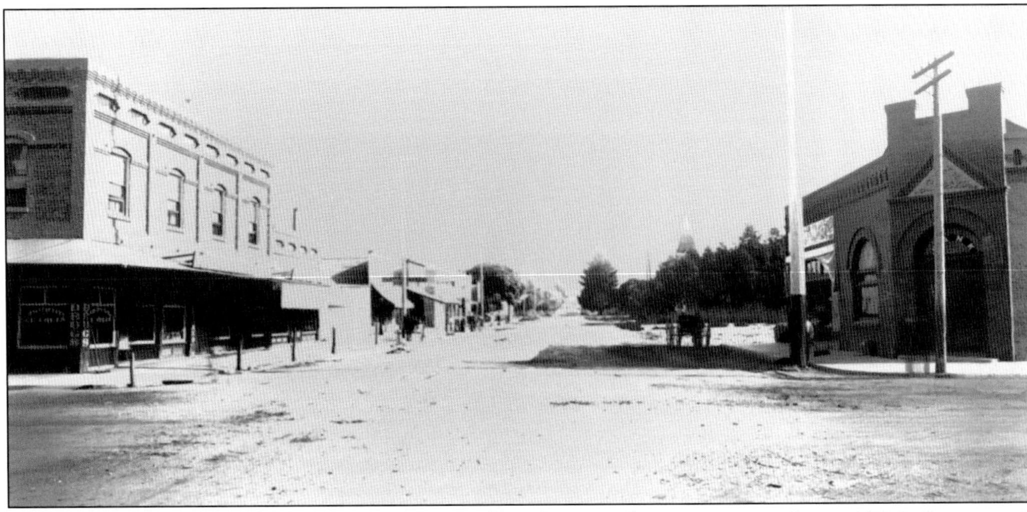

THE CORNER OF SIXTH AND D STREETS. Taken from a glass negative, the *c.* 1906 photograph shown above is looking north on Sixth Street. The building on the left housed Christopher's, which was a drugstore that also offered children delicious ice cream. Next to Christopher's hangs a sign where Doctor Savage, M.D., advertises his services. The building on the right is the Chino State Bank. The photograph below was taken looking south. The B. K. Galbreath Building can be seen at left. Next to it is the WCTU Fountain. Since Chino was a dry city, it was installed by the Women's Christian Temperance Union to provide drinks of water. The fountain was up a short time before being hit by a car whose owner claimed that his car did not stop when he said, "Whoa!" (Both, CN.)

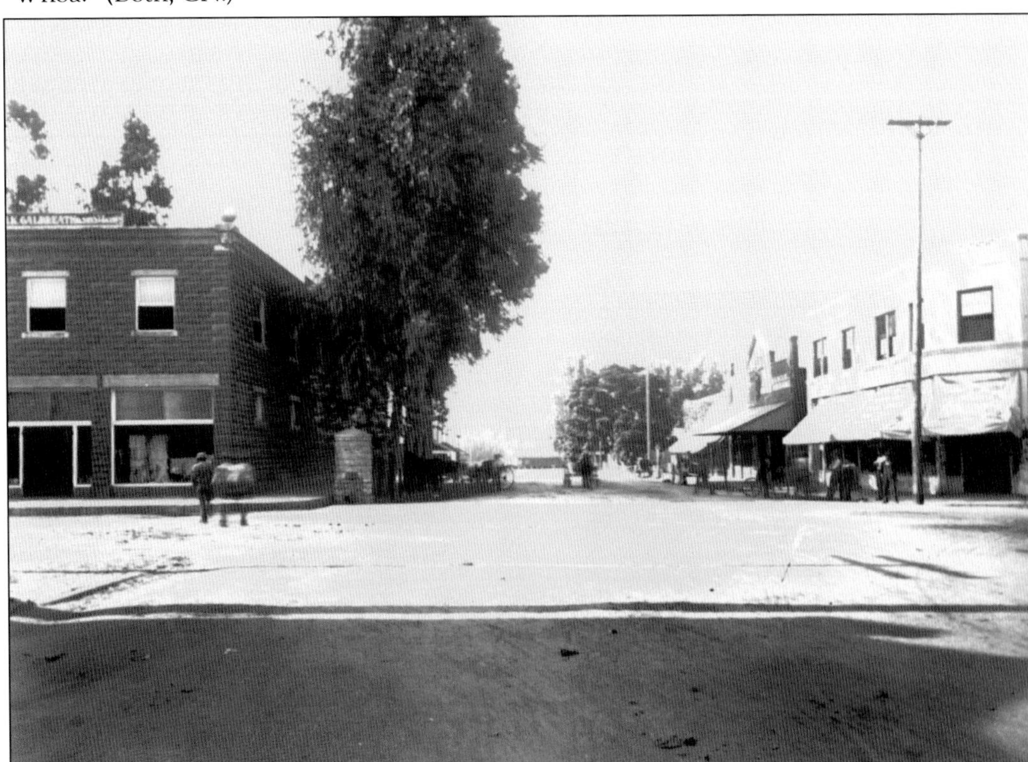

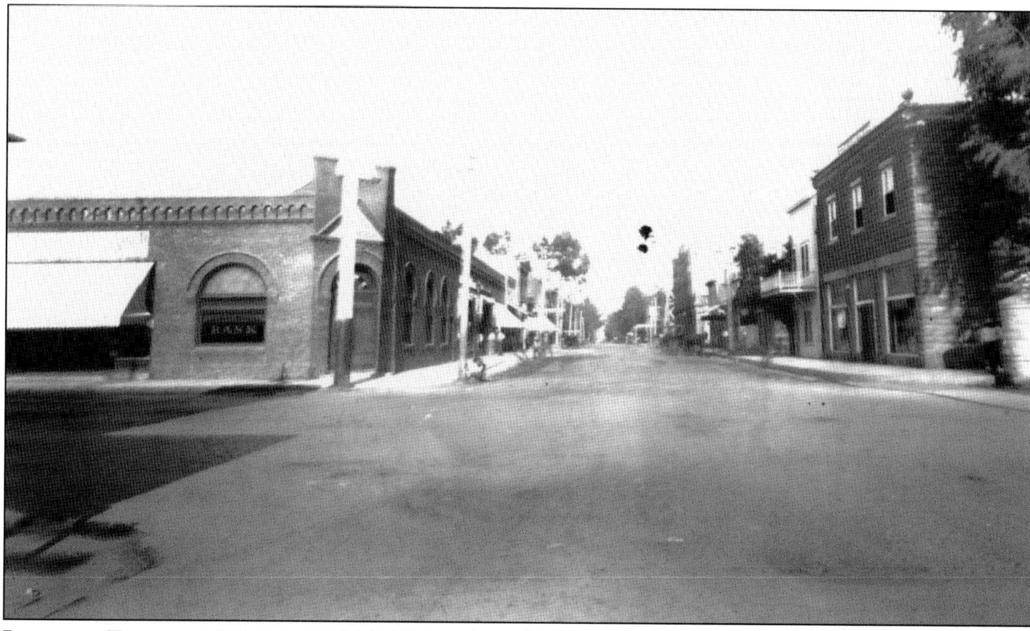

LOOKING EAST AND WEST, c. 1906. These four glass negatives were taken on the corner of Sixth and D Streets in downtown Chino shortly before the city was incorporated. In the above image, looking east on D Street, Chino State Bank is the building on the left. This building is now home to the current Chino Youth Museum. The Galbreath Building is on the right. In the image below looking west, the windows in the store on the left advertise "Clothing Etc., Stationary, Ice Cream, and the L.A. Examiner." In the window above the store, services are advertised for dentist E. S. Packson. Christopher's is in the building on the right. For nearly 50 years, this corner at Sixth and D Streets formed the hub of the city. (Both, CN.)

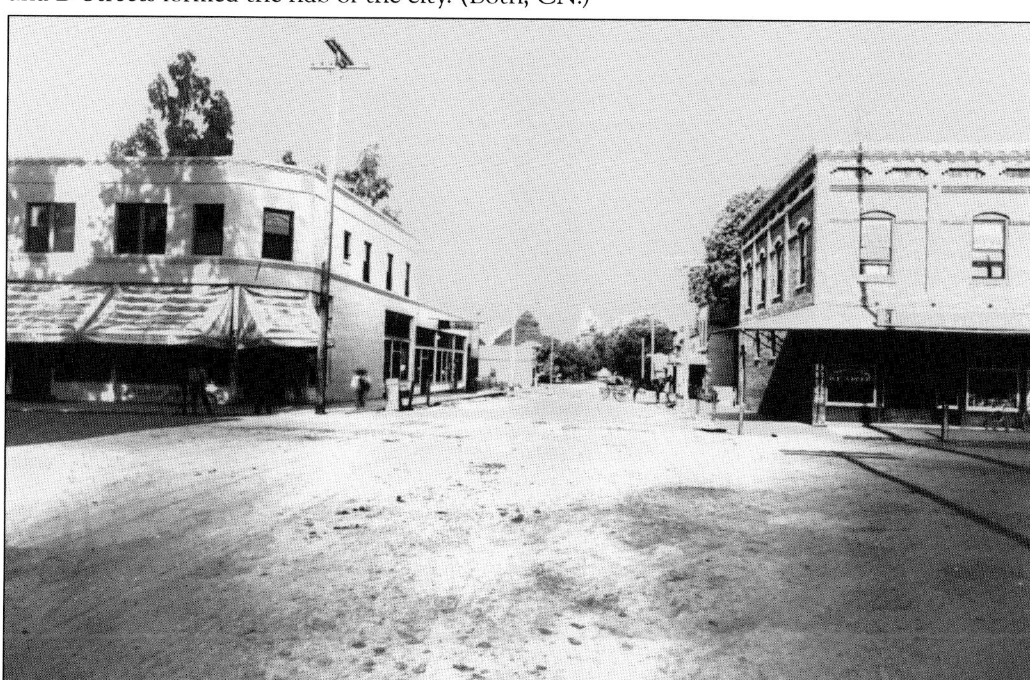

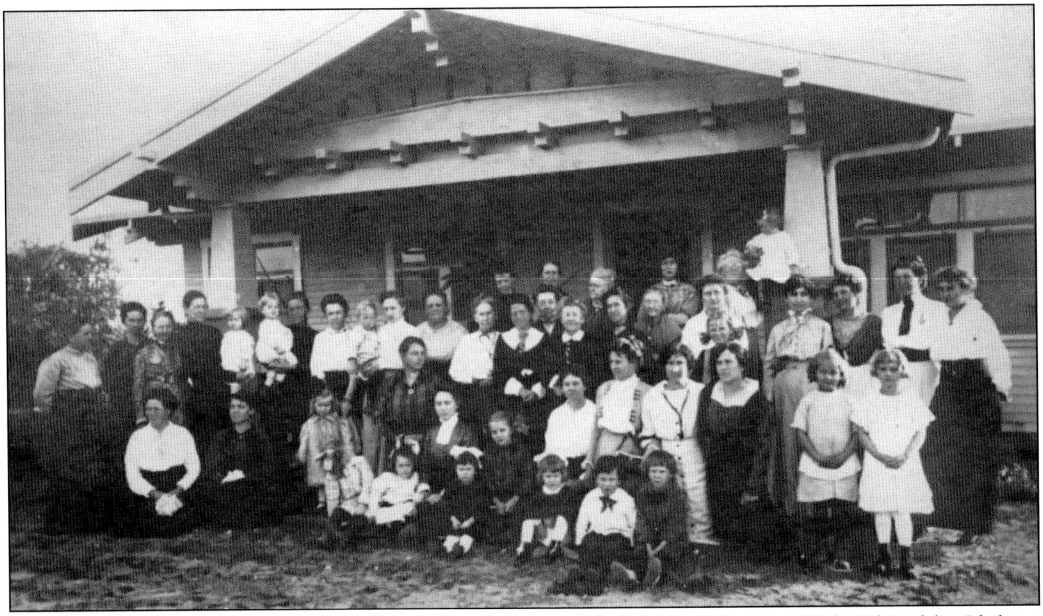

East Side Thimble Club. Mary Jane Riley (1871–1957) founded the East Side Thimble Club in 1907 to serve the community of Chino. By 1923, they had 75 members. Women volunteered to cook and sew for organizations such as the George Junior (Boys) Republic and the Casa Colina Convalescent Home for Crippled Children. Eva Henning Walters and Margaret Caulfield are in the photograph. (FW.)

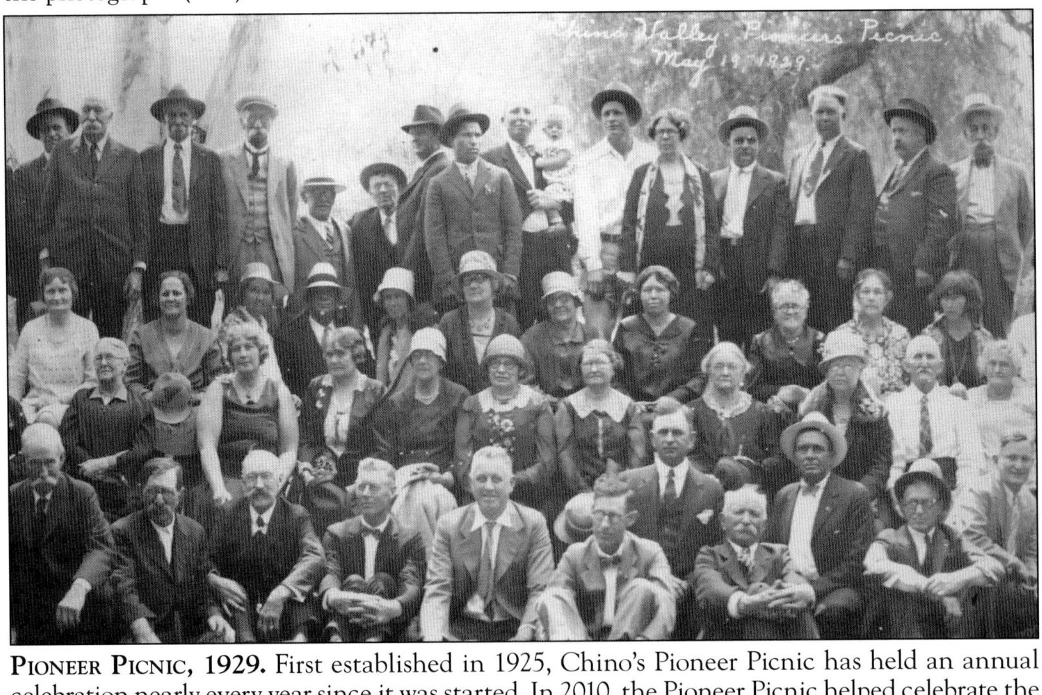

Pioneer Picnic, 1929. First established in 1925, Chino's Pioneer Picnic has held an annual celebration nearly every year since it was started. In 2010, the Pioneer Picnic helped celebrate the 100th anniversary of the city's incorporation. Held in May each year, the Chino Valley Pioneer Association as well as the Chino Valley Historical Society host this event where pioneer families and school chums reconnect. (GB.)

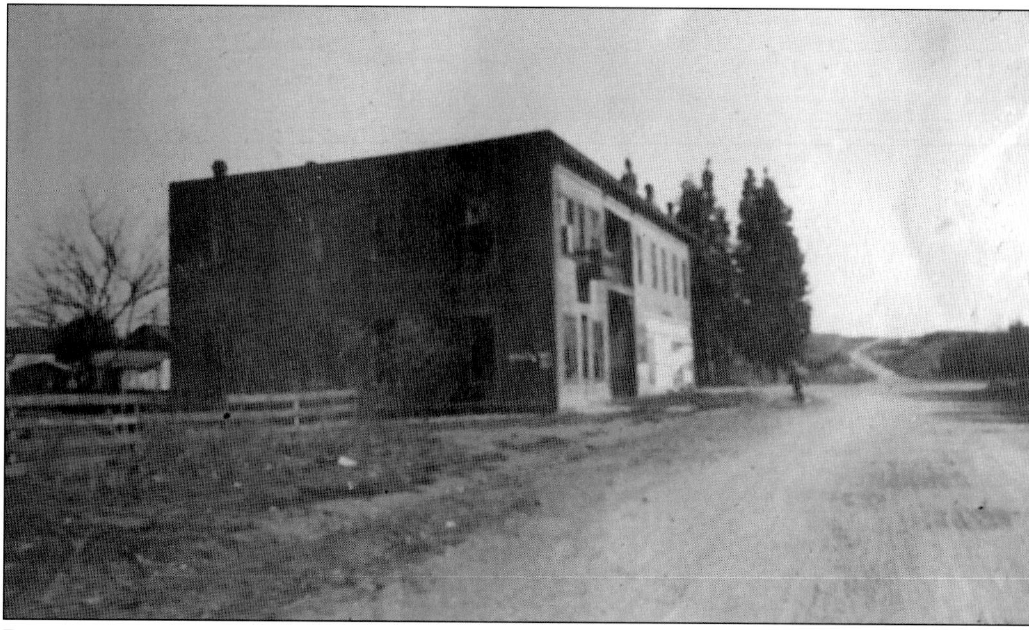

Prado Hotel in Early Days. Before the U.S. Army Corps of Engineers completed Prado Dam in 1941, the Prado Hotel offered overnight accommodations to weary travelers. Now underwater, it was lost as part of the project to protect Chino Valley from seasonal flooding, especially during winter months when heavy rains threatened homes, roads, railroad tracks, and farmlands of Chino. (GB.)

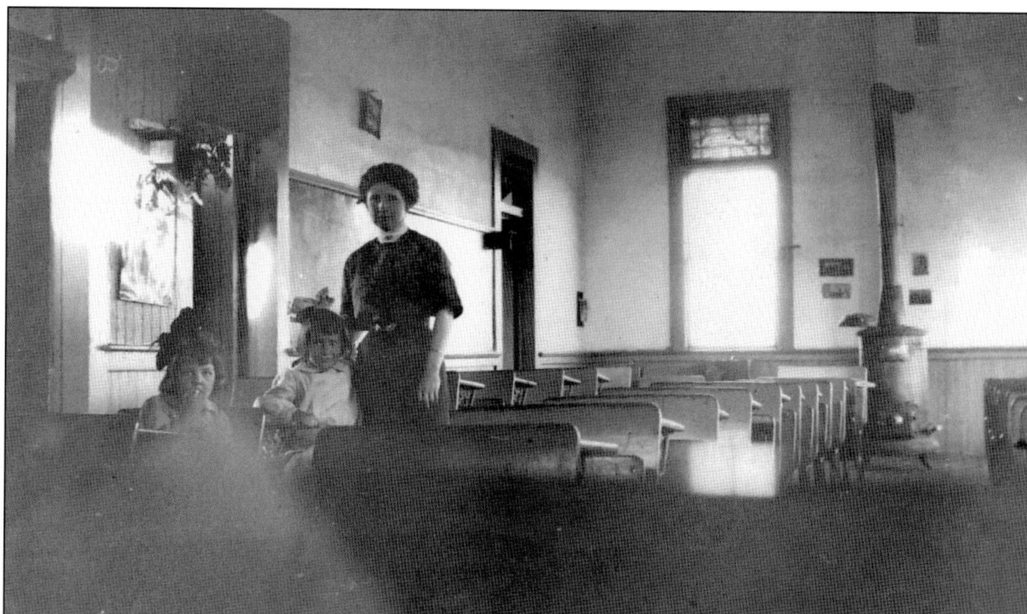

Early School in Prado. In 1911, before Alice Beck married Alfred Brown and raised their family in Chino, she taught in this one-room schoolhouse built on Prado Road in 1887. The school is now underwater. Alice graduated from Pomona High and the Los Angeles State Normal School, a teacher training school that was the predecessor of UCLA, the University of California, Los Angeles. (GB.)

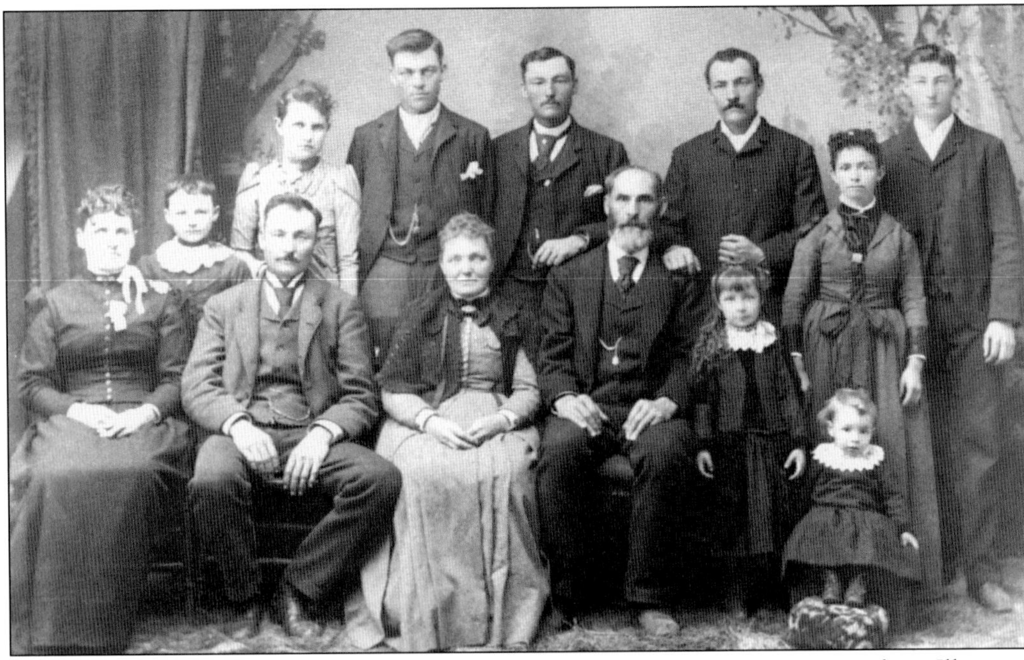

Samuel Pine Family, 1889. In the 1850s, Samuel Cook Pine led a wagon train from Illinois to Utah. Within the decade, he traveled to California and settled in what became San Bernardino. Eventually, Samuel and his wife, Jane Morrison Pine (both first row, center), and their five sons ranched along Pine Avenue in Chino. Samuel Jr. (seated left of his mother) was a San Bernardino County supervisor around 1920. (PF.)

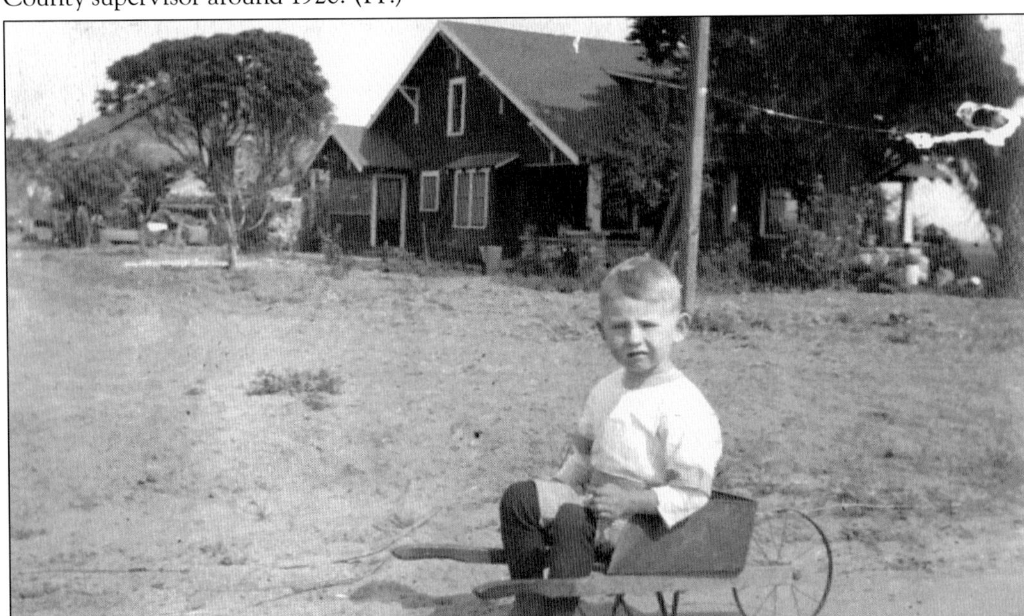

Gerald Brown in Wheelbarrow, c. 1916. In 1898, Alfred Brown arrived in Chino. Living near the present-day Chino airport at first, Alfred eventually purchased land here on Euclid Avenue, .5 miles east of Central Avenue. Sitting in this wheelbarrow is his son Gerald Brown. The barn in the background is still standing behind the horse auction. (GB.)

Two

Where Everything Grows

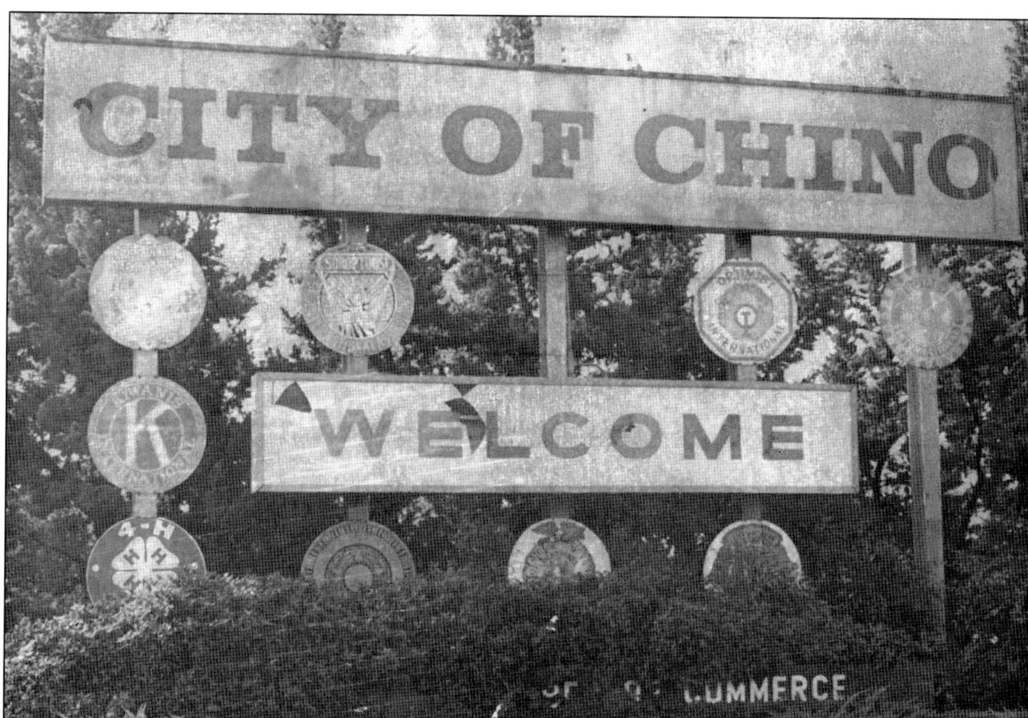

Welcome to Chino. Known as a city of opportunity, agriculture shaped Chino's history. Poultryman Gerald Brown described the crops grown near his farm on Central Avenue in 1939. The Fritz family had 10 acres of oranges, including a reservoir, two windmills, and an irrigation system. The Stantons had 10 acres of walnuts and 10 acres of peaches. They sold their peaches to the Moores who had a stand on Central Avenue. (CN.)

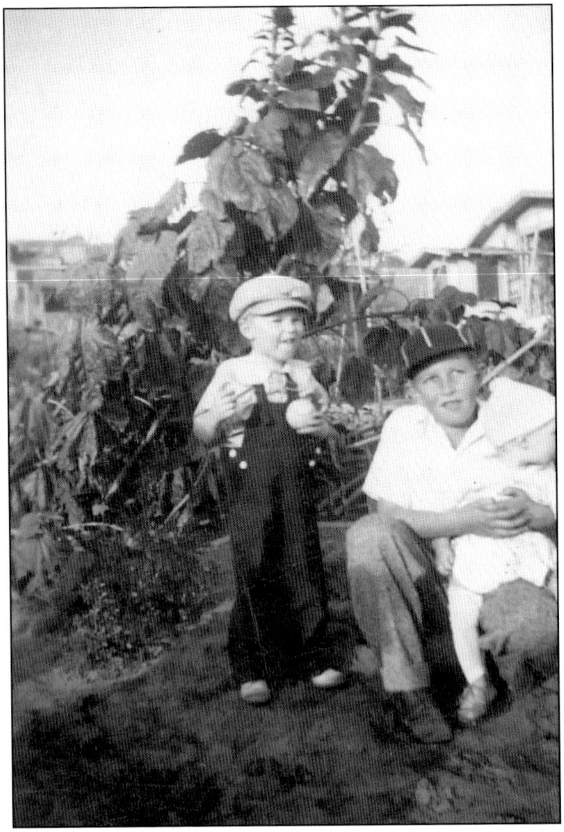

The Land of Sunflowers. Many of the fields in Chino were covered with sunflowers that grew taller than a man with stalks as thick as a person's wrist. When Charles Elmo (E. C.) Daniels came to Chino around 1910, he bought a quarter section lot between Chino and Schaefer that was covered in sunflowers. In this 1933 photograph are, from left to right, Gordon Daniels, Charles Gary Daniels, and Vann Daniels. (VAD.)

Farming the Land. Roy Brown rides a mower in this photograph. His nephew Gerald Brown remembered when farmers used teams. In the mid-1920s, Gerald Brown walked miles behind a one-horse cultivator. He could plow 2 acres a day with a two-way plow. Around 1931, however, a neighbor named George bought a Case tractor that could plow 10 acres a day. Local farmers then hired George to do the job. (GB.)

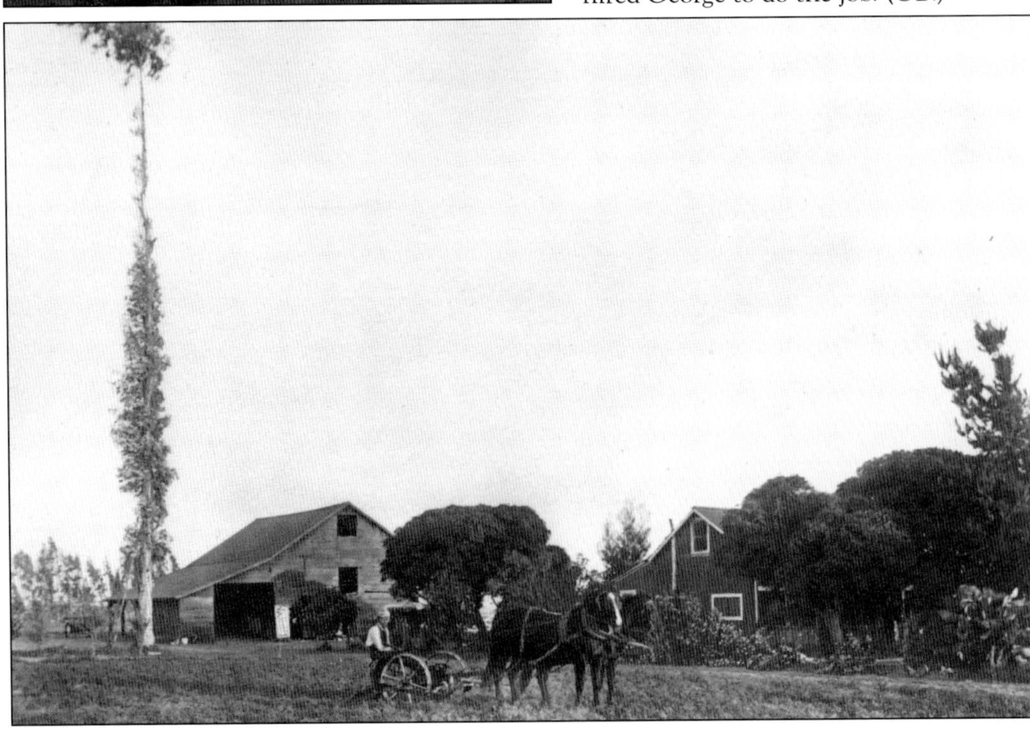

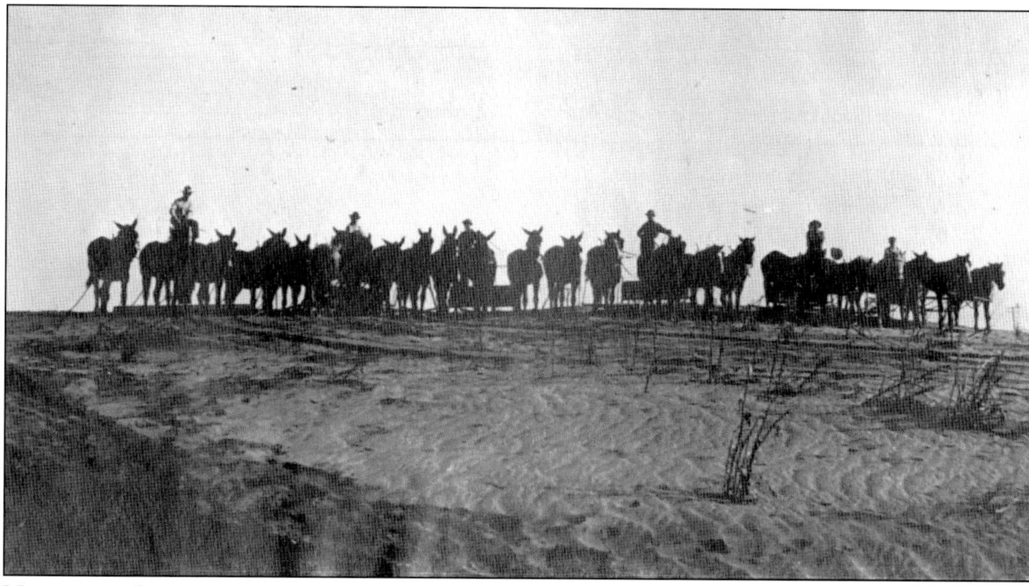

Neighbors Come to Help, 1913. Chino was divided into 10-acre lots with many farmers owning 10, 20, or 30 acres. Neighbors helped each other, such as shown in this picture where they are probably clearing the land for planting. By the end of the first decade of the 20th century, farmers installed permanent concrete pipelines to irrigate the land. Alfred and Roy Brown made their own pipe using gravel from a pit off Foothill Boulevard. (GB.)

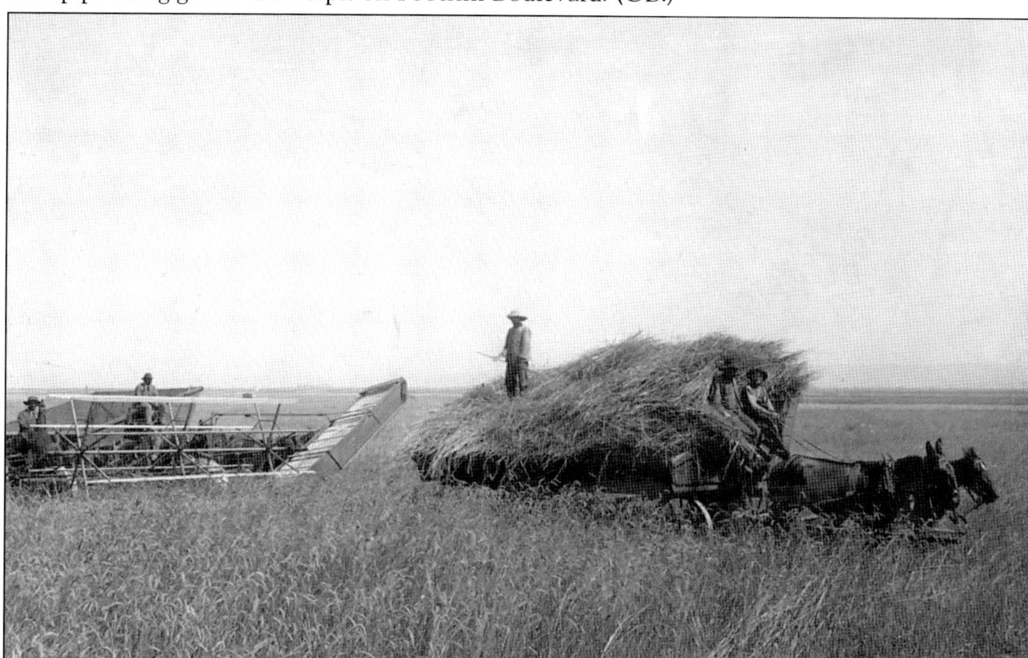

A Bountiful Harvest, 1910. E. C. Daniels bought his ranch because it was covered with sunflowers, projecting the land had underground water. He was right. He could throw a pick and strike water. The land was peat, which formed a cap for the water table. Opening a tap, water poured out, and he had an artesian well. E. C. Daniels burned the sunflowers, planted alfalfa, and reaped a rich harvest. (VAD.)

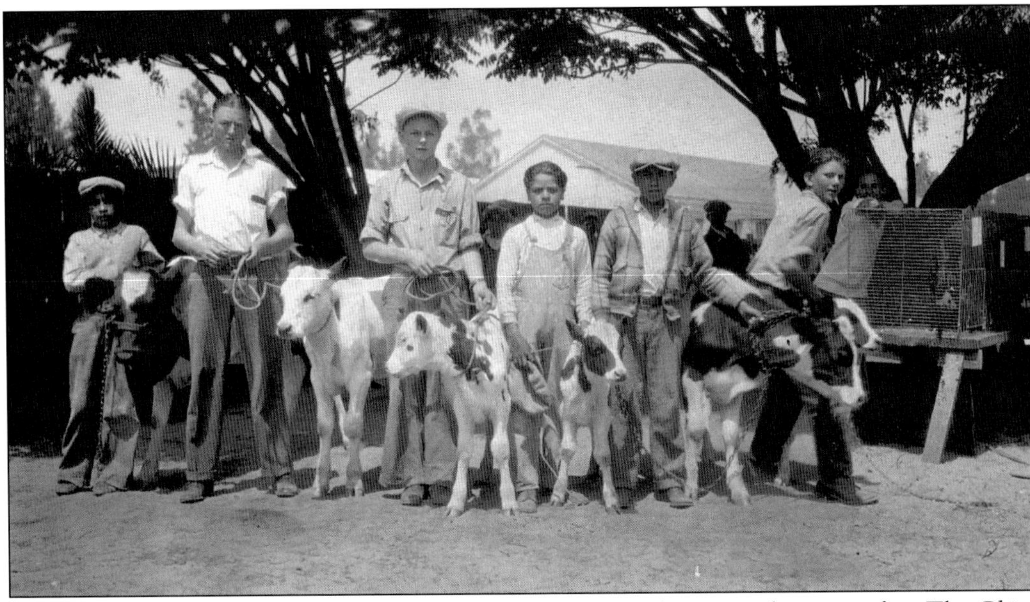

Calves at the Junior Fair. These future dairy farmers took part in the junior fair. The *Chino Champion* stated that, according to a report given by the San Bernardino County horticultural commissioner John P. Coy, Chino was a major producer of hay, growing three quarters of the alfalfa hay and two thirds of the grain hay produced in the county during 1926. (CN.)

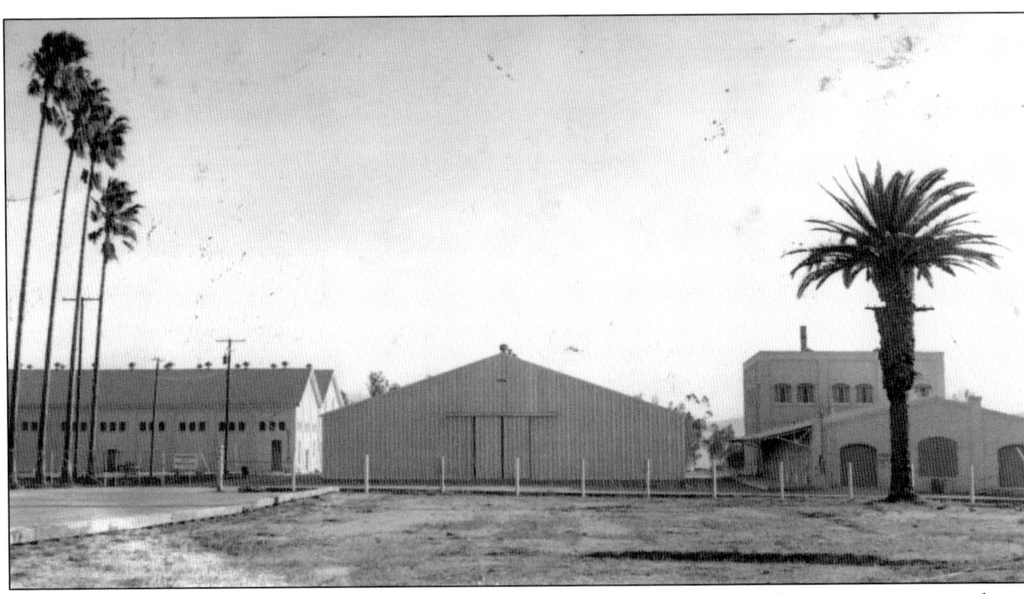

The Chino Sugar Mill. The American Crystal Company operated Chino's major agricultural and industrial business at the beet sugar plant from 1891 to 1917. Chino's Crystal Club was formed for leaders of the factory to connect and keep current on updates and news regarding the sugar manufacturing industry. (CN.)

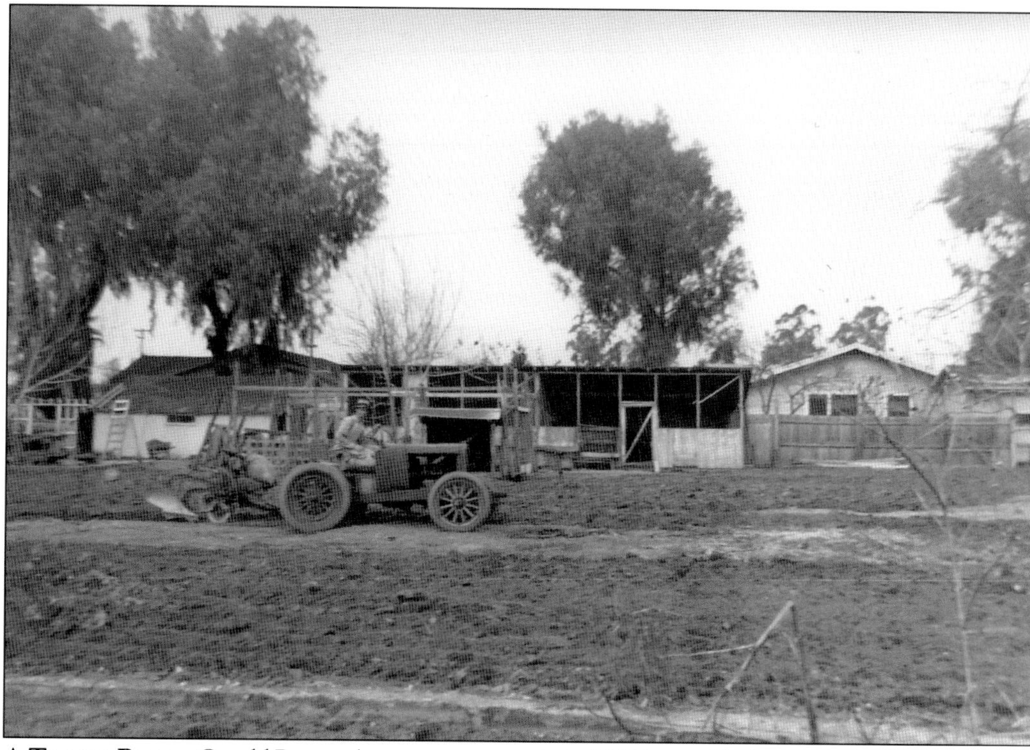

A Time to Plant. Gerald Brown drove a tractor made in 1935 from a Dodge truck. With an irrigation system, farmers could raise row crops such as potatoes, sweet corn, and black-eyed beans. This brought in more income than they could make from dry farming. Dry-grain crops would use open-ditch irrigation, as they had done before the creation and installation of concrete pipelines. (GB.)

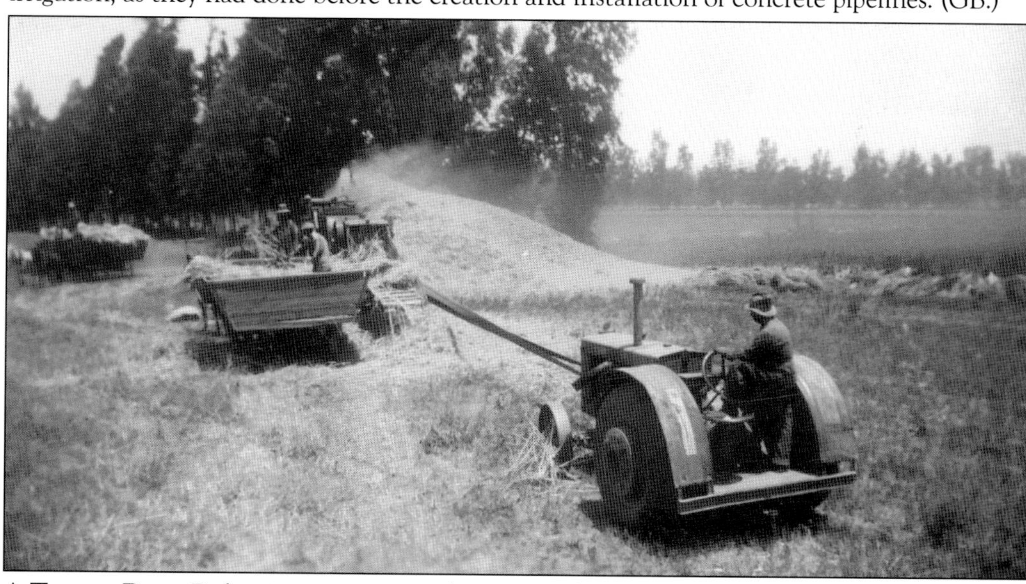

A Time to Reap. Before irrigation, many farmers in Chino raised barley and wheat, known as dry farming. During harvest, the stationary threshing machine owned by Mr. Rabb went from farm to farm in the neighborhoods. It was powered by an iron-wheeled tractor and hooked up to run with a long belt. Neighbors helped each other thresh so they did not have to hire work crews. (GB.)

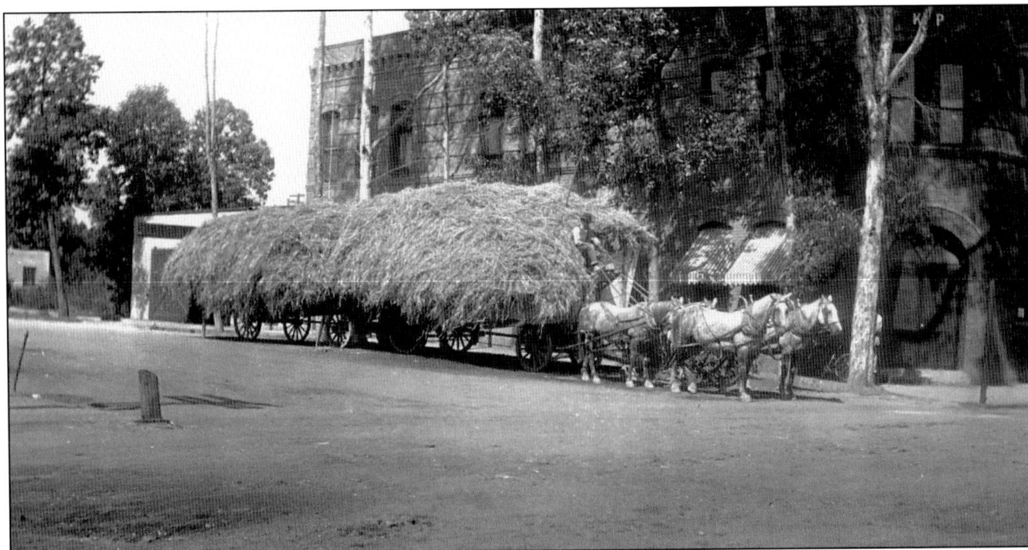

Alfalfa, a Profitable Crop. When E. C. Daniels harvested his first crop of alfalfa, he sold it in Downey. Paying just $1 down in the early 1900s to purchase his ranch at what is now Benson and Oaks Avenues, he was able to pay off his property by the end of the first year for a total of $4,400. (CN.)

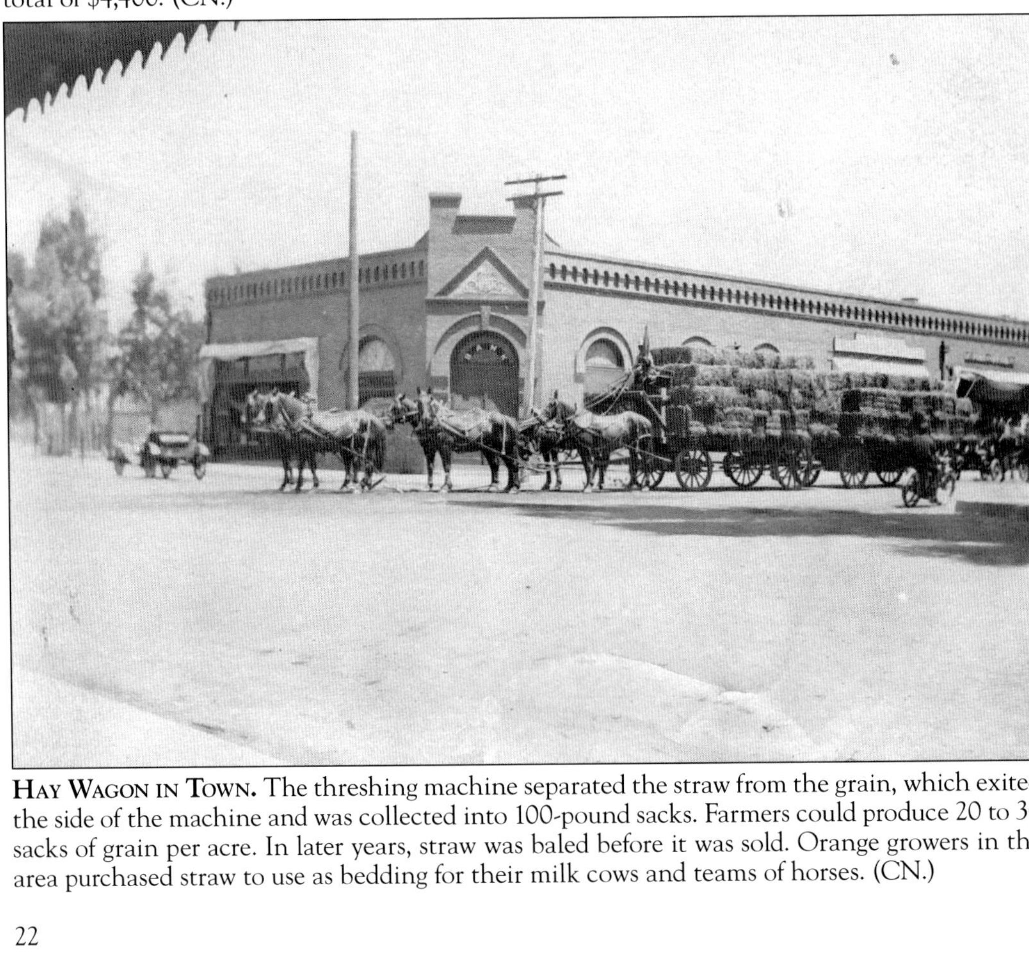

Hay Wagon in Town. The threshing machine separated the straw from the grain, which exited the side of the machine and was collected into 100-pound sacks. Farmers could produce 20 to 30 sacks of grain per acre. In later years, straw was baled before it was sold. Orange growers in the area purchased straw to use as bedding for their milk cows and teams of horses. (CN.)

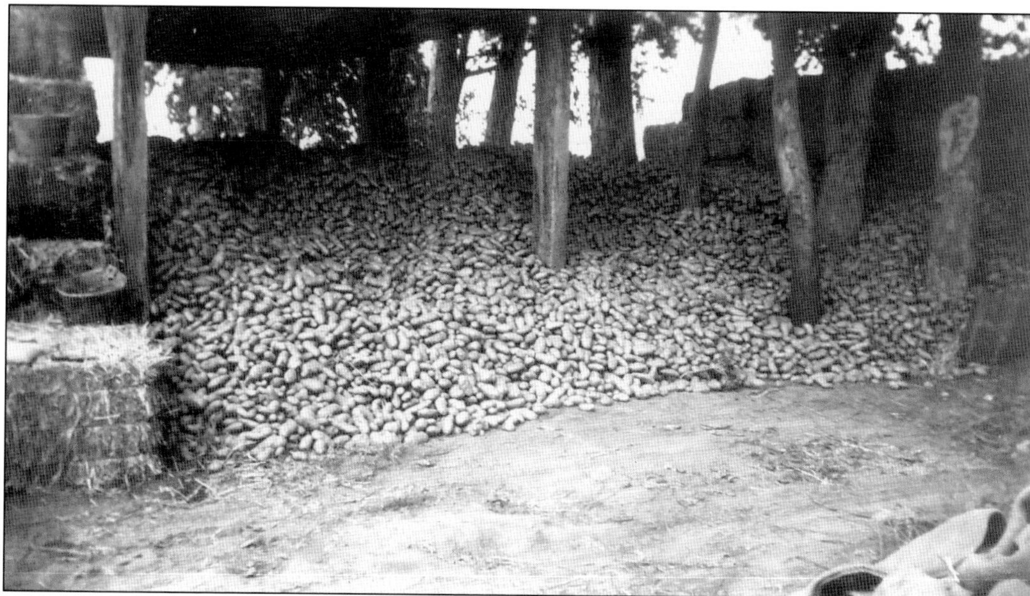

World War II Potatoes. Farmers such as Gerald Brown grew potatoes during World War II as food for the soldiers. Crops of potatoes and corn used a large amount of water, which was supplied by the Chino Irrigation Water Company. At one time, the water company serviced 1,000 acres north of Philadelphia Avenue. Most of these farms had peach and plum orchards along with walnut groves. A few grew citrus. (GB.)

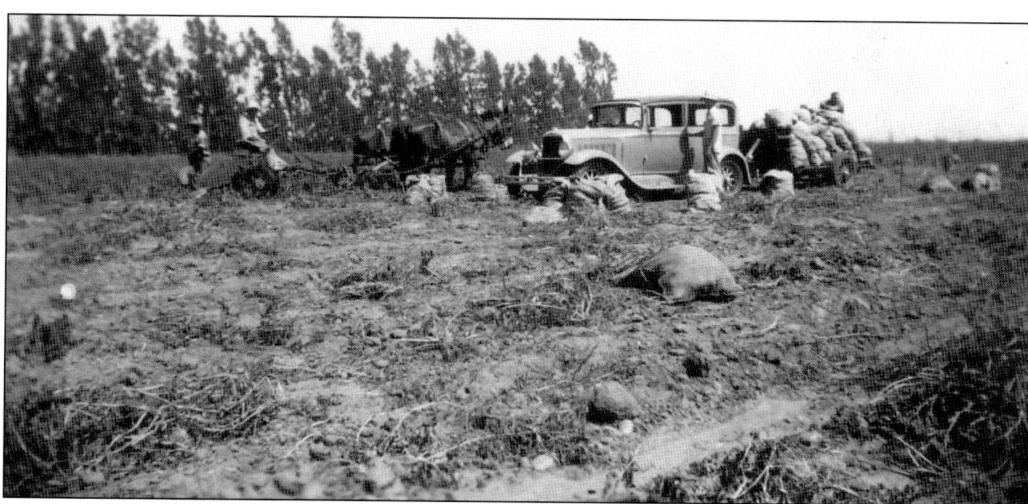

Harvesting the Potato Crop. Bill Rehkopf and Gerald Brown grew a potato crop together. They did not make much profit, so Gerald decided to plant peach trees instead. He planted Sims, a white freestone peach, to sell to Hunts Cannery in Fullerton. Seedlings cost 25¢ each and were planted 20 feet apart. He planted crops in between the trees. (GB.)

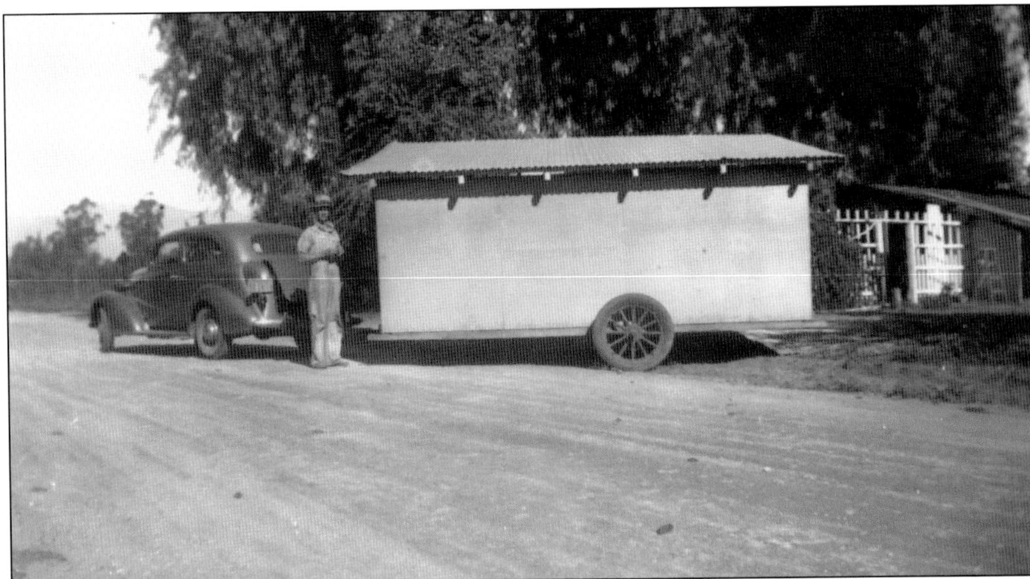

Moving the Chicken House. Gerald Brown is shown moving structures he built on a vacant lot adjacent to his parents' house at Tenth and D Streets. His grandmother Elizabeth Beck helped with the move. When Sterns Cannery sold labor camp buildings in the late 1930s, Gerald Brown purchased a community kitchen for $5 to store chicken feed. Local dairymen purchased three-room houses for workers helping at the dairies. (GB.)

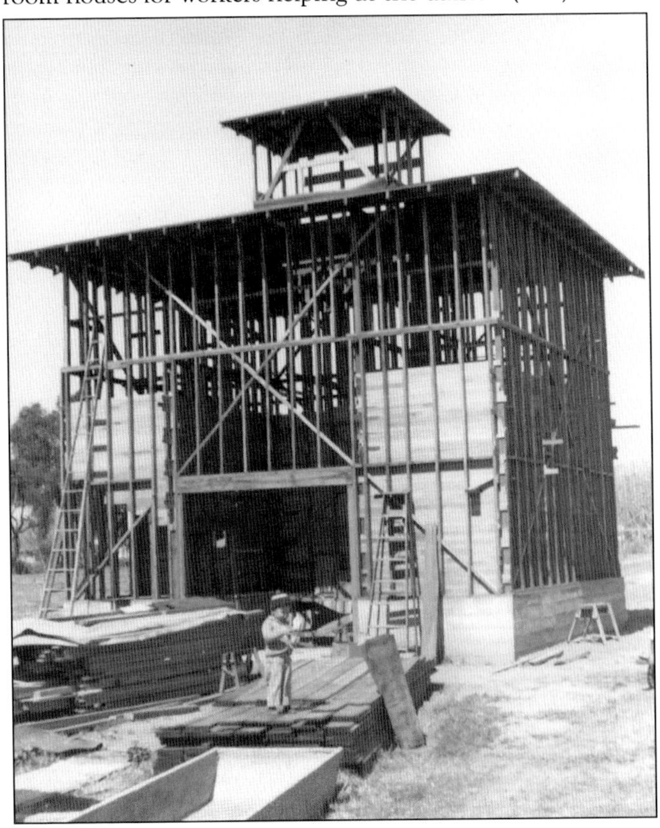

Building a Granary. Before World War II, grain was stored in sacks. During the war, however, burlap sacks were in short supply. Farmers had to adjust to handling bulk storage, as Gerald Brown did by building a granary in 1944. Lumber was rationed, but farmers were given first choice. Gerald Brown's granary had seven bins and could hold 100 tons of grain. (GB.)

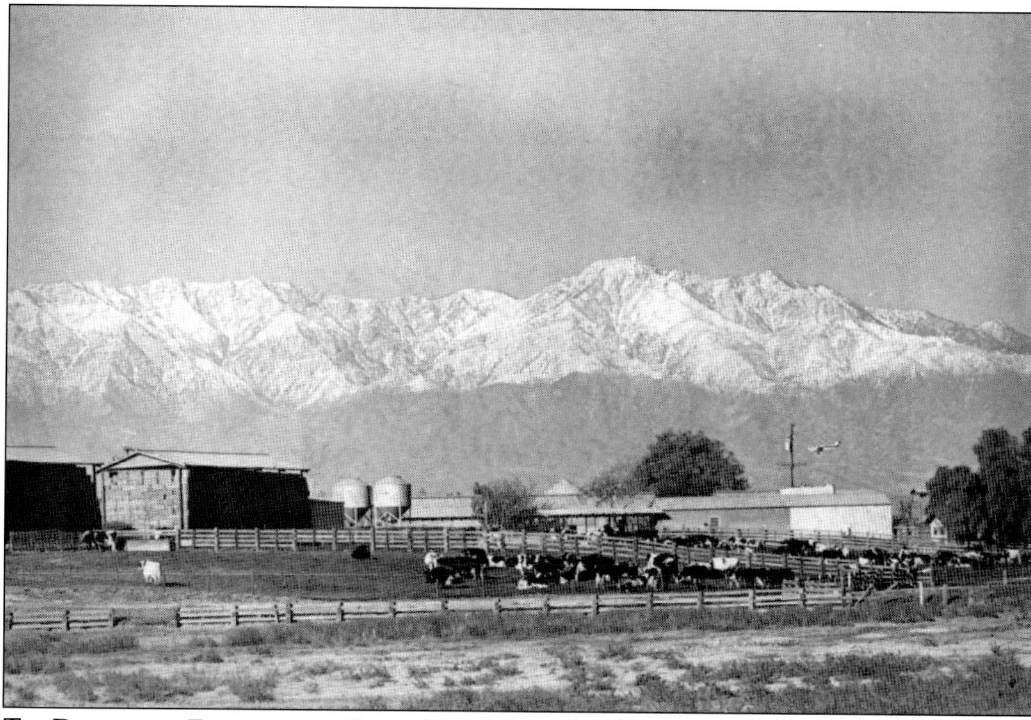

The Dairies are Established. The early 1920s brought a housing boom to Los Angeles, so dairies moved from what Southern Californians called the Los Angeles "milkshed" out to Chino. In this photograph can be viewed what became a common winter scene in Chino, beautiful snowcapped mountains as a backdrop for Chino's newest and very productive dairy industry. By 1926, there were over 150 dairies in the area. (CN.)

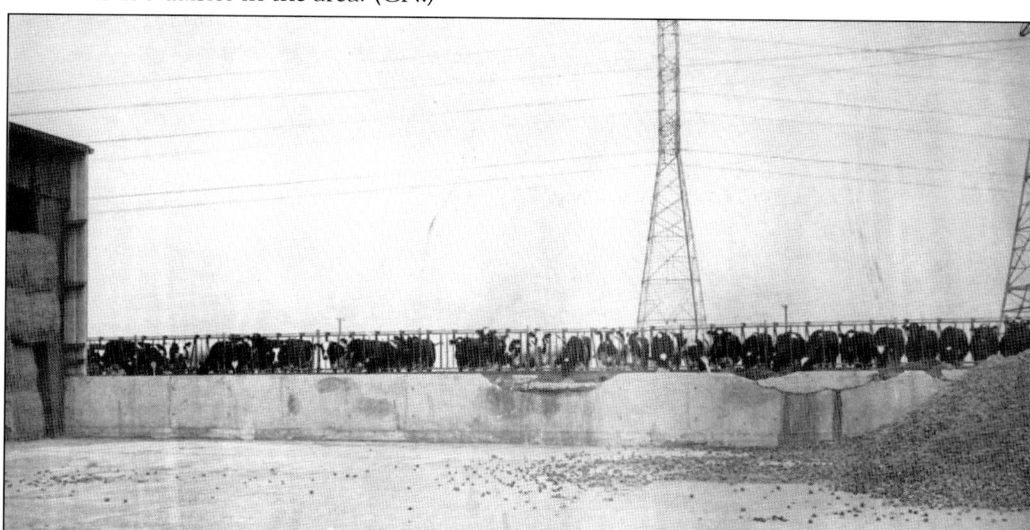

San Bernardino County Dairy Preserve. A variety of ethnicities, including African Americans and immigrants from Mexico and Asia, have been among Chino's dairy owners and farm laborers. The 1920s brought Swedes and Swiss. Dutch and Portuguese arrived after World War II. The Dairy Preserve was one of the world's largest concentrated dairy regions, operating over 400 dairies. Today many of the dairies have moved due to urban development. (CN.)

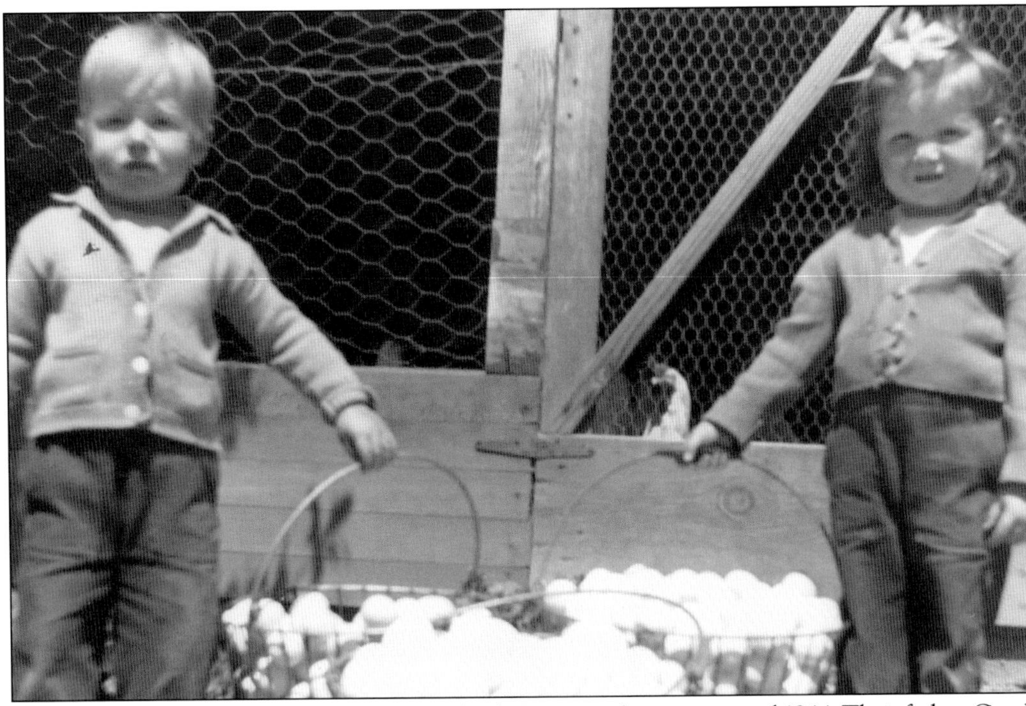

BASKETS FILLED WITH EGGS. Michael and Melinda Brown gather eggs around 1944. Their father, Gerald Brown, was always expanding his chicken farm. He had a running bill at the lumberyard. The bank would only give him $200 at a time, and only if his father cosigned it. After Melinda was born, however, the bank president, Mr. Latham, said, "You don't need that anymore. You're a family man." (GB.)

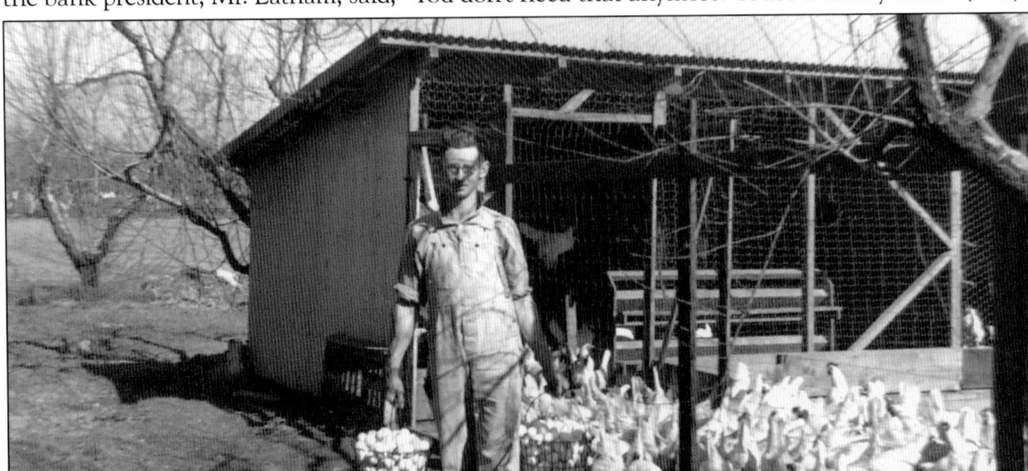

GERALD BROWN, POULTRYMAN. In February 1939, Gerald Brown bought this farm at 11565 Central Avenue, just prior to his marriage. Gerald Brown and his wife, Clara, raised chickens while farming the land. By 1944, they had room for 4,000 birds. In the background of the photograph, an orchard of peach trees can be seen. (GB.)

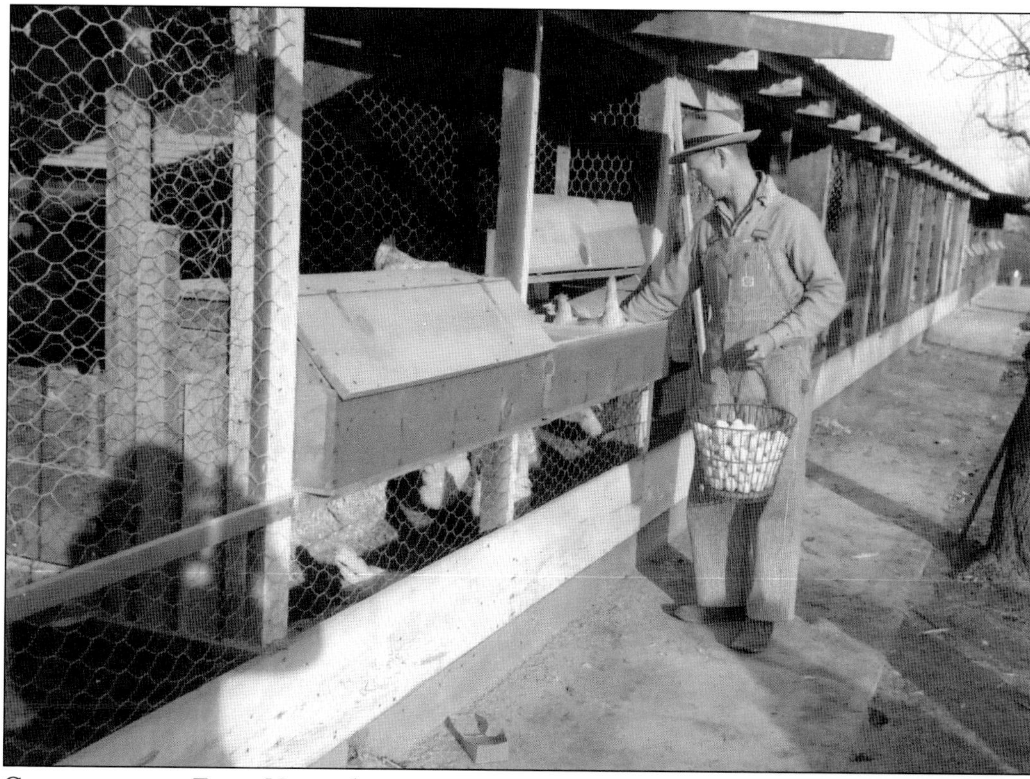

Collecting the Eggs. Up until 1966, Gerald Brown raised all his own chickens. He had outdoor gas brooders and pullet-growing facilities under the walnut trees in inexpensive tar paper buildings. New baby chicks hatched every 10 weeks. These spent six or seven weeks under the brooders before they were moved under the walnut trees. (GB.)

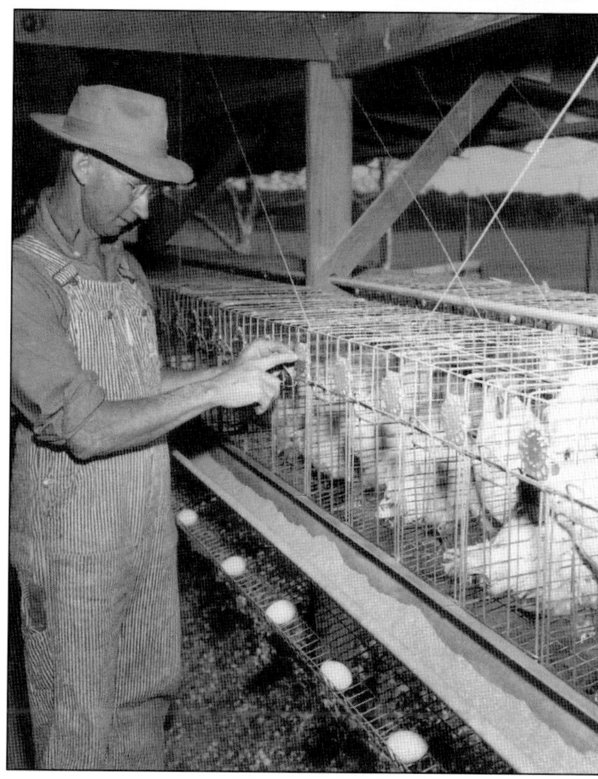

Raising Chickens in Cages. The poultry industry changed in the 1960s with an all-in-all-out policy where all the chickens were the same age and all had been vaccinated at the same time. By now, Gerald Brown had converted all his facilities to laying facilities. With the use of cages, he was able to commit to 45,000 birds. (GB.)

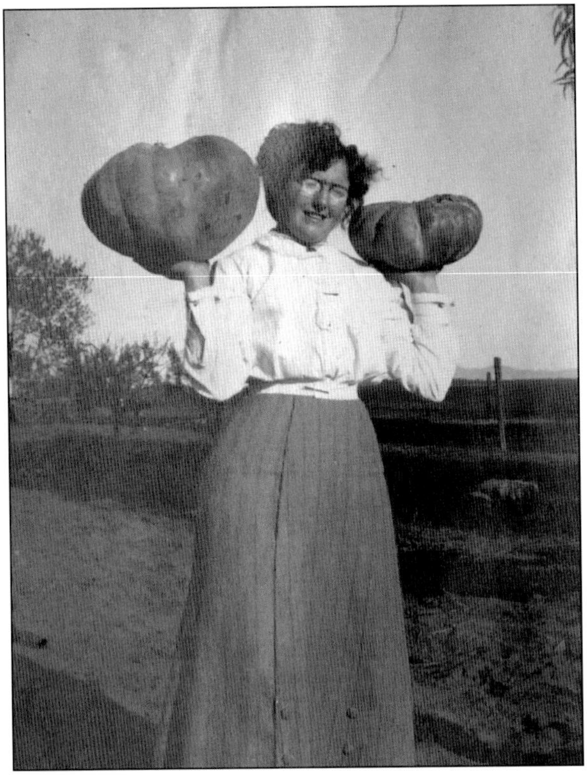

Pumpkins and Vegetables Galore, 1912. Edna Riley LaForge proudly holds up pumpkins from her ranch. Chino was known as the place that grew the salads for the tables in Los Angeles. On Gerald Brown's land, the Nakamotos farmed truck crops such as turnips and radishes. The Chacons raised tomatillos. The Bairs grew yams. Field crops were not limited to vegetables, however. Julian Martinez raised roses for rootstock. (GB.)

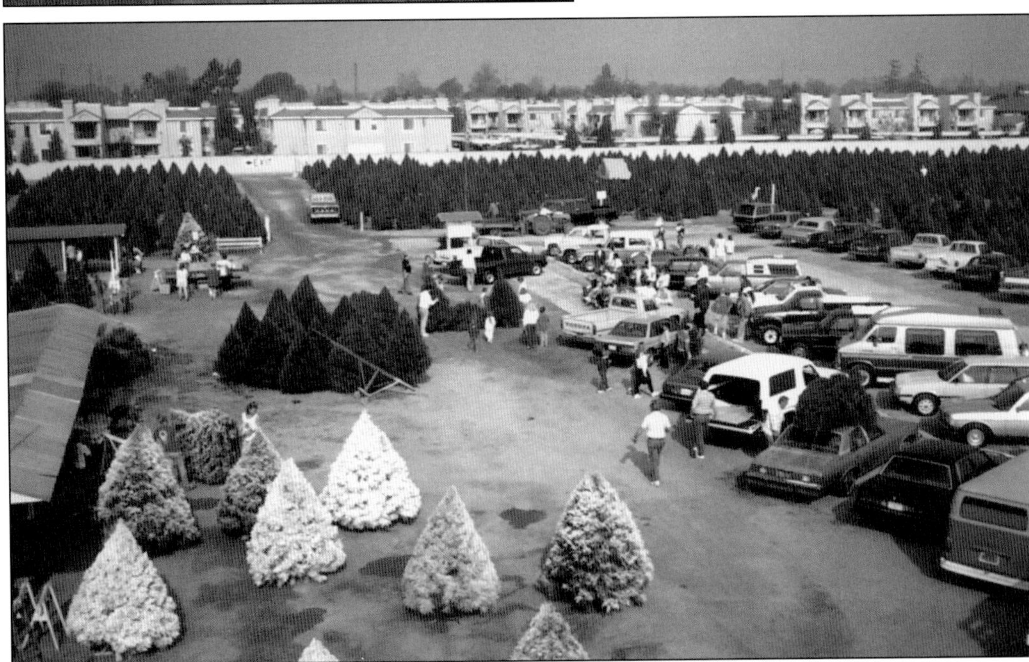

Christmas Tree Farm. On November 20, 1982, Smith and Brown Tree Farm celebrated its opening day of the season. Originally started in 1969 with his longtime employee, friend, and partner Ken Smith, the tree farm was intended to screen the street from the chicken farm. People flocked to Central Avenue to purchase Christmas trees that were locally grown. (GB.)

Three

Industry and Progress

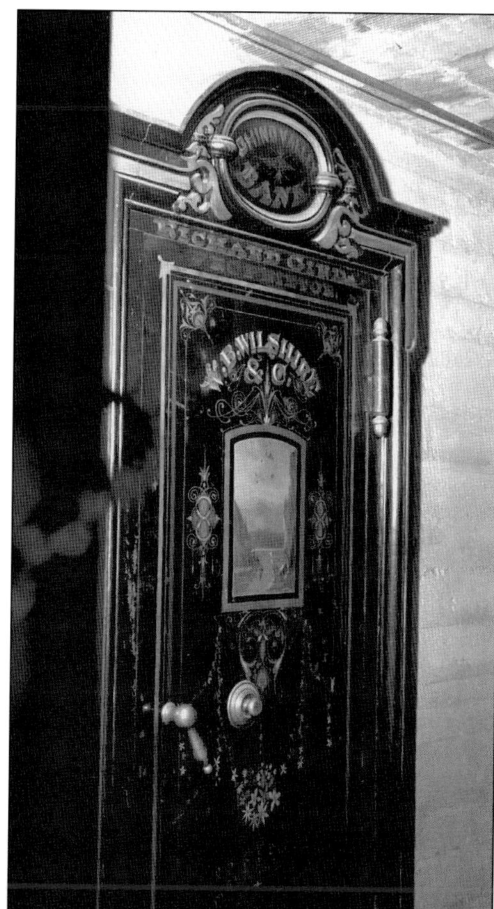

Chino Valley Bank Vault, c. 1911. This historic vault is from the Chino Valley Bank, one of the earliest banks in Chino. Other early banks included the Chino Savings Bank and the First National Bank of Chino, both of which Edwin Rhodes served as vice president in 1925, according to *Chino Champion*'s column, "100 Years of Chino." (CN.)

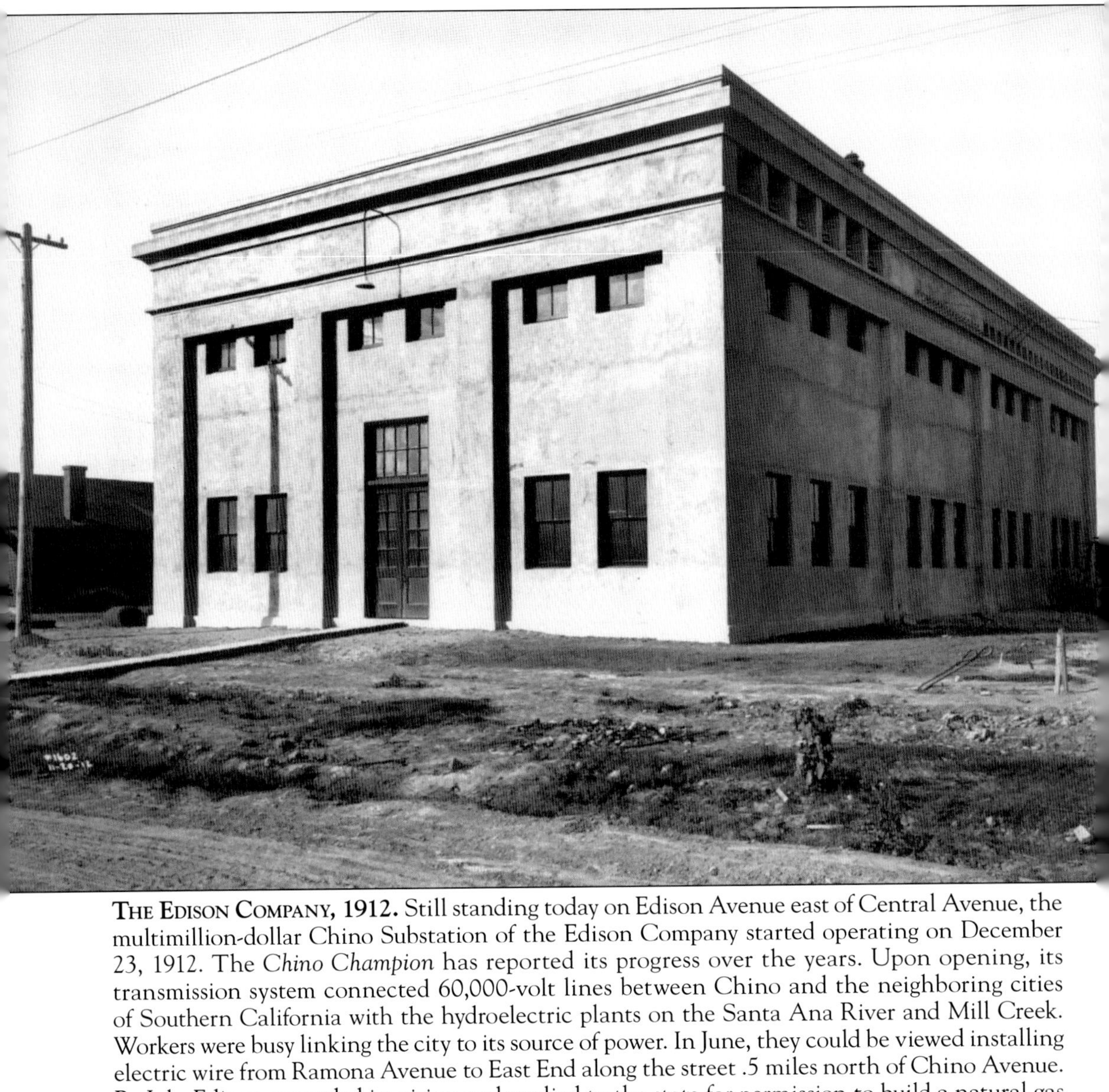

THE EDISON COMPANY, 1912. Still standing today on Edison Avenue east of Central Avenue, the multimillion-dollar Chino Substation of the Edison Company started operating on December 23, 1912. The *Chino Champion* has reported its progress over the years. Upon opening, its transmission system connected 60,000-volt lines between Chino and the neighboring cities of Southern California with the hydroelectric plants on the Santa Ana River and Mill Creek. Workers were busy linking the city to its source of power. In June, they could be viewed installing electric wire from Ramona Avenue to East End along the street .5 miles north of Chino Avenue. By July, Edison expanded its vision and applied to the state for permission to build a natural gas distribution system in Chino along with electric power. Bringing electricity to Chino, as well as Southern California, the Chino Substation of the Edison Company celebrated a historic day on June 6, 1939, when power surged through its wires from Hoover Dam. (CN.)

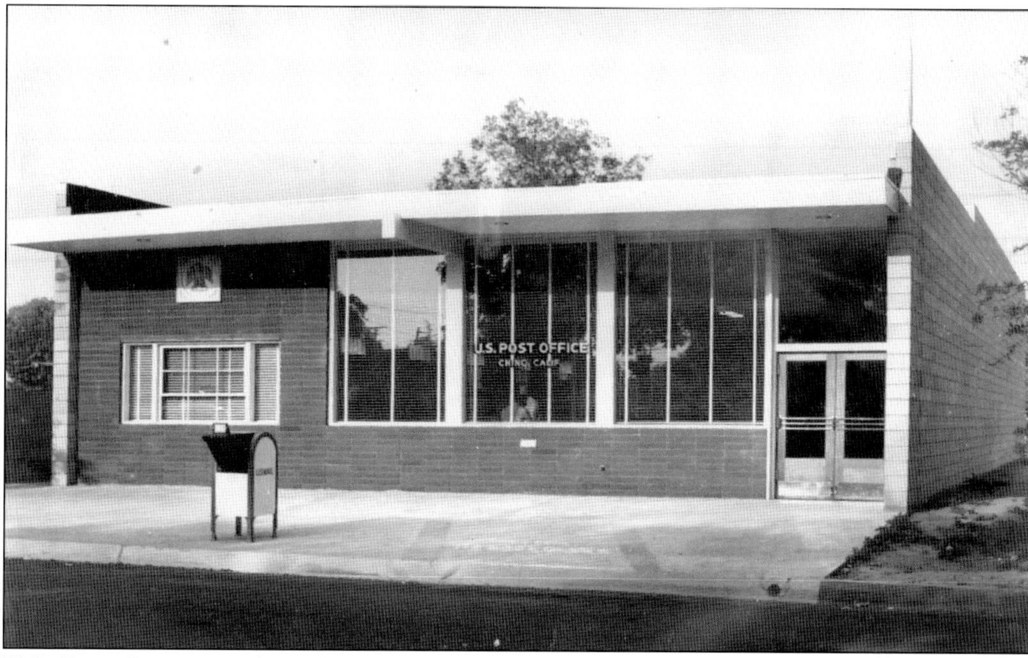

U.S. Post Office. In the early days of Chino, there were no town mail carriers. Gerald Brown remembered that one of his boyhood chores was to go the post office on Sixth Street, south of D Street, to collect the mail. Families were each assigned a mailbox with their own combination. Chino's first postmaster was John Wasson. (CN.)

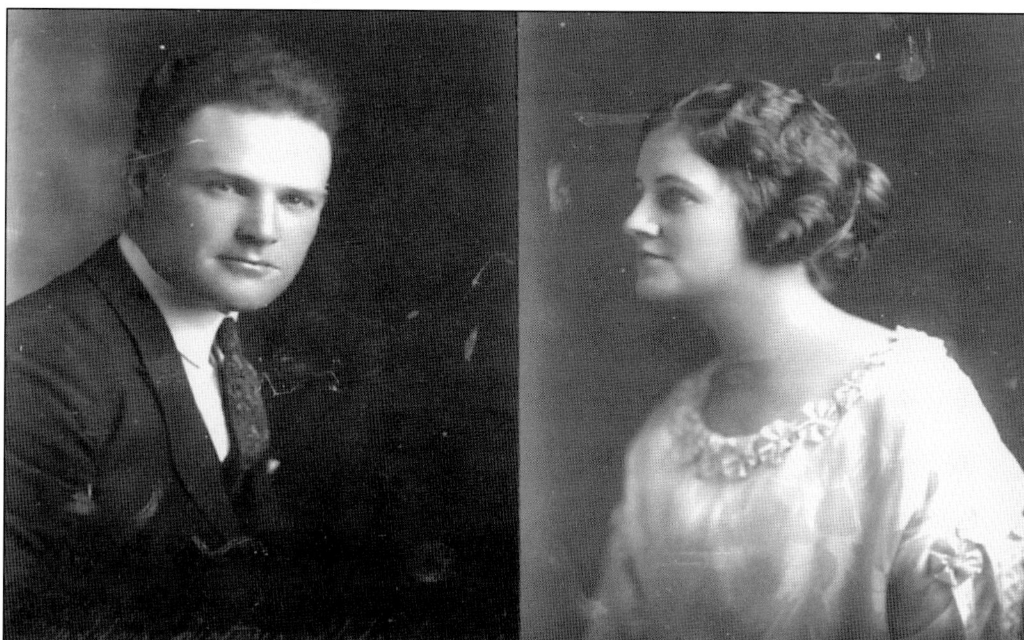

First Letter Carrier. This is the 1920 wedding picture of John A. and Ferneena Daniels. John A. (J. A.) Daniels was the first letter carrier for the postal service in the city of Chino. Ferneena Daniels was an elementary teacher in Chino. Among her students were two future Chino mayors, Zeke Cortez and Ruben S. Ayala. Ayala went on to become the senator of California. (VAD.)

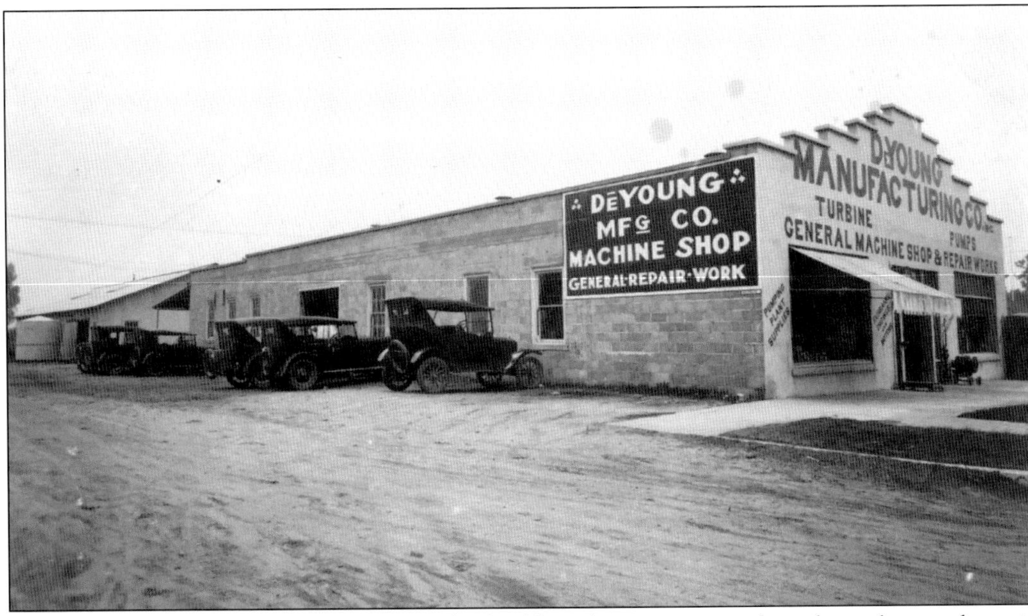

DEYOUNG MANUFACTURING COMPANY. This building, boasting general machine shop and repair, was located in Chino at Central Avenue, north of D Street, which is where the current medical building now stands. In 1929, the name of Chino was painted atop its roof so airplane pilots flying overhead could recognize the city. (CN.)

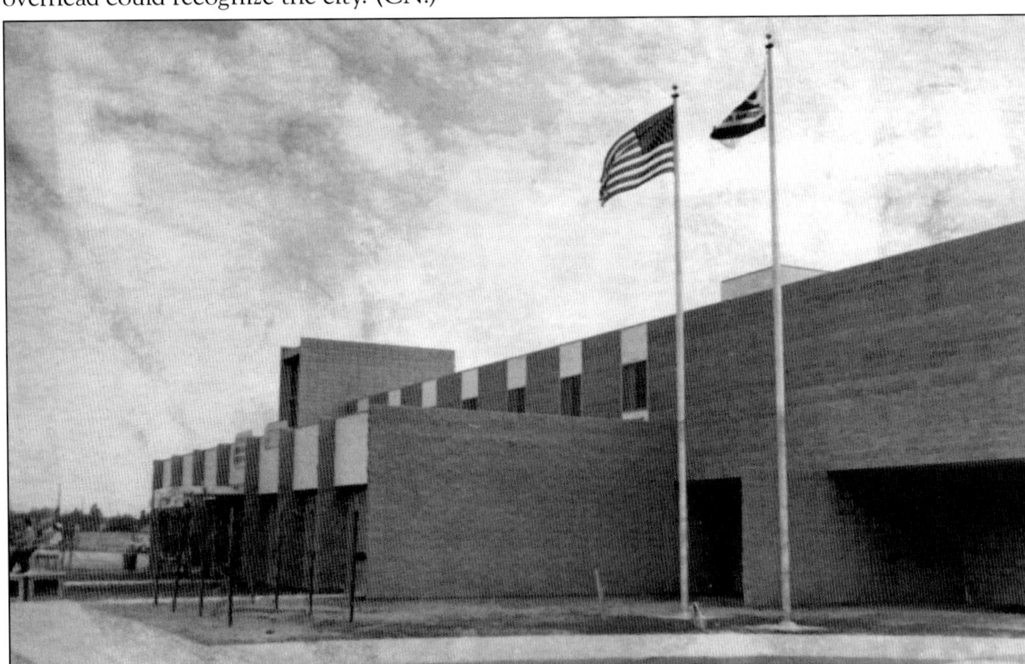

CHINO VALLEY MEDICAL CENTER. In October 1972, Chino Valley Medical Center opened its doors. This 126-bed community hospital is located next to the Chino Post Office. Before the construction of the community hospital took place, early Chino families availed the services of pioneer doctors such as Elgar Reed. Armando Dominguez was also called upon but was not licensed. He was known by Chino pioneers as the Miracle Man. (CN.)

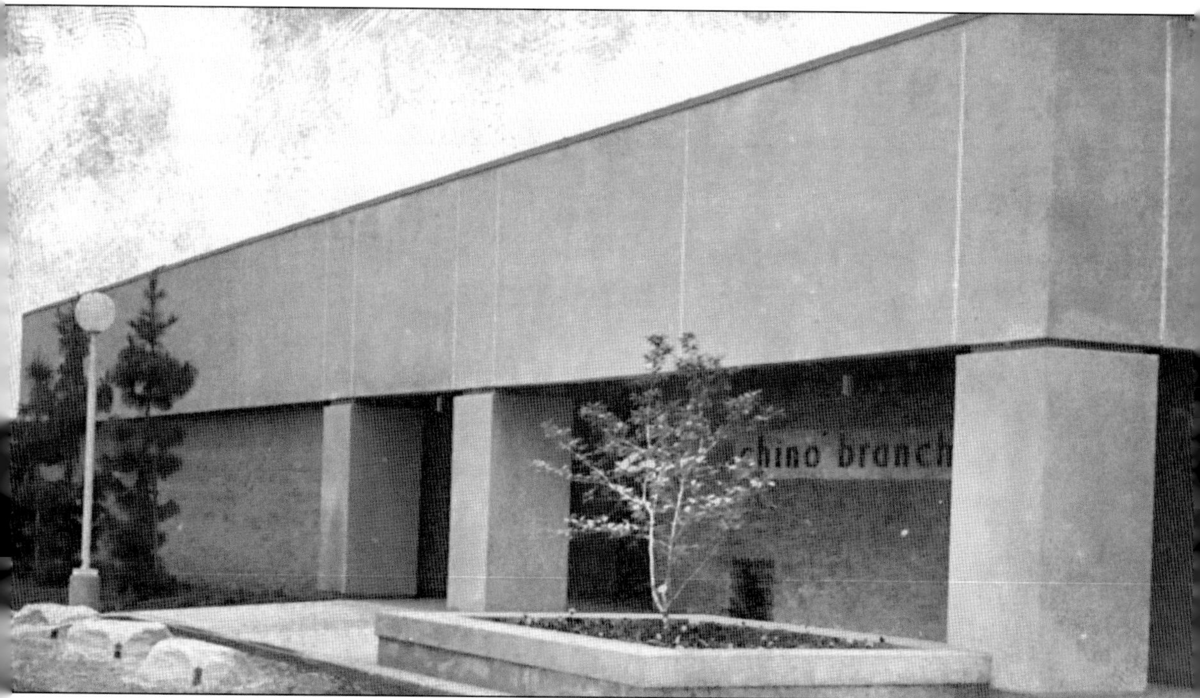

CHINO BRANCH LIBRARY. The *Chino Champion* reported in its column, "100 Years of Chino," that it was the St. Cecilia Club that spearheaded the drive to institute a free public library in a room at Chino's city hall. In 1913, city hall was located at Seventh and D Streets, where the current library's parking lot is now paved. In May 1913, the Chino Public Library opened its doors with a celebration, including music played on a phonograph. The next day, library patrons were welcomed at the library, with Mrs. J. T. Schroeder receiving the first library card and checking out the first library book. She had 440 books to choose from for her selection. Rick Erickson's *History of the San Bernardino County Library 1913–1988* reports that, by 1915, the Chino Branch Library's 1,500 books filled a large room in city hall. In 1943–1944, the library reported it was working with the children of the Hispanic population in Chino to display their artwork. Helen Pine served as librarian from 1951 to 1968. (CN.)

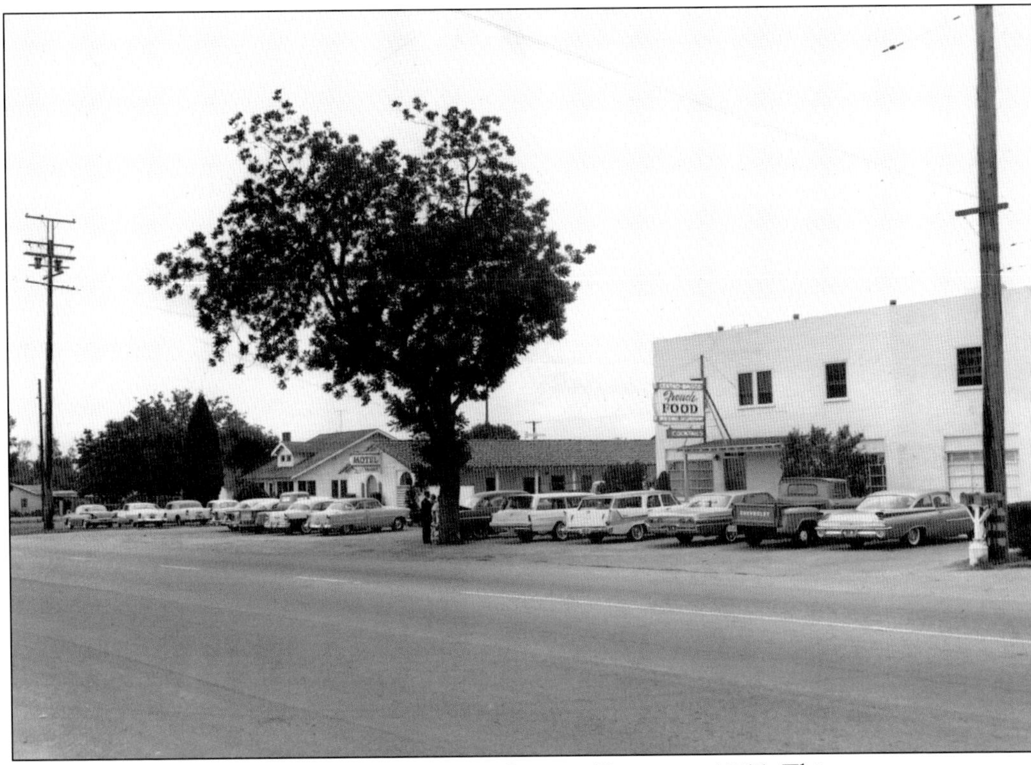

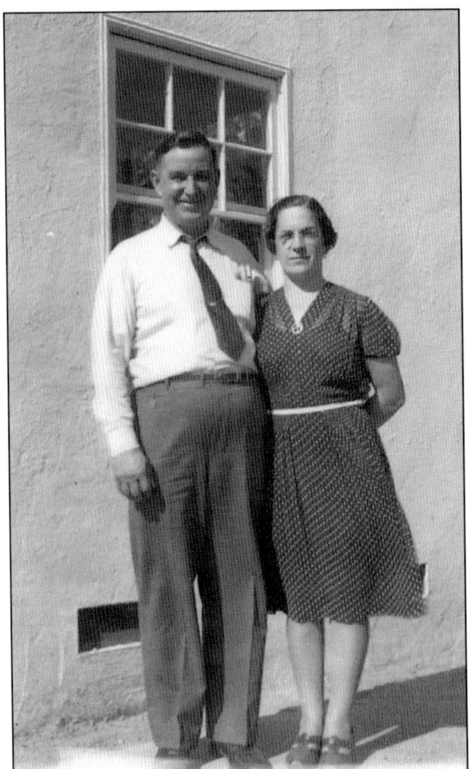

CENTRO BASCO, C. 1955. This restaurant, located in the downtown area at Central and Chino Avenues, has continuously served the community since 1940. It specializes in Basque-style food and offers a daily three-course meal, including homemade soups and traditional lamb dishes. These meals are served family-style on platters and in tureens. Guests seated at long tables pass these dishes to one another. (BF.)

JOHN AND GRACE ROBIDART, C. 1940. The Robidarts were the original owners of the Centro Vasco Hotel complex, which included the Centro Basco Restaurant and a recreational outdoor handball court. The hotel, still in operation, was initially used as a lodging place for seasonal Basque shepherds who tended flocks in the nearby hills. The Berterretche family acquired the restaurant in 1970. (BF.)

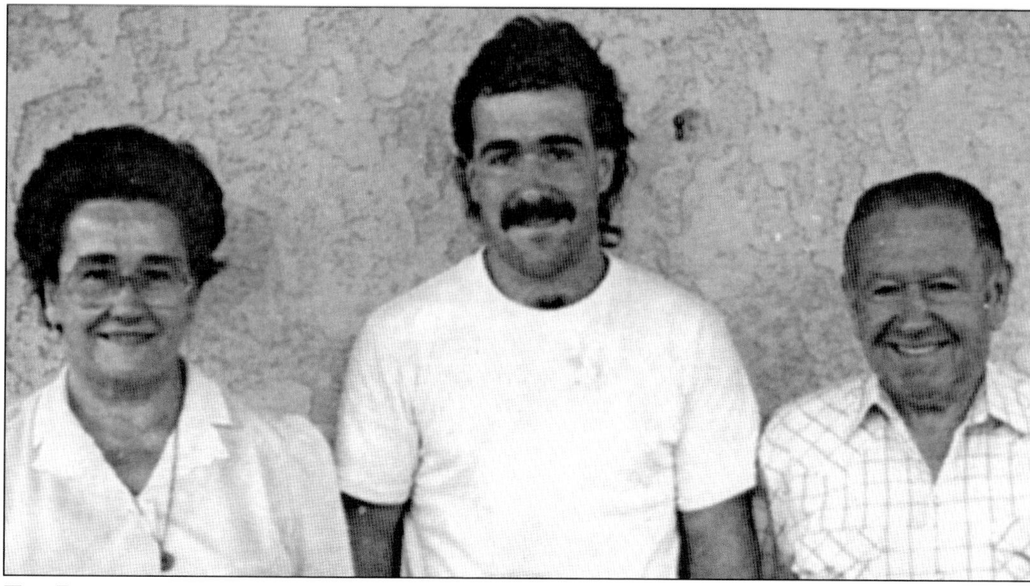

THE BERTERRETCHE FAMILY. Pierre Berterretche (right) emigrated from the Basque Pyrenees to Wyoming in the 1950s as a sheepherder. Monique (left) arrived in 1955 as a camp cook for the lambing season, when the pastoralists brought in their flocks. After the two married, they moved to Chino in 1958. Here they raised their son Joseph (center) and daughters Jeanne, Marie, and Bernadette. (BF.)

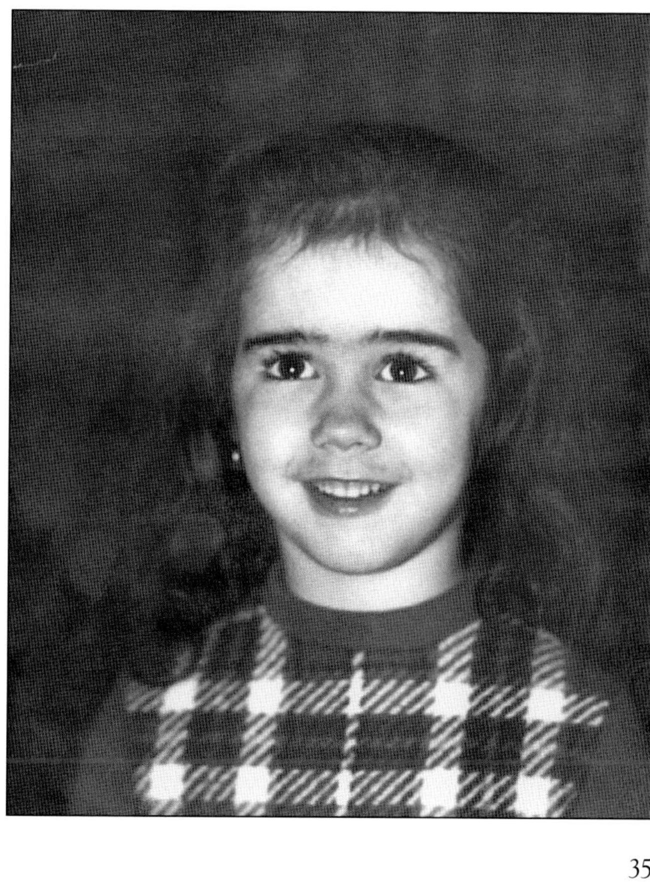

BERNADETTE BERTERRETCHE, C. 1965. After 12 years of milking cows in the local Chino dairies, Pierre saved enough pay to purchase Centro Basco, where Monique then re-created the savory dishes of her French hometown, located near St. Jean Pied de Port. Under Bernadette's management, the restaurant continues to be a family-run enterprise and is one of the oldest Basque cuisine establishments in Southern California. (BF.)

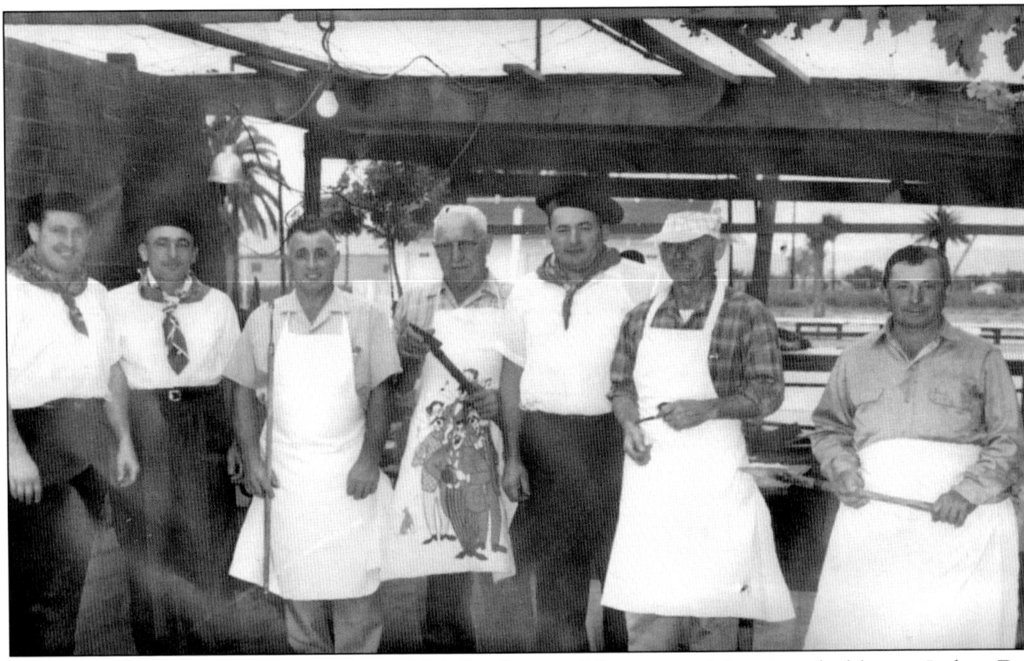

BARBEQUE AT CENTRO BASCO, C. 1965. The Basque Heritage celebration, held over Labor Day weekend, always commences on that Sunday with various cultural events. It ends on the subsequent Monday with a big barbeque held at Centro Basco. The handball court, located behind the restaurant, plays host to a flotilla of outdoor grills commandeered for the activity. (BF.)

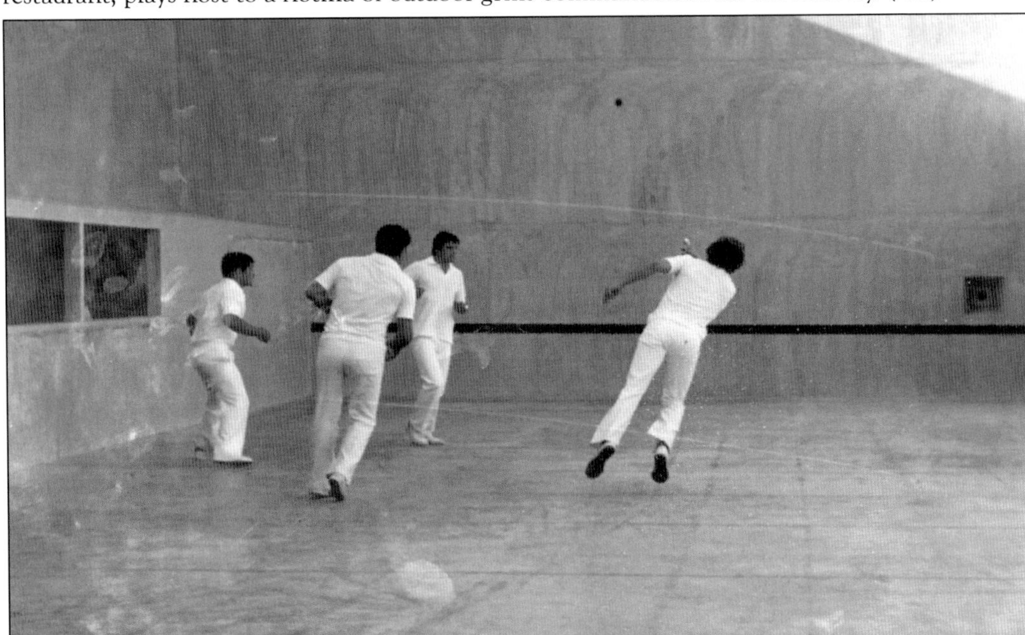

INDOOR HANDBALL COURT. Outdoor or indoor, the sport of handball has a high degree of popularity among the Basque population. The court shown above is of the indoor variety. As the dairies of Chino grew in size and prosperity, their owners expanded or rebuilt farmhouses to include various comfortable amenities such as this handball court found at the Aphessetche Dairy. (BF.)

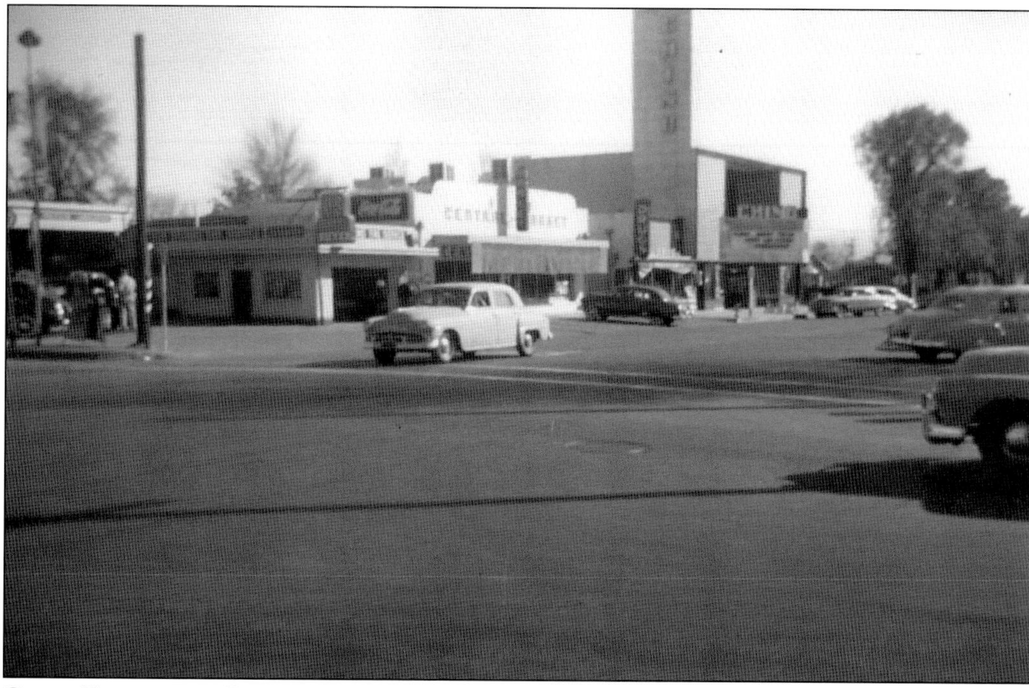

CHINO THEATER ON CENTRAL AVENUE. The community of Chino has had a variety of theaters in its lifetime. The *Chino Champion* stated that the new Dawes movie theater opened in 1910, the year of the city's incorporation. The Edison Company provided power for the theater. Today 100 years later, the neon sign of Chino Theater has been relit and is a symbol of historic Chino. (GB.)

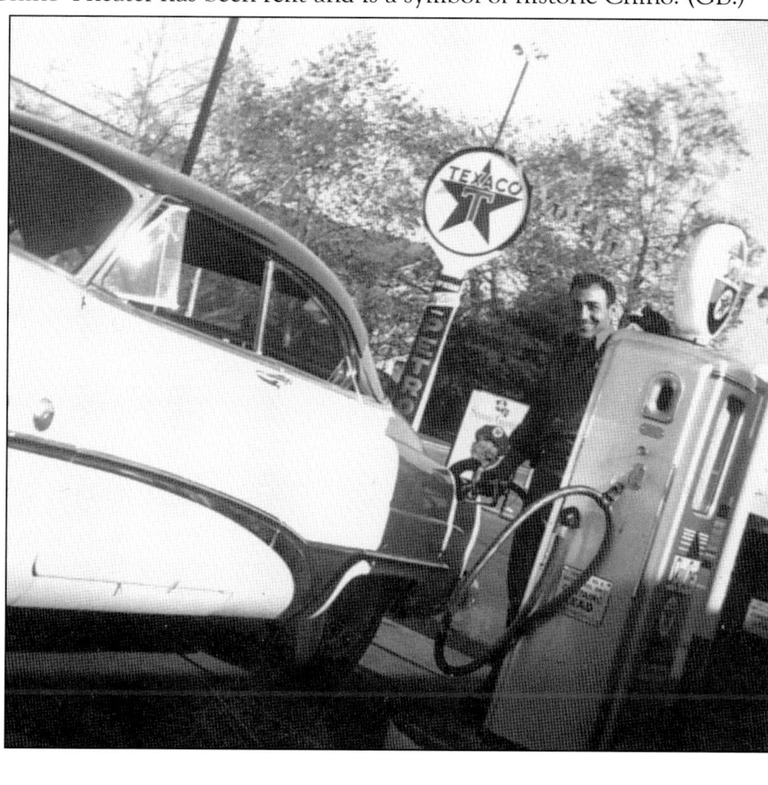

DAVE AND TYE'S TEXACO, C. 1956. For nearly 30 years, David George and his brother Tye owned and operated a Texaco service station in Chino, on Riverside Drive. The George family moved to Chino in the early 1930s, and both brothers graduated from Chino High. In his senior year, David George starred as No. 27 on the football team, kicking field goals and scoring many touchdowns. (DG.)

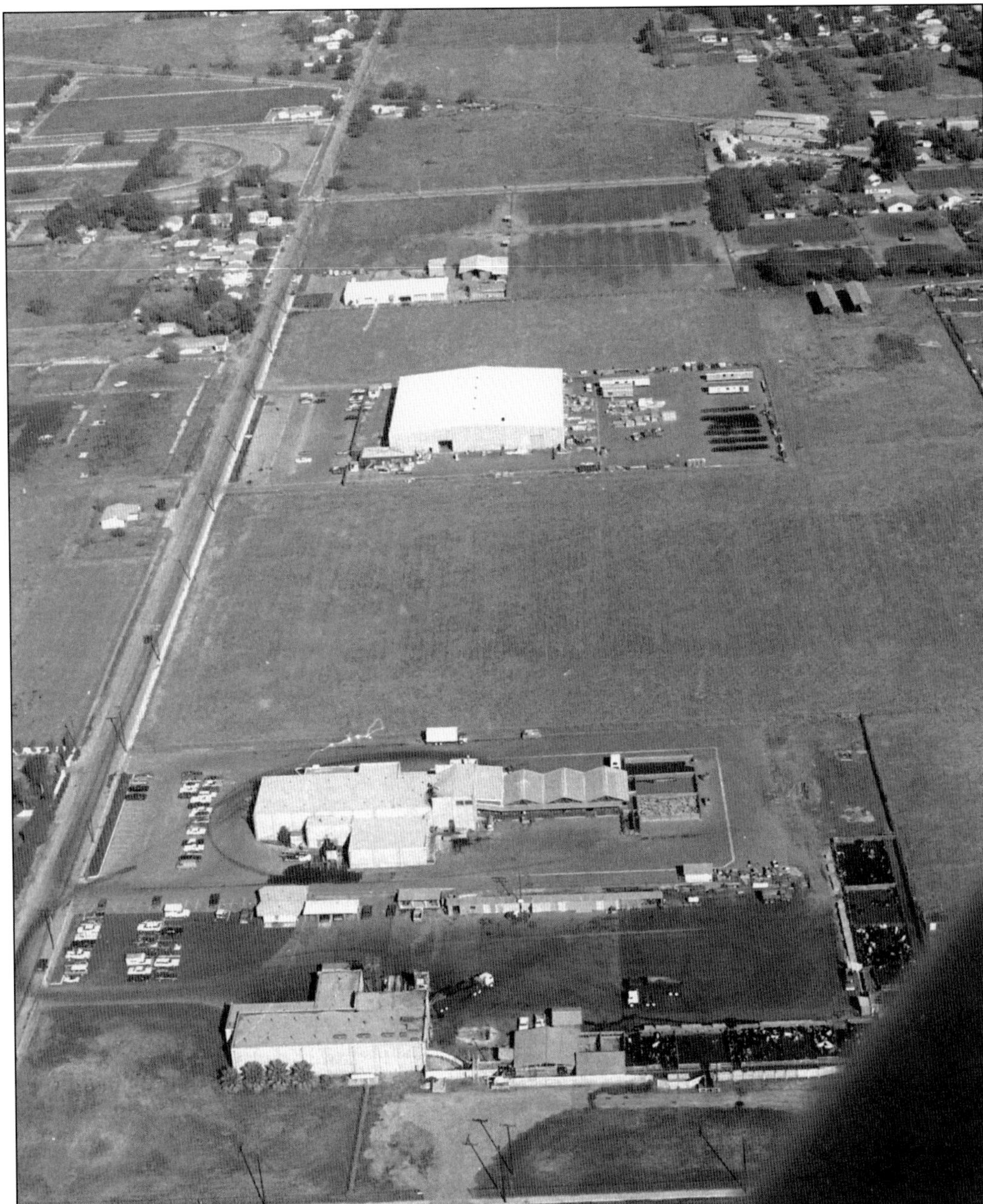

Aerial of Schaefer Avenue. According to the memoirs of Sophia Schaefer Lako shared in the book *Chino Valley: Where Everything Grows*, in 1891, W. Jacob Schaefer and his family moved into their shanty in Chino on what is currently Cypress Avenue. W. Jacob Schaefer raised beets to sell at the Sugar Beet Factory. The company provided him with seeds to plant, and an agricultural expert from France instructed all the farmers on successful methods of growing beets. Following these instructions carefully, W. Jacob Schaefer produced a fine harvest his first year, enabling him to purchase 40 more acres on what is now Oaks Avenue. In this photograph, Schaefer Avenue, the street named after the W. Jacob Schaefer family, is running from left to right along the bottom. Yorba Avenue is the street running from top to bottom along the left. (CN.)

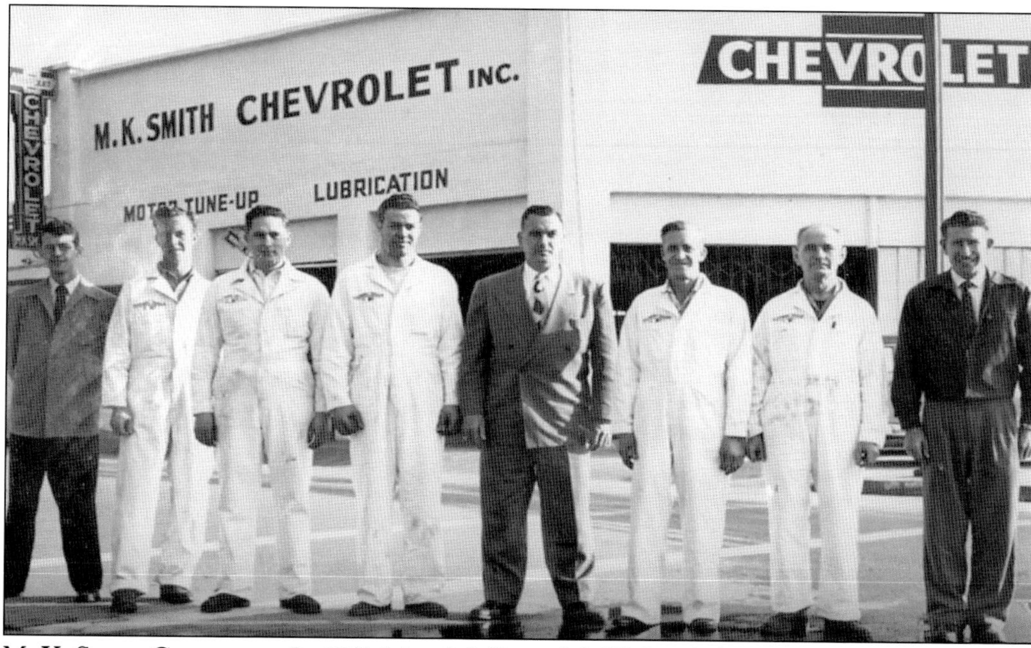

M. K. Smith Chevrolet. In 1941, Meredith Kopp (M. K.) Smith (center) stands with the seven original employees of M. K. Smith Chevrolet. Originally on the southeast corner of Seventh and D Streets, where White's Garage now stands, the landlord leased the building to M. K. Smith on a handshake alone, with no written lease. (MKS.)

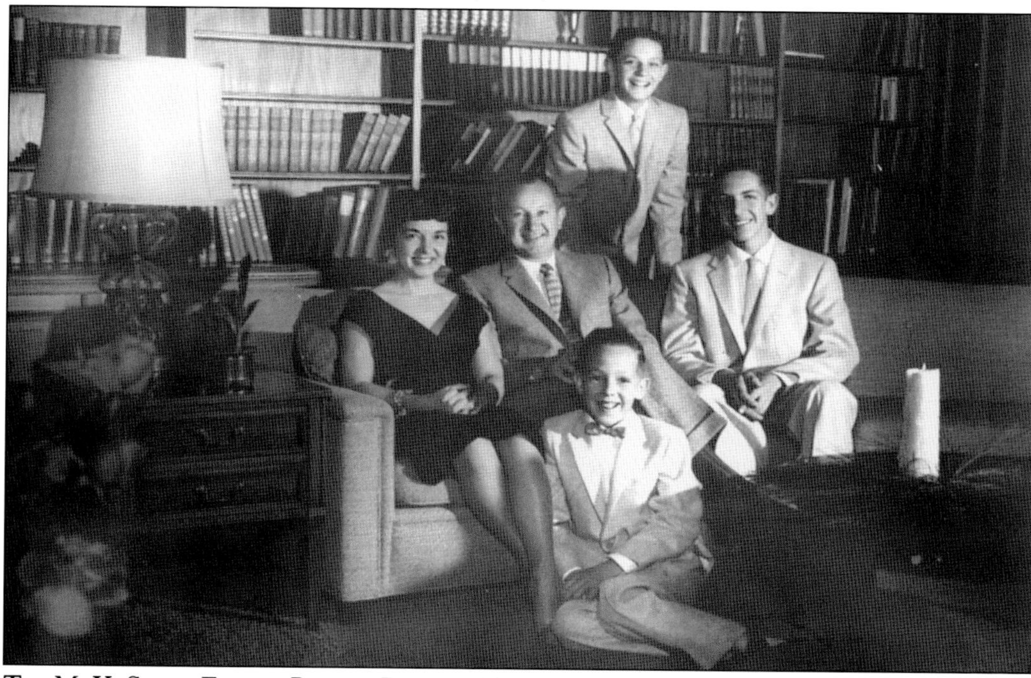

The M. K. Smith Family. Born in Dayton, Ohio, in 1902, M. K. Smith attended Pasadena High School in the 1920s. In 1939, he worked at the Chevrolet Motor Division for two years before becoming a dealer in Chino. Here he is pictured with his wife, Helen Morissey Smith, and sons Ken (standing), Doug, and Bob (seated on the floor). (MKS.)

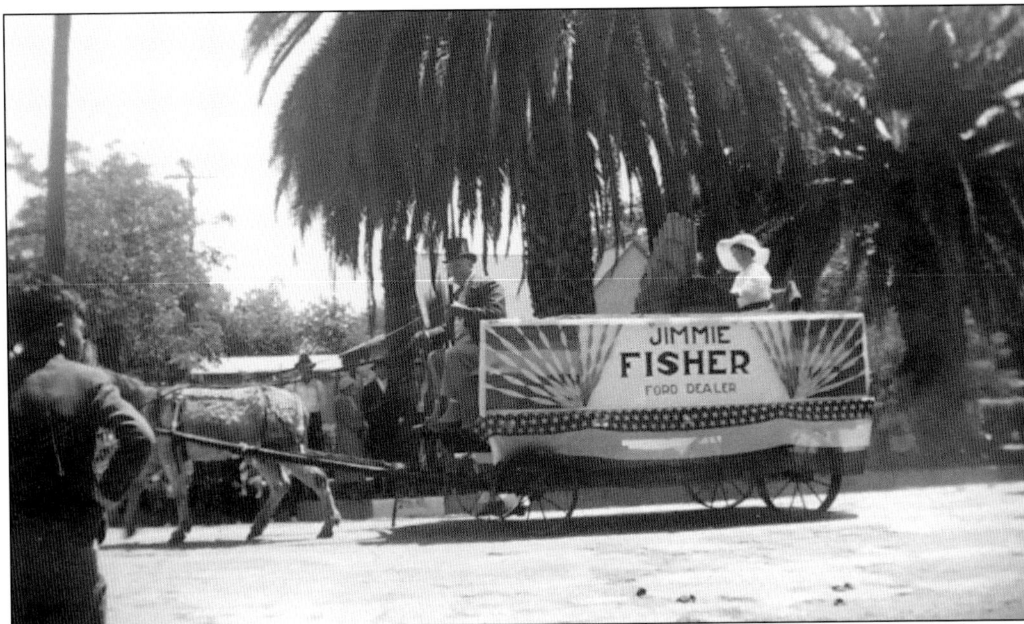

FORD DEALERS IN CHINO. Citizens of Chino transitioned from horse-and-buggy days to automobiles at a pace comparable with the rest of the nation. To provide service and supply Chino with a selection of automobiles, various businesses opened and operated within the community. On the northwest corner of Central and D Streets, J. M. Fisher managed his Jimmie Fisher Ford dealership. In 1936, about the time of the photograph of his float in this parade, he purchased, with plans to offer the community a full service station, two lots across the street. Shown in the photograph below is another business that supplied automobile service to the community, the John Engel Ford Dealer. (Both, CN.)

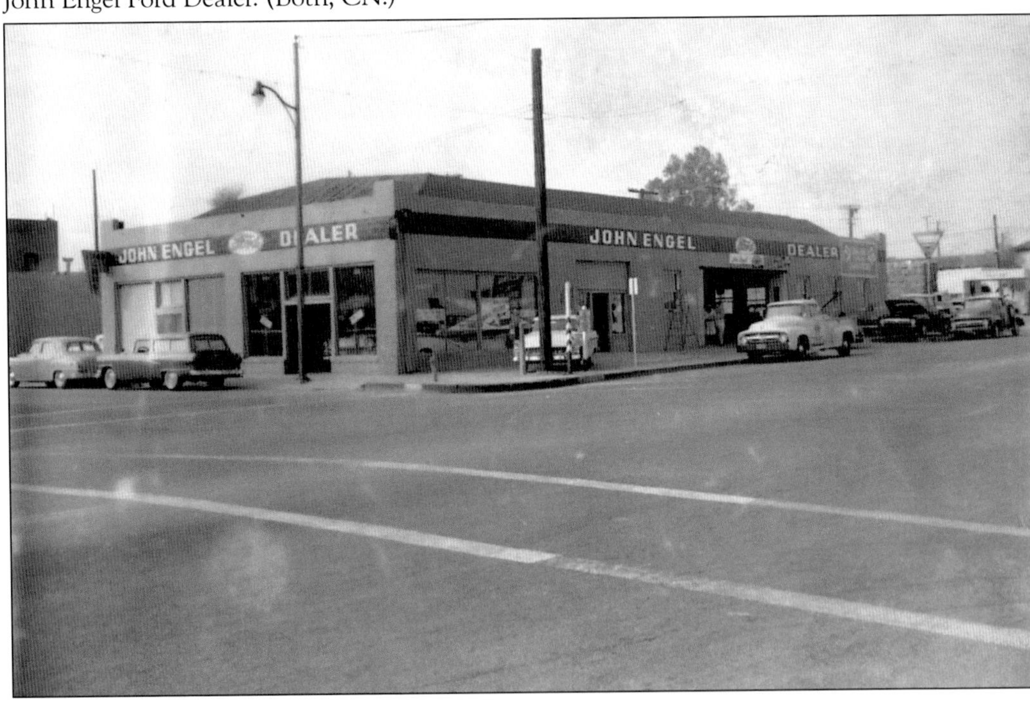

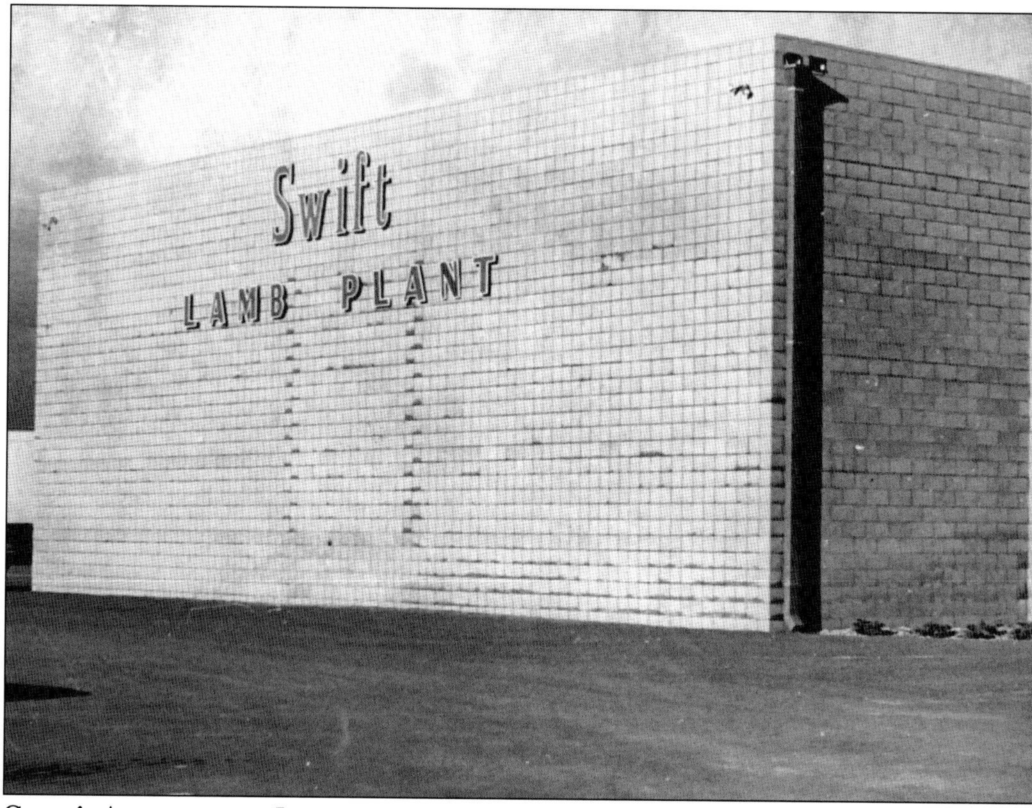

Chino's Agricultural Industry. Since its earliest days with the Beet Sugar Factory, Chino's main industries have revolved around its agricultural resources. The Swift Lamb Plant and the Chino Valley Meat Packing Company are just two of the local industries that have supplied work for the community. Another important industry in the community was the Chino Walnut Growers Association. The walnut packinghouse was located next to the railroad tracks at Chino Avenue and Monte Vista. Harwell Furniture Company is now using the old building. In the 1920s, after the beet industry failed, walnuts became Chino's main agricultural industry, earning annual returns in the millions. (Both, CN.)

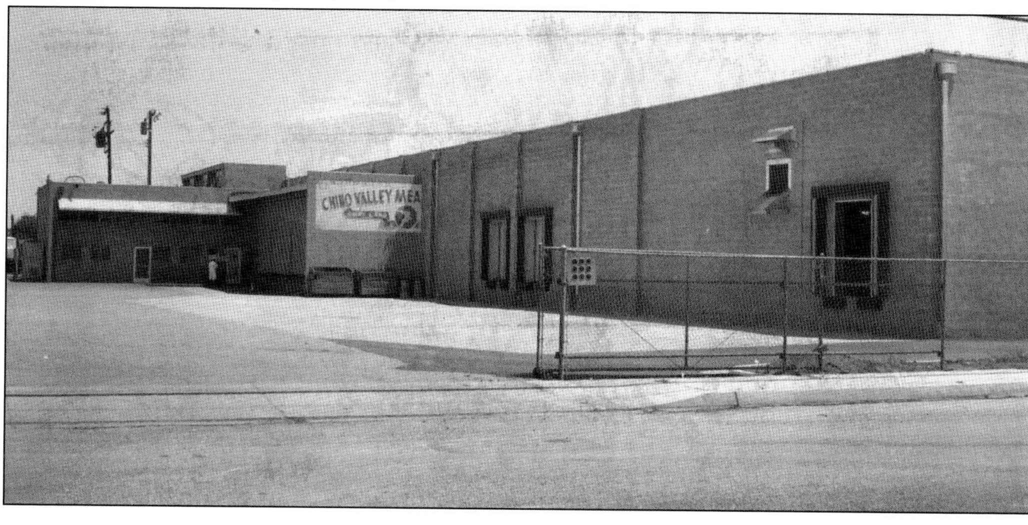

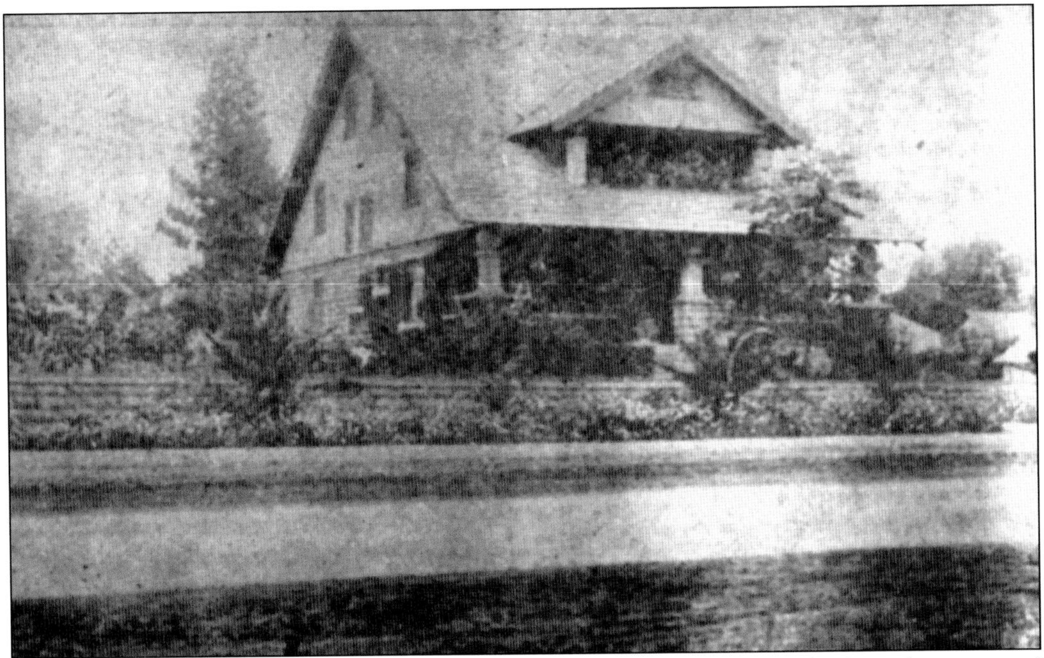

The B. K. Galbreath Home, 1913. The home of B. K. Galbreath was built at the corner of Central Avenue and C Street, located near the store that he managed on the southeast corner of Sixth and D Street. Along with being a well-known merchant in Chino, he was active in community affairs such as laying the foundation for Chino's first fire department. He was president of Chino Fire Company No. 1. (CN.)

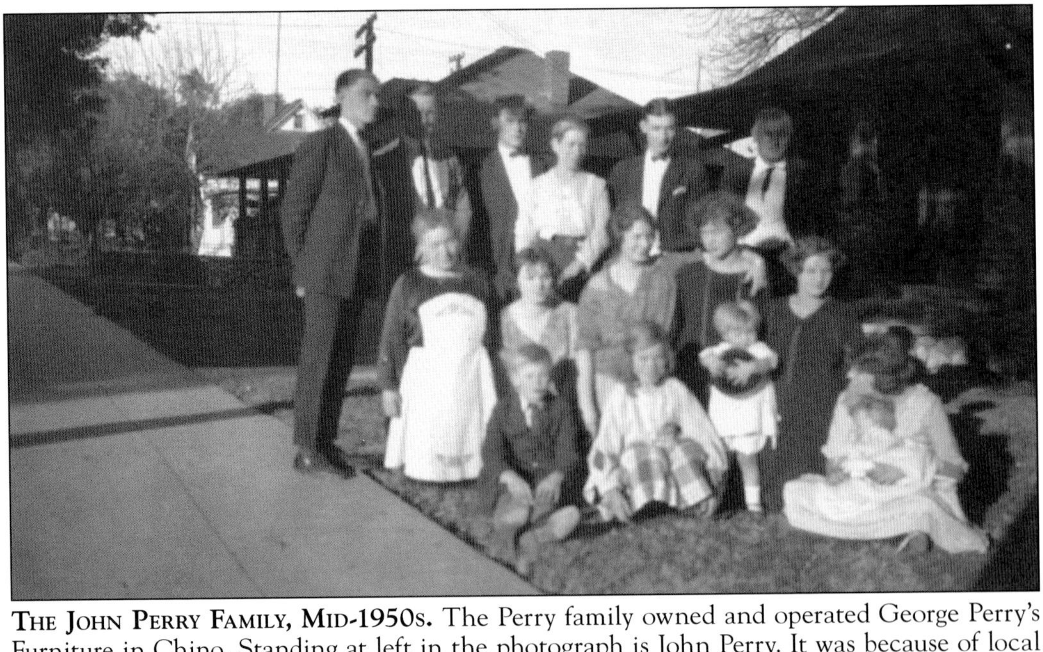

The John Perry Family, Mid-1950s. The Perry family owned and operated George Perry's Furniture in Chino. Standing at left in the photograph is John Perry. It was because of local families such as the Perrys, who established important businesses within the city to meet the people's needs, that Chino grew to be a successful and thriving community. (FW.)

Four

From Here to There

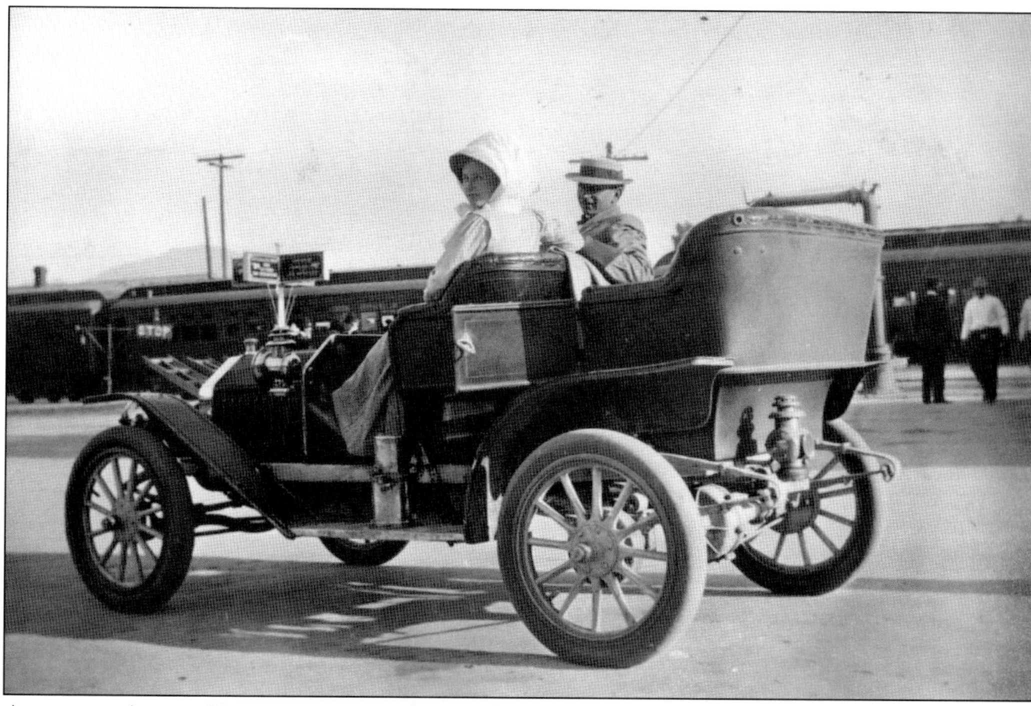

Alice and Alfred Brown, c. 1910. This Buick held the distinction of being the first motorized car on the east side of Chino. This young couple, not yet married, enjoyed a fashionable ride through town. Several years later in 1919, Alfred Brown got his first Model T Ford. He cranked it to start it. In 1921, he purchased a new Model T Ford, and that one had an electric self-starter. (GB.)

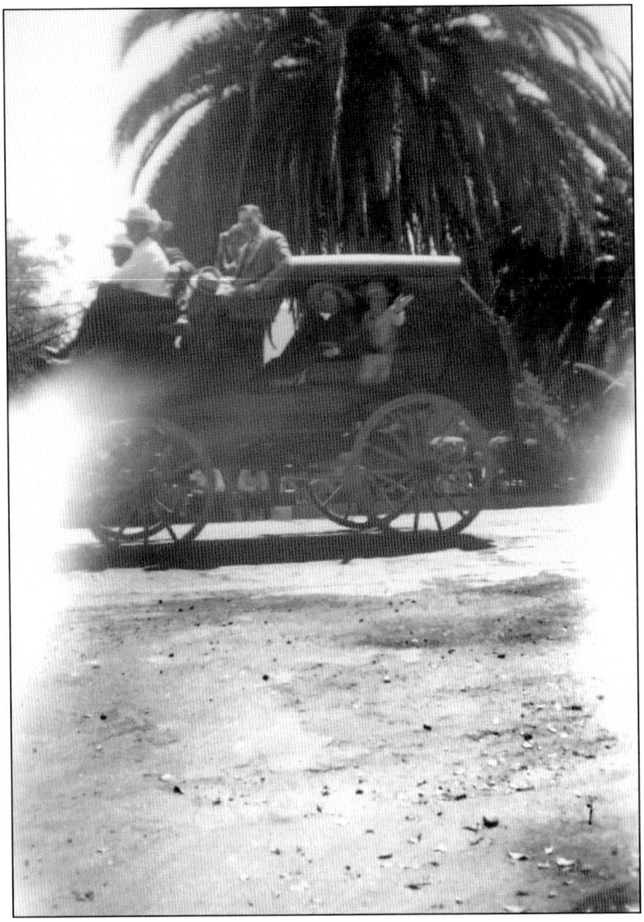

THE BUTTERFIELD STAGE COMPANY, MID-1930S. The sight of a horse-drawn stagecoach in this parade is reminiscent of days gone by. In 1856, Robert Carlisle acquired the Chino Ranch and leased it to the Butterfield Stage Company. Consequently, the ranch became an official station for the Overland Mail on its route to the City of the Angels. Passengers alighted to sample the local fare while the coach changed out its last team of horses for the final leg of the journey. Carlisle continued to live on the premises as stationmaster. The Butterfield stage route was closed during the Civil War, and Wells Fargo reopened and operated it after the war until the transcontinental railroad made travel by stage impractical. In the photograph below, the Butterfield sisters, Nellie Butterfield (second from left) and Florence Butterfield (far right), enjoy visiting with friends. (Both, CN.)

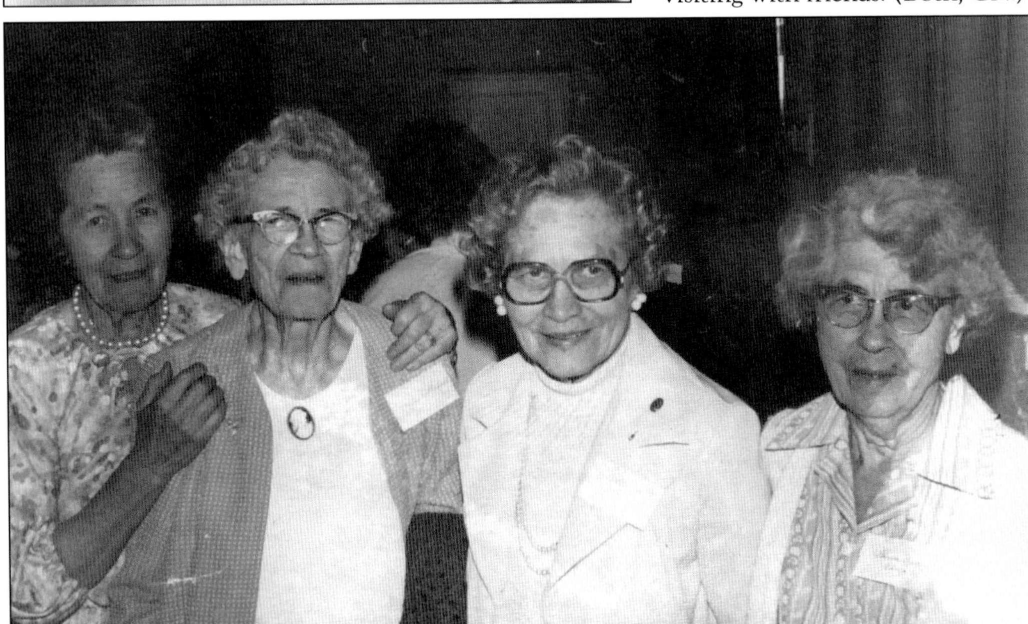

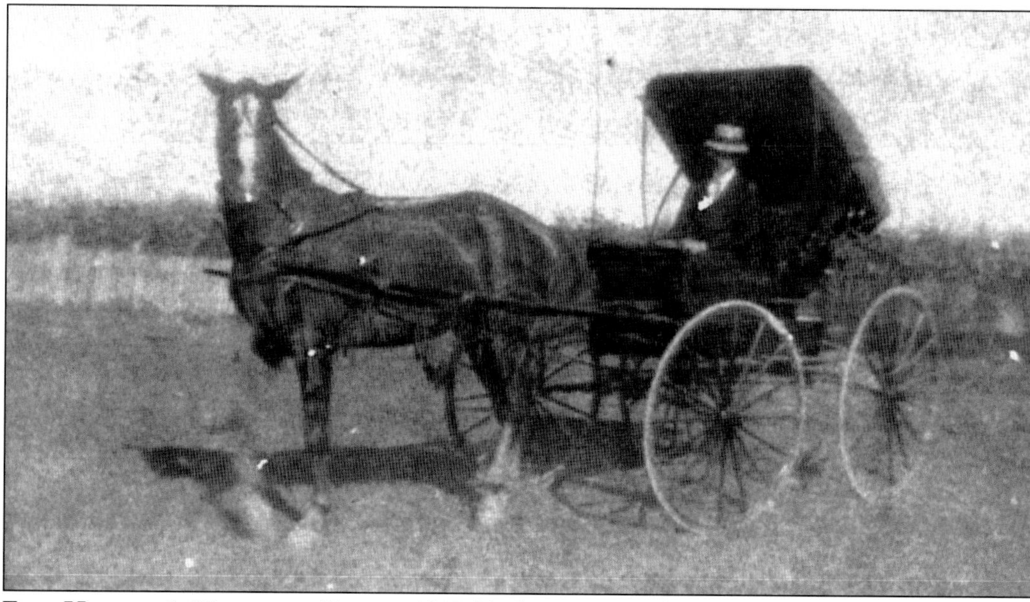

FRED HENNING'S HORSE AND BUGGY, 1917. Fred Henning is driving to the Pomona train station to pick up the Thompson family, his new neighbors arriving from Panama. The Thompsons built their ranch next to the Hennings' ranch. For a time, there were only three houses on Riverside Drive between Oaks and Magnolia Avenues. The houses belonged to Fred and Margaret Caulfield Henning, Fred and Eva Henning Walters, and the Thompsons. (FW.)

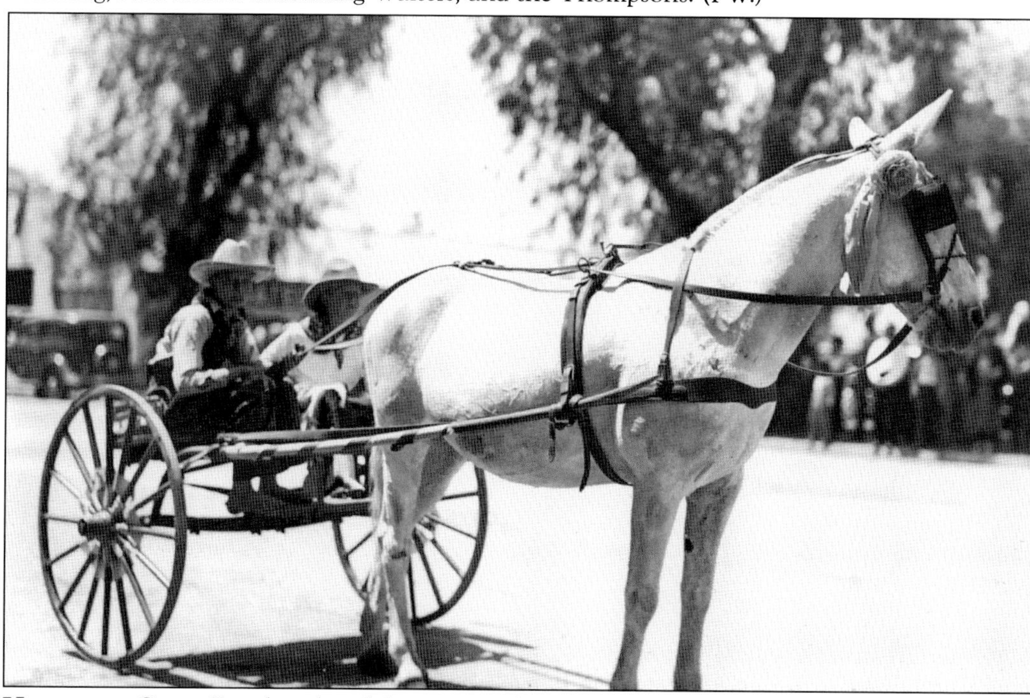

HORSE AND CART. Families that did not own a buggy often got around Chino in a simple horse and cart such as the one shown in this mid-1930s photograph of a parade in Chino. Gerald Brown, born in Chino in 1913, had faint memories of his parents having a horse and buggy as their sole means of transportation. It was just a small buggy, with no top. (CN.)

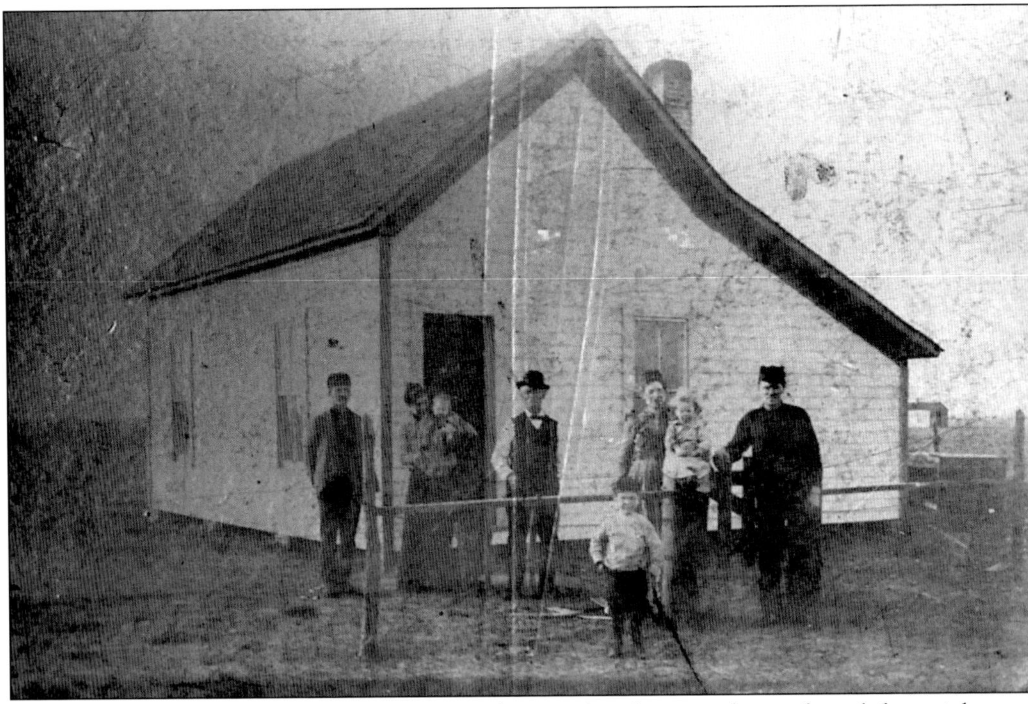

Engineer Fred Walters and Family. Standing in the photograph are, from left to right, two unidentified people, Fred Henning, Eva Henning Walters, and Fred Walters. The children are unidentified. Engineer Fred Walters drove a train between Ontario and Chino, along tracks that ran up and down on Euclid Avenue. He is shown wearing his railroad hat. This photograph was probably taken at the Henning Ranch on Riverside Drive. (FW.)

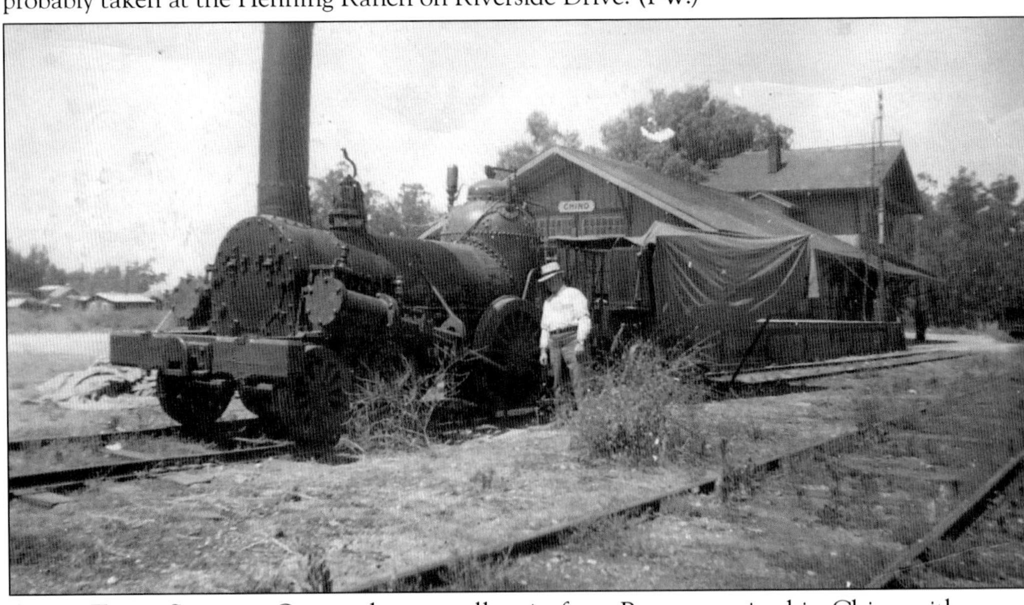

Chino Train Station. Once a day, a small train from Pomona arrived in Chino with one or two cars. Local stores ordered in goods from their distributors, and deliveries would arrive by rail. A small trucking firm called a transfer business then delivered the goods to the stores. The Galbreath Store was one of its steady customers. (GB.)

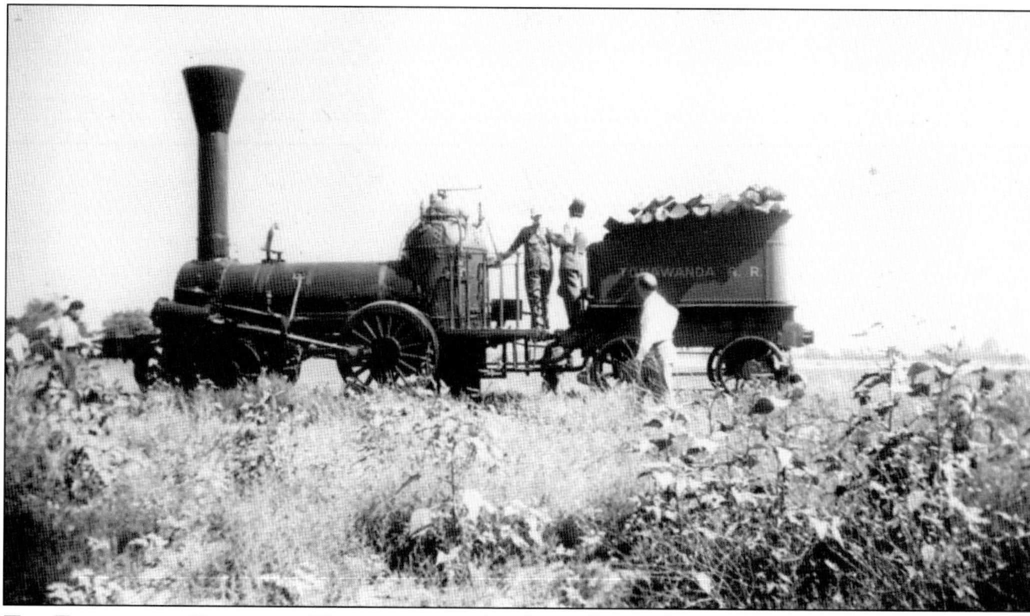

The Tonawanda Railroad. This train was a familiar sight in Chino. Usually, Southern California's hot, dry weather posed no problem to the railroad, but in 1910, there was exceptionally high precipitation. Flooding was an issue, especially along the railroad tracks. Residents in Chino sent a petition to the board of supervisors to solve the problem along what is now Chino Avenue, between Sixth Street and Central Avenue. (GB.)

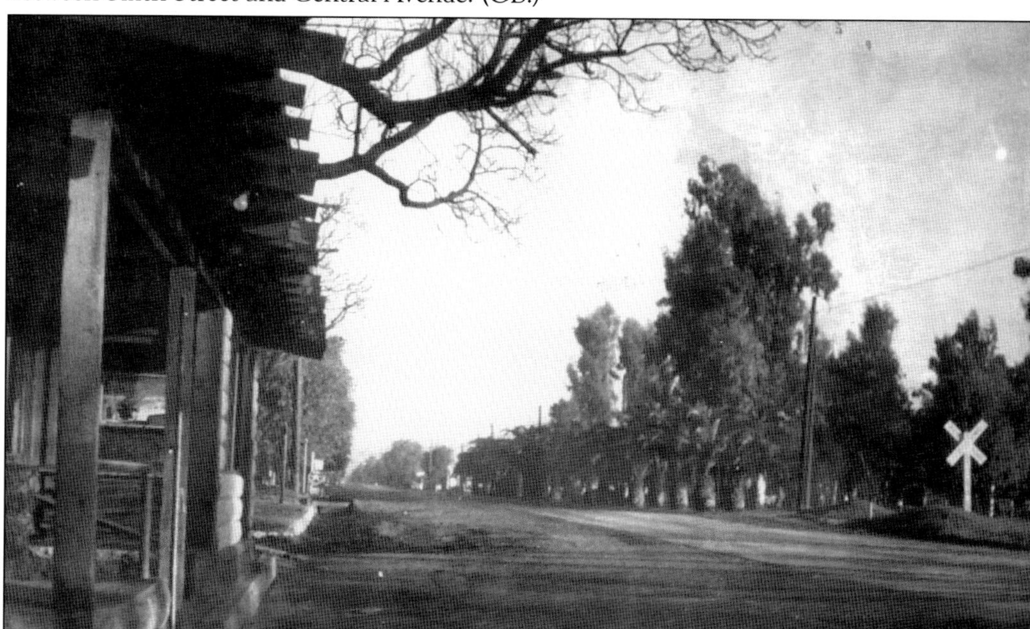

Chino Railroad Crossing. The railroad was an important part of Chino. In beet season, farmers drove their crops to a loading facility on G Street. The beets were loaded onto open gondola railcars that had small cracks between the sidings for better airflow. Gerald Brown remembered when they were still loading with a wagon and eight mules. Occasionally, the driver would throw a beet at the lead mule. (CN.)

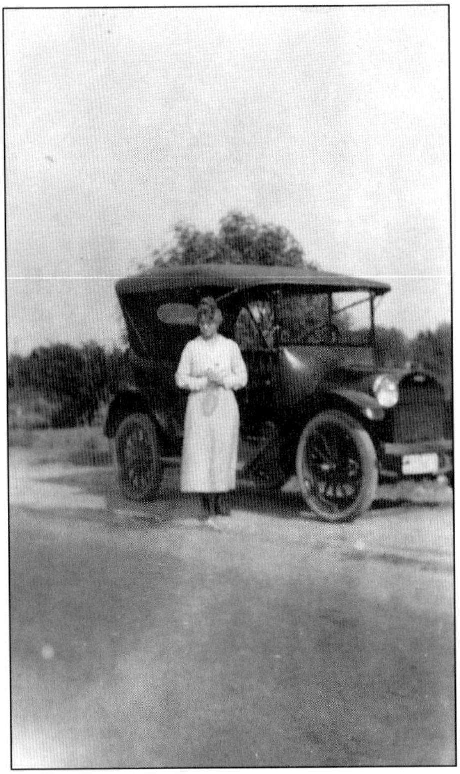

Model T Ford. Before Ferneena Austin (Daniels) married, she drove this Model T to El Segundo by way of Buena Park. She was friends with Walter Knott's mother and would stop by to enjoy homemade ice cream and pie. Continuing on her trek, she drove to the oil fields where brothers J. A. Daniels (her future husband) and Joe Daniels were working. (VAD.)

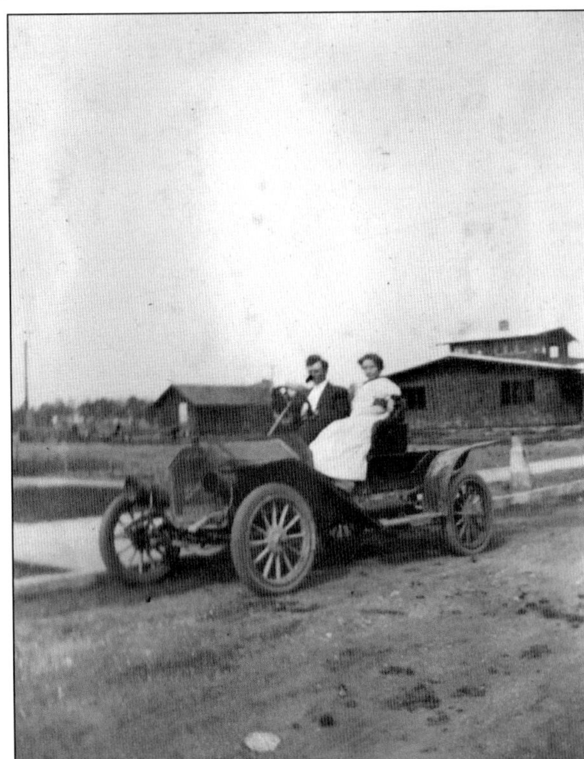

Riding in Buick, 1913. Alfred and Alice Brown are seen riding in their Buick. Before tires had changeable rims, any tire problems had to be changed on the wheel, with tire irons and all. That meant the driver always needed to carry along tire equipment and patching material. The Browns did not get a car with stick shift until 1928. (GB.)

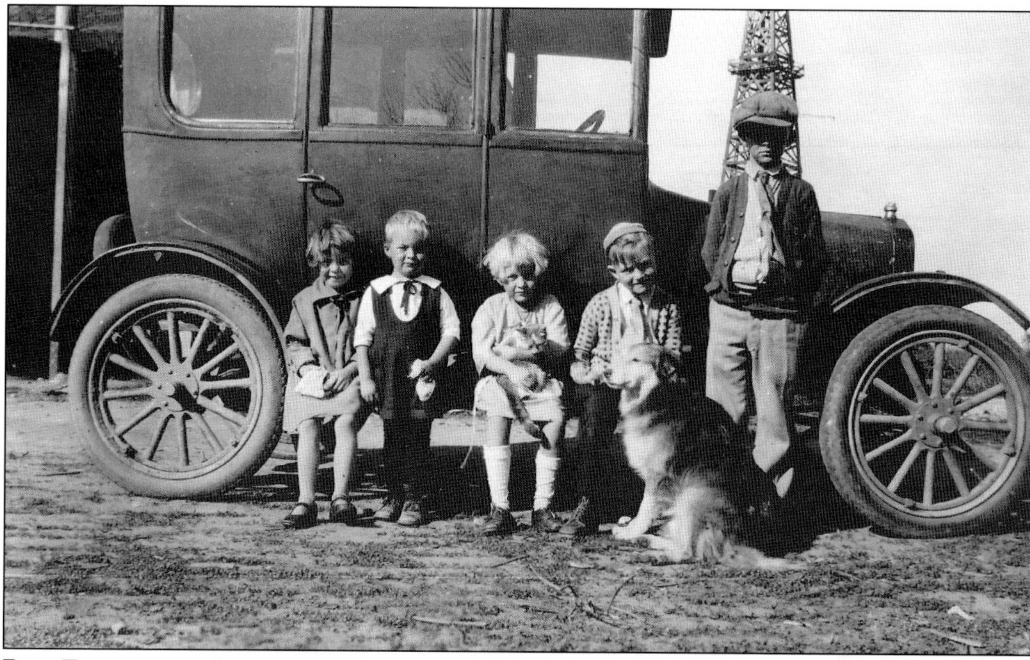

Pine Family with Car, 1926. These children of Roy and Ruth Pine pose with their dog and cat in front of their car. The children are, from left to right, Margaret, Walter, Lillian, Edward, and Frank. During the 1920s, Euclid Avenue was extended from the stage line (now Mission Boulevard), south to Pine Avenue, west between the Pine family ranches, and then north to connect with Central Avenue. (PF.)

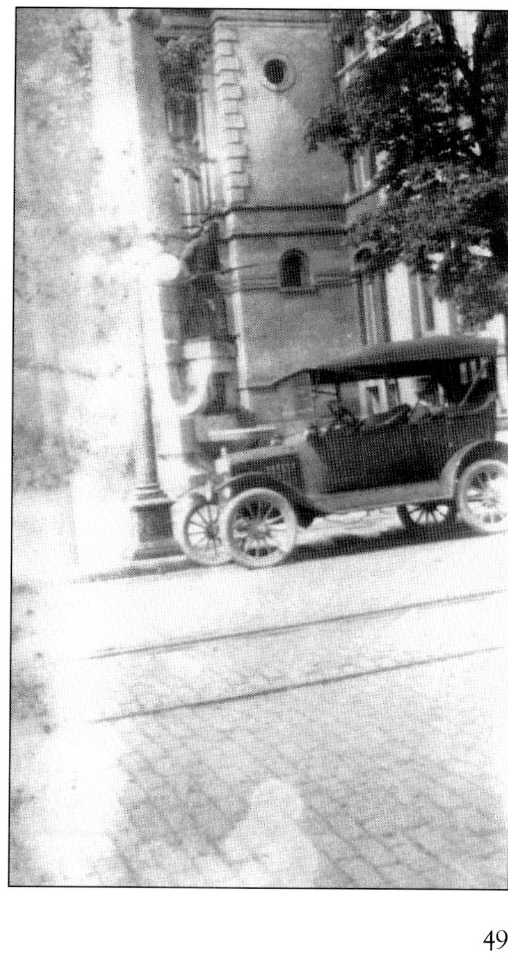

Ford Touring Car, c. 1930s. By the early 1930s, cars began to be seen regularly along the streets in Chino. This car probably belonged to Fred Walters, owner of the Feed and Fuel in downtown Chino. The building in the background was probably located in the beautiful neighboring city of Pomona. (FW.)

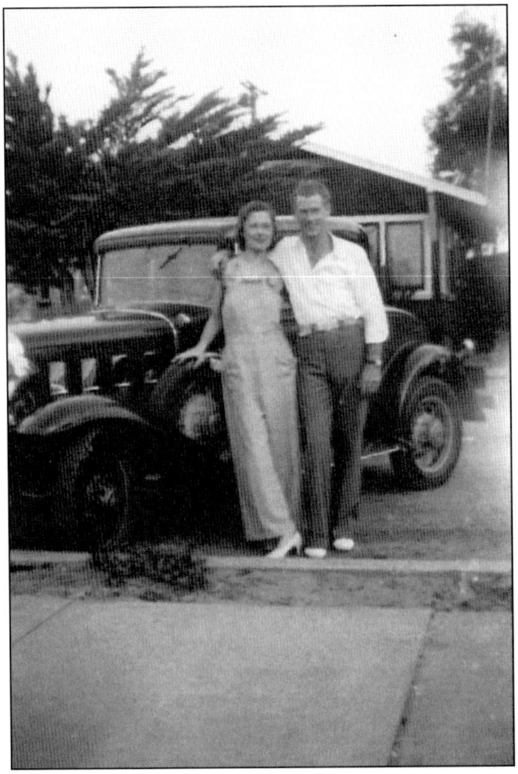

Evelyn Waters Bennett and George Bennett. Traffic had become such an issue in Chino that five years before this 1933 photograph was taken the Automobile Club of California had put in 62 stop signs at intersections along Riverside Drive, Central Avenue, and Chino Avenue. It would be over 50 years before most of these stop signs were eventually replaced with traffic signals. (FW.)

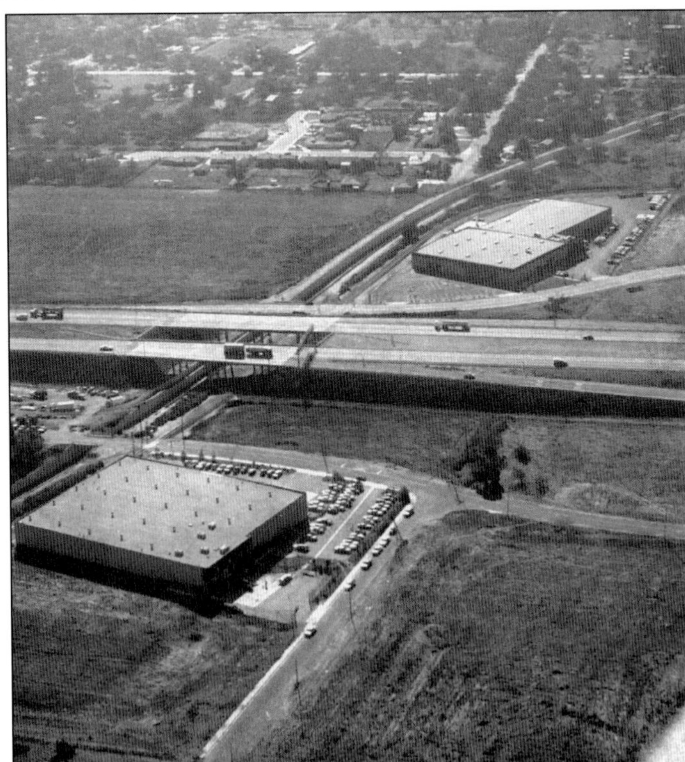

Aerial Shot of Freeway. Construction of freeways marked the next step of progress regarding transportation in Chino. According to local news reported in the *Chino Champion*, during the 1970 construction of the 60 Freeway, Central Avenue was widened, destroying the walnut trees, palm trees, citrus trees, and 70-year-old pepper trees that once lined the street. (CN.)

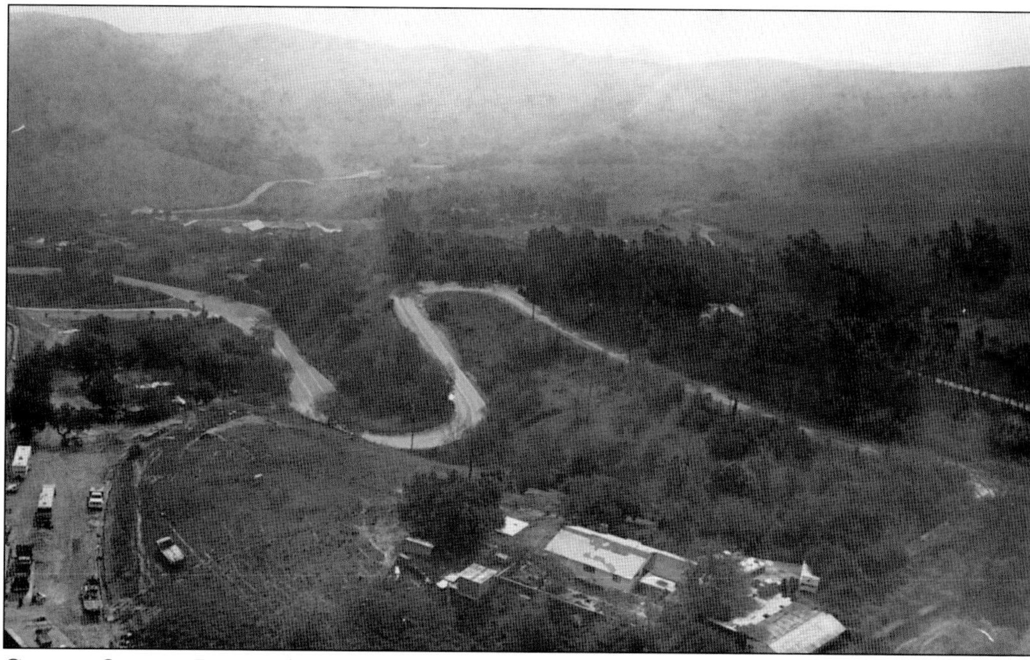

Carbon Canyon Road. The scenic drive along Carbon Canyon Road can be viewed in this aerial photograph. In 1927, as reported in the *Chino Champion*, the city council approved a petition to pave Ramona Avenue to connect with the street now known as Chino Hills Parkway. This was done to provide ease of access to Carbon Canyon. Finances for the project added up to $4,000. (CN.)

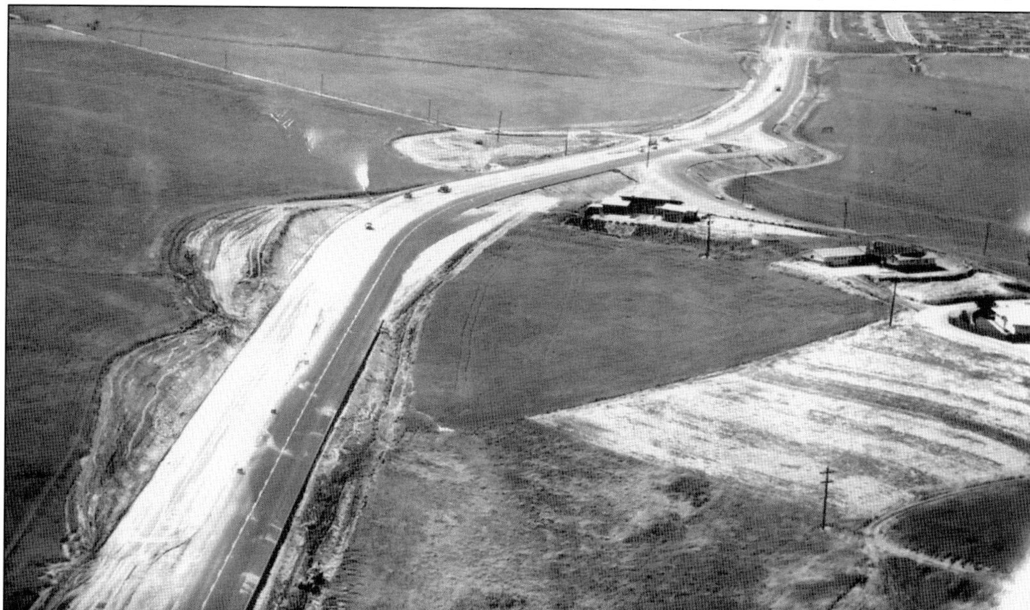

Construction of Highway 71. This 1957 photograph shows construction of Highway 71 along Garey Avenue, south of Riverside Drive. The following year, the first link of the freeway opened in May. The *Chino Champion* reports that Highway 71 was initially referred to as the Temescal Freeway, then the Corona Freeway, and finally the Chino Valley Freeway. Local residents simply call it the 71. (CN.)

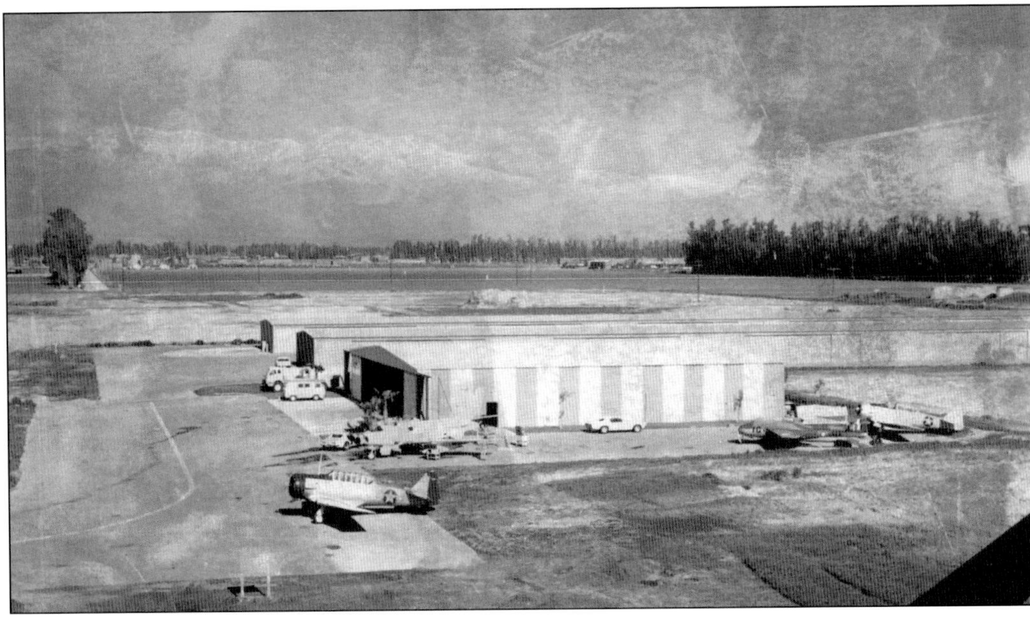

Chino Airport in Southern California. Air travel established Chino's presence even stronger on the map. In 1940, Cal Aero Field was built as a training facility for World War II pilots. Now known as Chino Airport, it celebrated its 70th birthday in September 2010. Located on more than 1,000 acres of land, the airport currently boasts three runways that serve private, business, and corporate needs. Within its complex, it houses over 600 based aircraft, 100 businesses, 2 aircraft museums, and Flo's Café, which is a perennial favorite with locals and pilots alike. The above photograph taken on December 20, 1973, shows hangars against the backdrop of snowcapped mountains. The aerial photograph shown below was taken of Chino Airport in 1980. (Both, CN.)

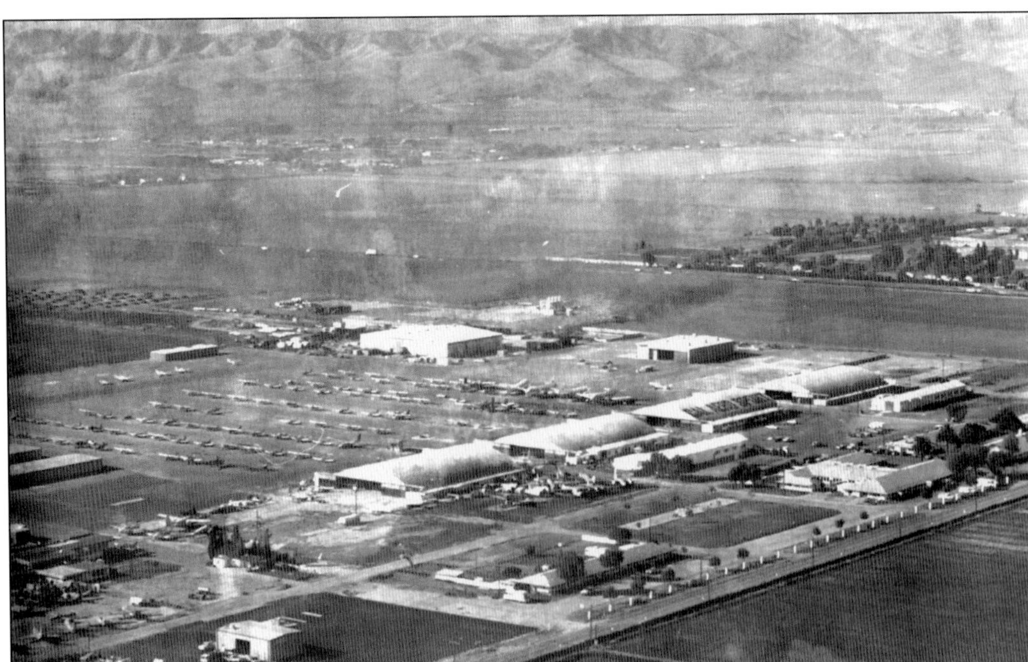

Five

Serving the Needs

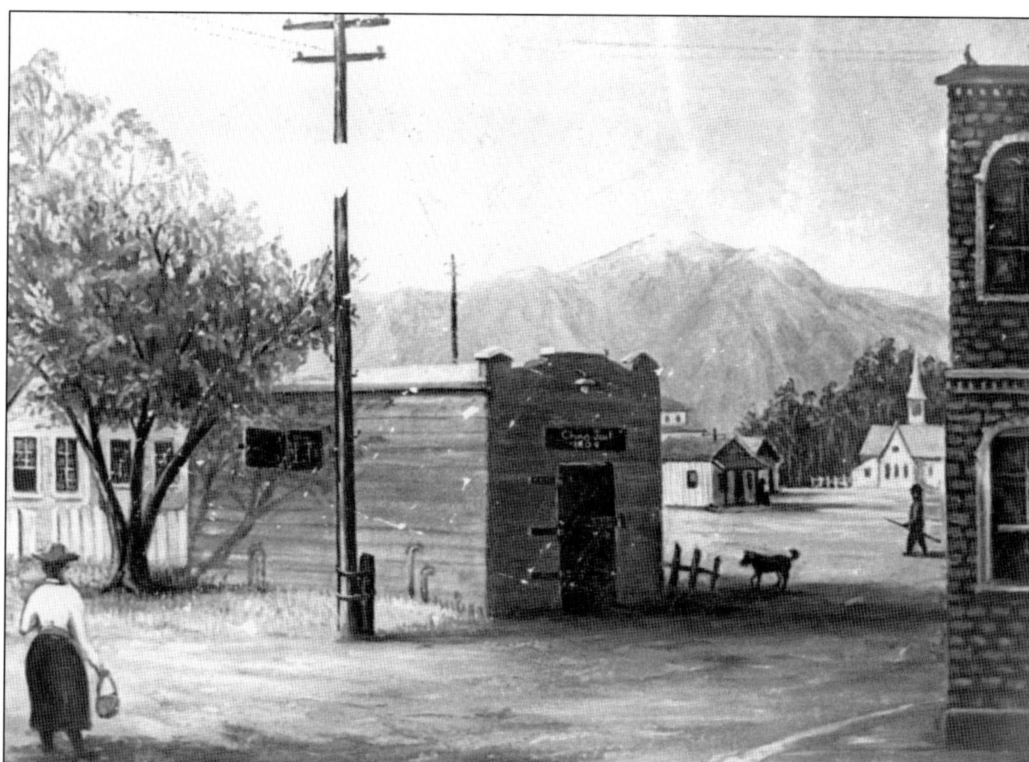

The Old Jail. The Chino jail is depicted in this painting from around 1909. The size of the structure and its somewhat dilapidated appearance on the unpaved streets of early-20th-century Chino betoken a quieter era. The relative security of the area may have been an added incentive for building the California Institution for Men in 1938. The jail is currently used as storage on the site of the Community Building. (CN.)

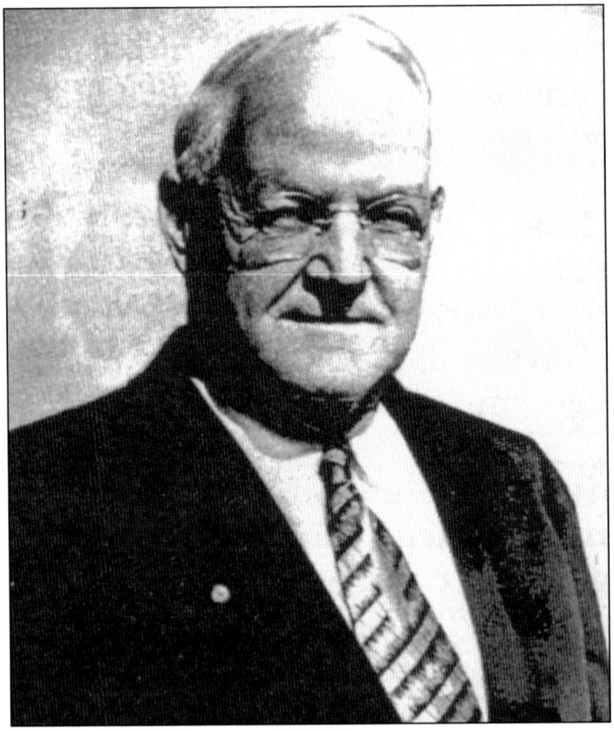

Kenyon J. Scudder (1890–1977). From 1941 to 1956, Kenyon Scudder was the first superintendent of the California Institution for Men (CIM) at Chino. Scudder espoused the philosophy that "prisoners were also people" and that they benefited more from vocational training than from punishment in their rehabilitation programs. An inmate machine shop and cannery were among Scudder's many innovations. (CIM.)

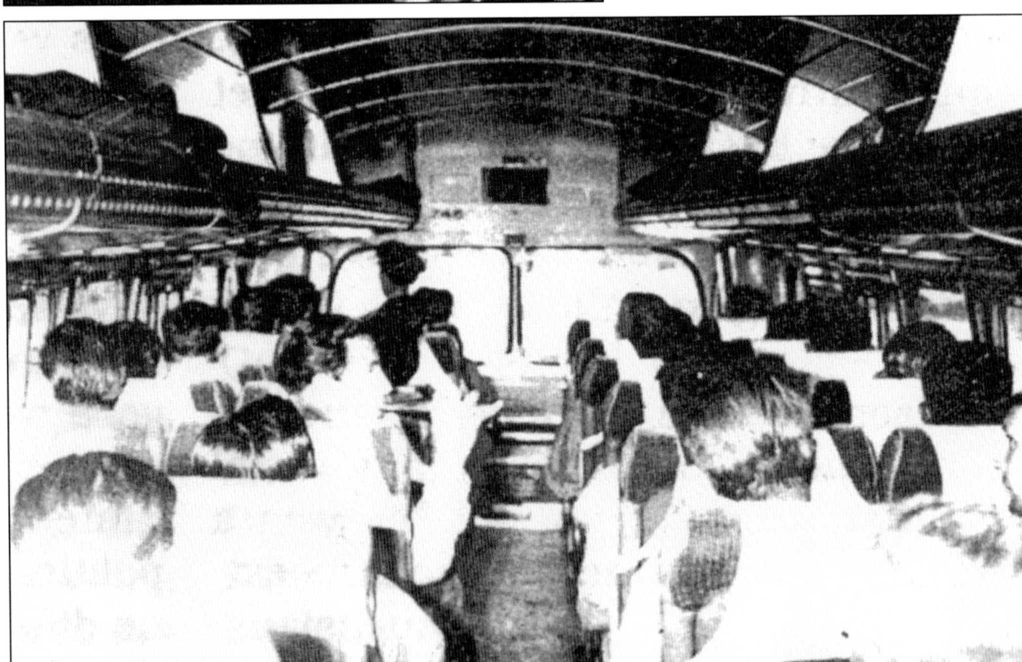

The First Bus Load of Inmates. Following a screening process, 34 prisoners of differing racial backgrounds were transported from San Quentin to the California Institution for Men. Kenyon Scudder and his associate Robert Wood accompanied the men on their journey, which took place on July 10, 1941. Box lunches, sodas, and cigarettes were provided for the inmates in accordance with Scudder's novel correctional techniques. (CIM.)

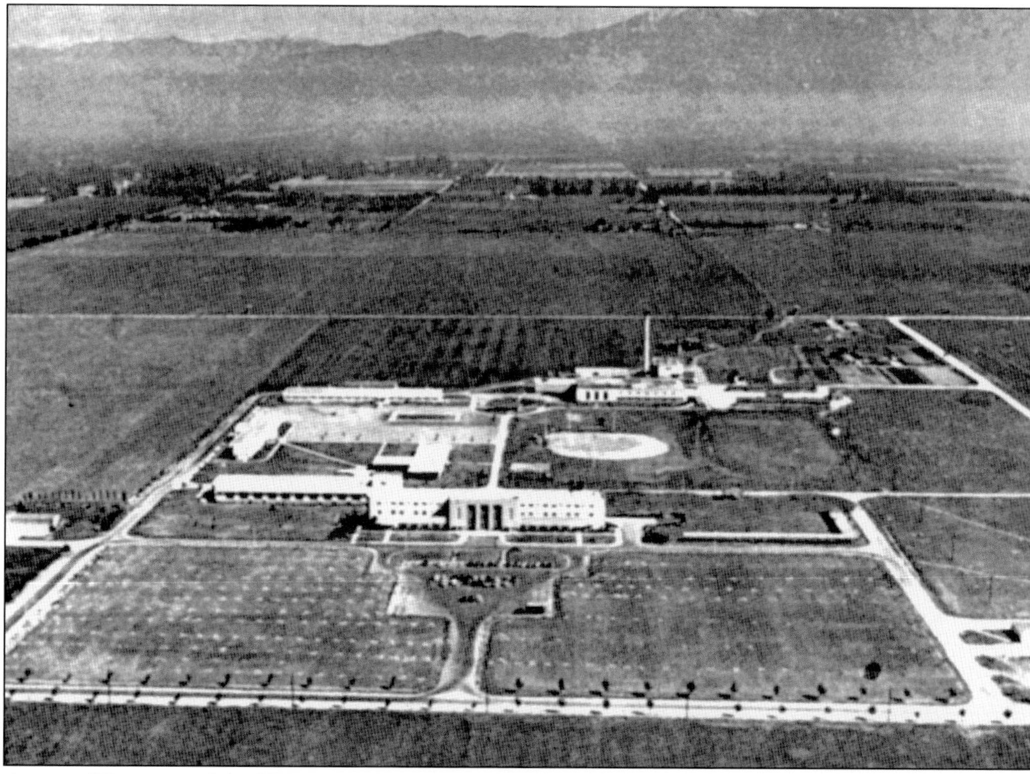

Aerial View, c. 1941. Taken shortly after it opened, this is one of the earliest aerial shots of the California Institution for Men. Shown to the left of the photograph are the 285-cell West and South Dorms. Lacking from the view are such later structures as the single-story dwellings, educational classrooms, the furniture-building facility, the firehouse, and the gym. (CIM.)

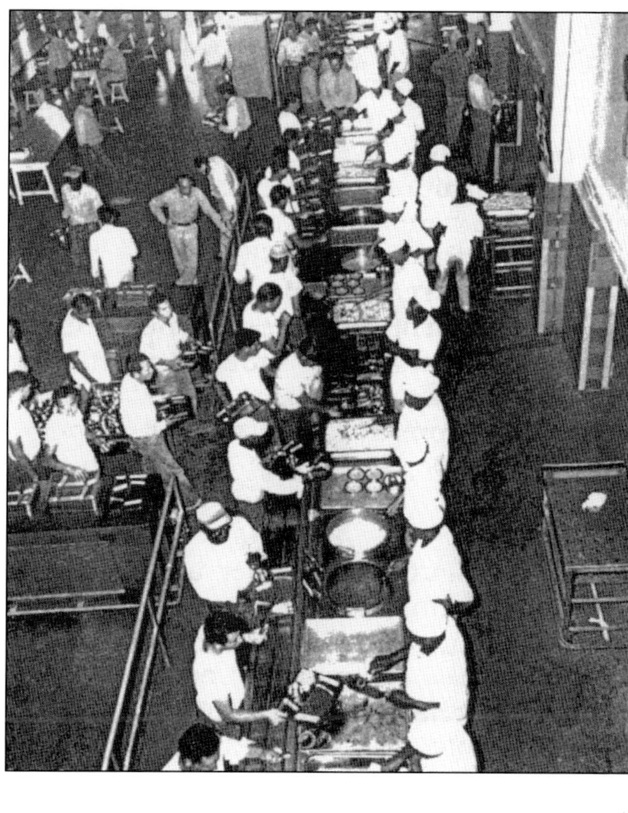

Cafeteria-Style Dining. Although not the first to offer cafeteria-style dining for the inmates (San Quentin and Folsom actually started the practice), the California Institution for Men refined the process. It offered fresh items grown locally on its ranch and farm and improved the sanitary conditions surrounding the preparation and serving of the meals. (CIM.)

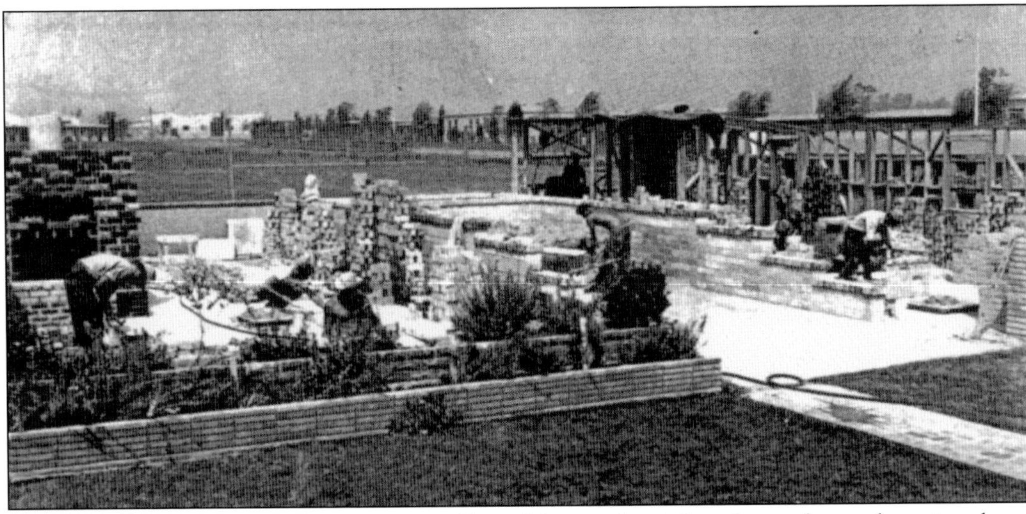

Vocational Education Department. Supt. Kenyon Scudder planned an educational and training program for inmates prior to the opening of the California Institution for Men and budgeted $150,000 for building a vocational shop. When World War II began, additional federal funding provided inmates with training in welding, tool and die, piping, and machinery to aid the war effort. This photograph shows the department under expansion to include landscaping and masonry. (CIM.)

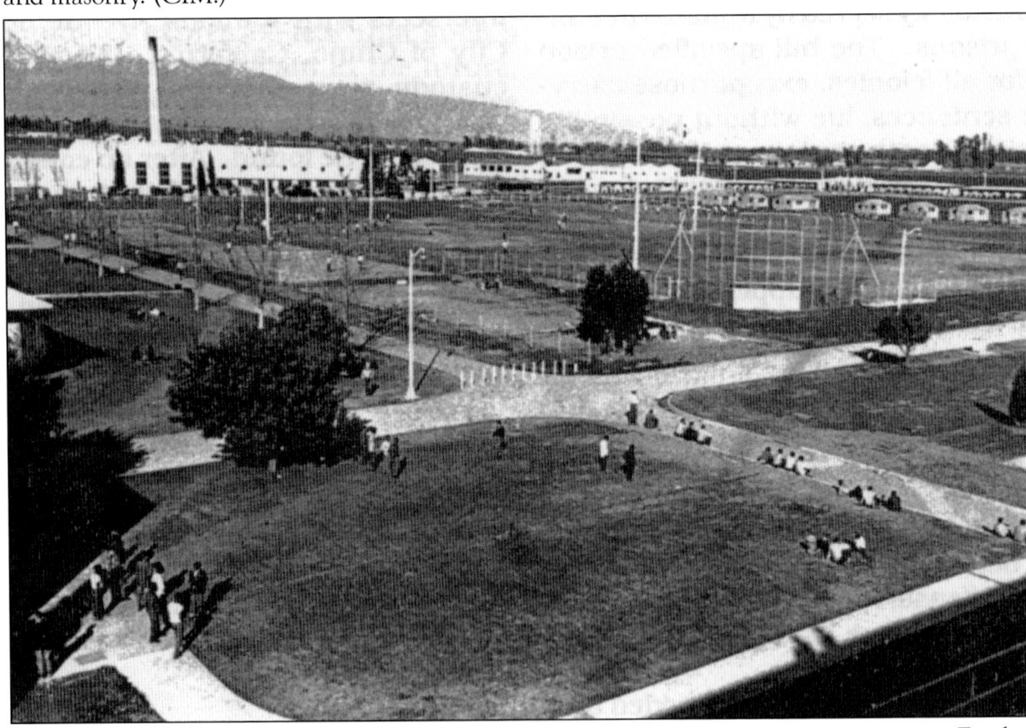

Northeastern View of the Yard. The California Institution for Men's Minimum Facility offers minimum custody housing for general population inmates. It also provides educational and vocational training programs, housing for older or infirm prisoners (minimum 45 years of age), and acts as a transfer point for Northern Californian inmates who are part of the reentry program, awaiting pickup by Parole Services. (CIM.)

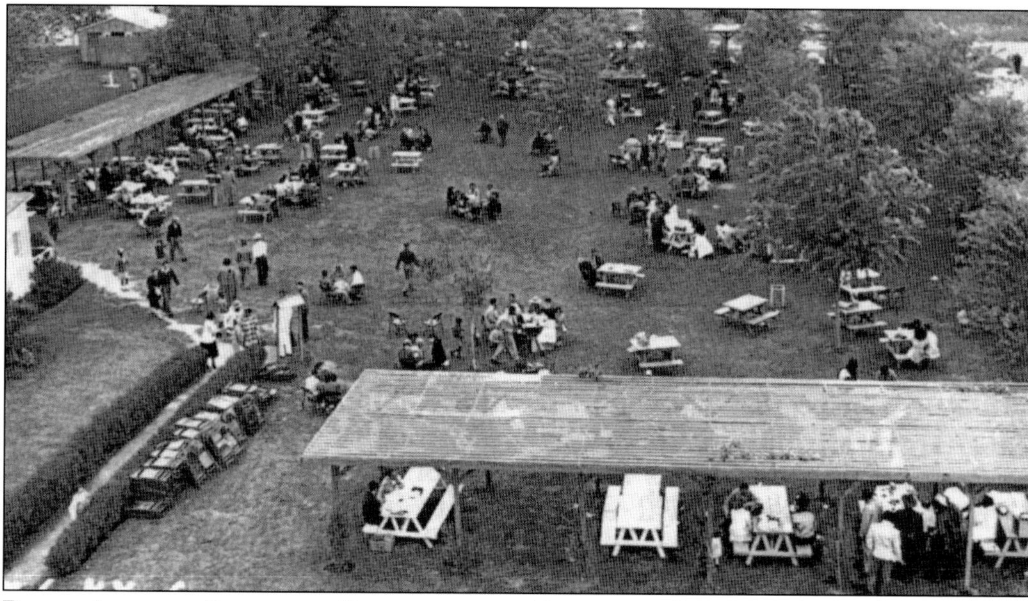

Picnic Area for Successful Rehabilitation. Pursuant to Supt. Kenyon Scudder's visionary concepts, the Chino Institution for Men pioneered visiting procedures, which were radically different from the "no contact" rules practiced by California's other penal institutions. Picnic tables scattered about the grass allowed inmates a relaxed and enjoyable time with family and friends in an informal atmosphere, which was a necessary building block to the success of a prisoner's final rehabilitation. (CIM.)

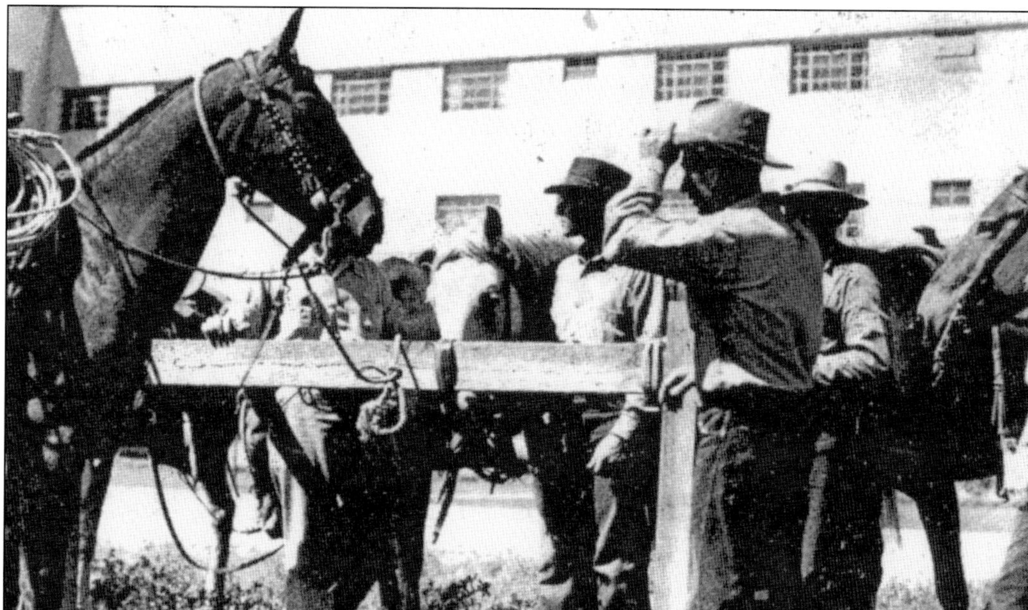

Hitching Post and Ranch Hands. A fully operational ranch was established at the Chino Institution for Men. The ranch that inmates worked on boasted a herd of 700 Hereford cattle, dairy sheds, a beef shed, a slaughterhouse, poultry coops, and sheep enclosures. In addition to local forage, 2,000 acres of pastureland, near Mount Palomar, were leased for grazing. This hitching post was located in front of the Administration Building. (CIM.)

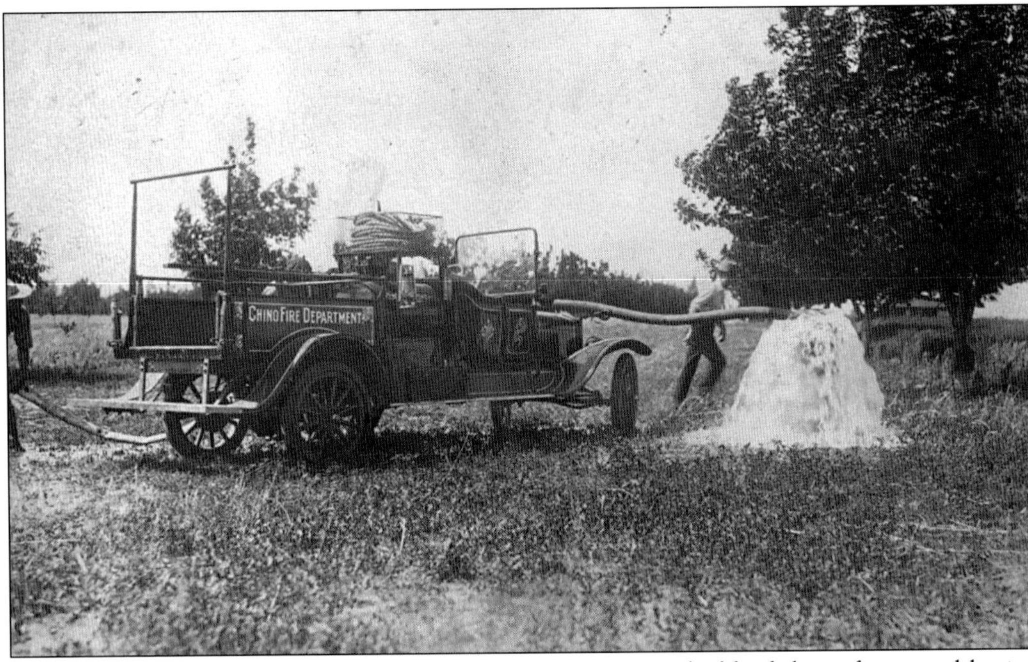

TESTING CHINO'S FIRST FIRE PUMPER. Attracting a large crowd of firefighters from neighboring communities, the City of Chino tested its new fire engine at a location currently known as Lake Los Serranos. Chino's first fire chief was L. F. Deyo. The city's first fire commissioners were Bill Tebo, Bill Houlihan, and J. C. Reher. Chino's first paid firefighter was Frank Payne. (CN.)

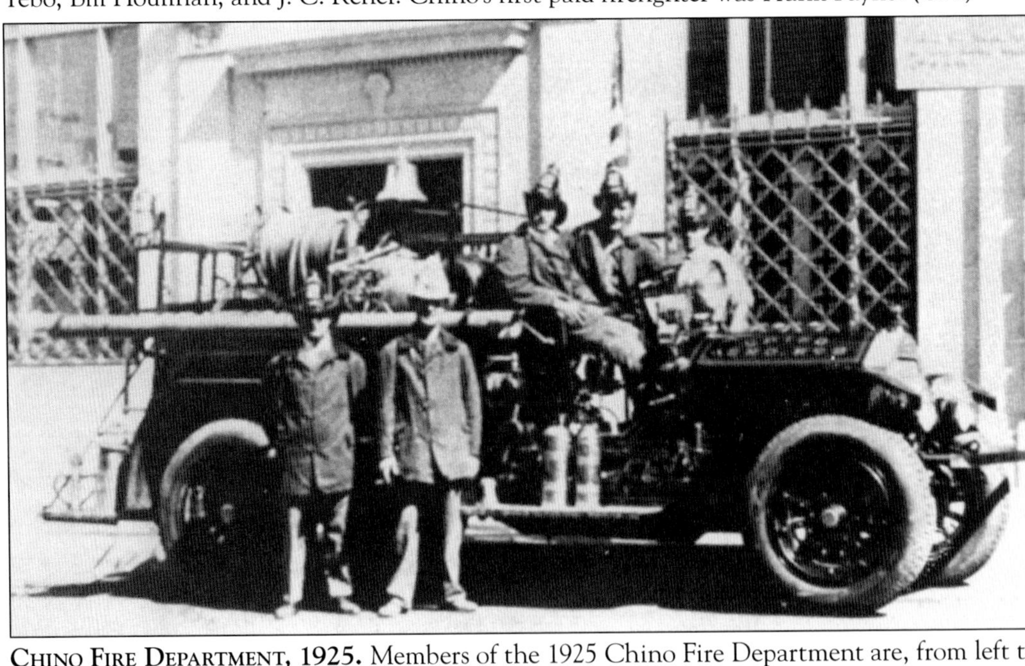

CHINO FIRE DEPARTMENT, 1925. Members of the 1925 Chino Fire Department are, from left to right, Les Cline, Curly Reynolds, Art Wagner, Jim Andrews, and R. B. Dickerson. These firefighters are proud to serve their community using this American LaFrance pumper, Chino's second fire engine or Engine No. 2. Fire chief Art Wagner is remembered as having brought Chino's firefighters from a rural volunteer brigade to a full-time professional fire department. (CN.)

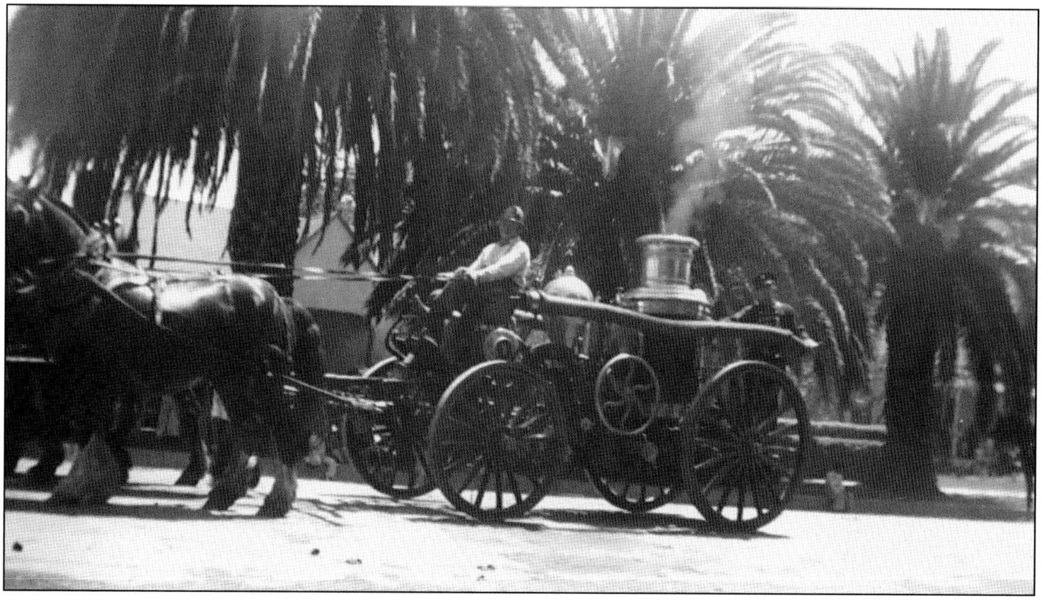

Horse-Drawn Fire Pumper. Before Chino's fire department formed, neighbors ran to the rescue when "Fire!" was cried. Chino founder Richard Gird had positioned several fire hydrants complete with hoses at key locations within the city. In 1895, Chino Fire Company No. 1 was formed with B. K. Galbreath as president. Plans were made to purchase a hook-and-ladder cart. (CN.)

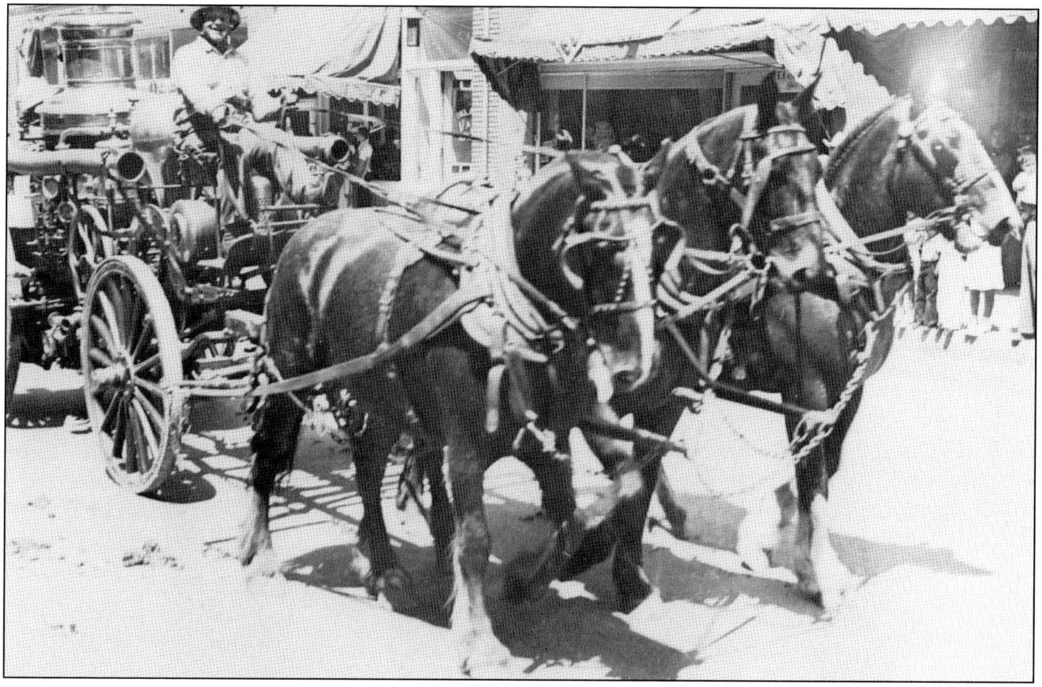

Fire Pumper in Parade, c. 1937. The fire department joins the parade festivities by driving this fire pumper along the parade route. Early members of the Volunteer Fire Department included Bill Milam, Arthur Ernst, Guss Milam, Charlie Krause, Bert Newman, Norman Goog, Dell Clark, Homer Hill, Elmer Jertberg, Harry Stark, Fred Ruiz, George Gunn, Claude Staples, Dewil Jones, Jesner Sholander, and Bill Houlihan. (CN.)

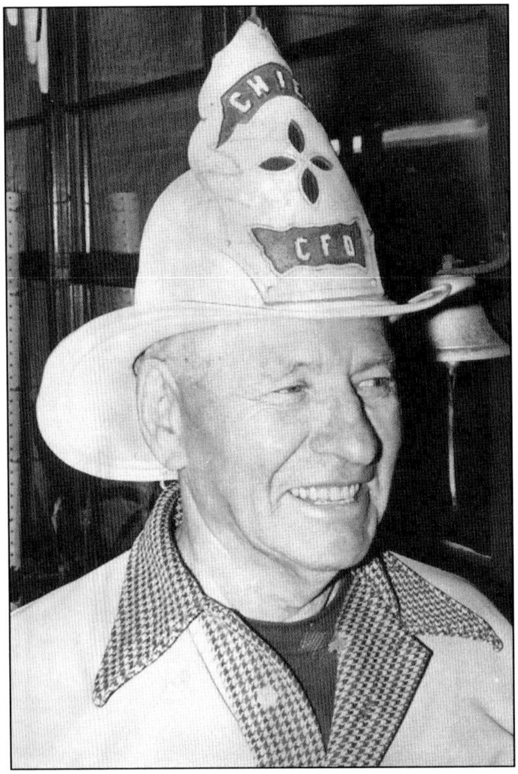

ART WAGNER, FIRE CHIEF. The "Father" of the Chino Fire Department, Art Wagner, served the city of Chino for 32 years. In the 1930s, his wife, Ruth Wagner, answered emergency phone calls in their home and sounded the alarm. Chief Wagner saw Chino's fire department grow from a truck and 24 volunteers to six units of fire equipment with nine full-time firefighters and 20 volunteers. He resigned in 1956. (CN.)

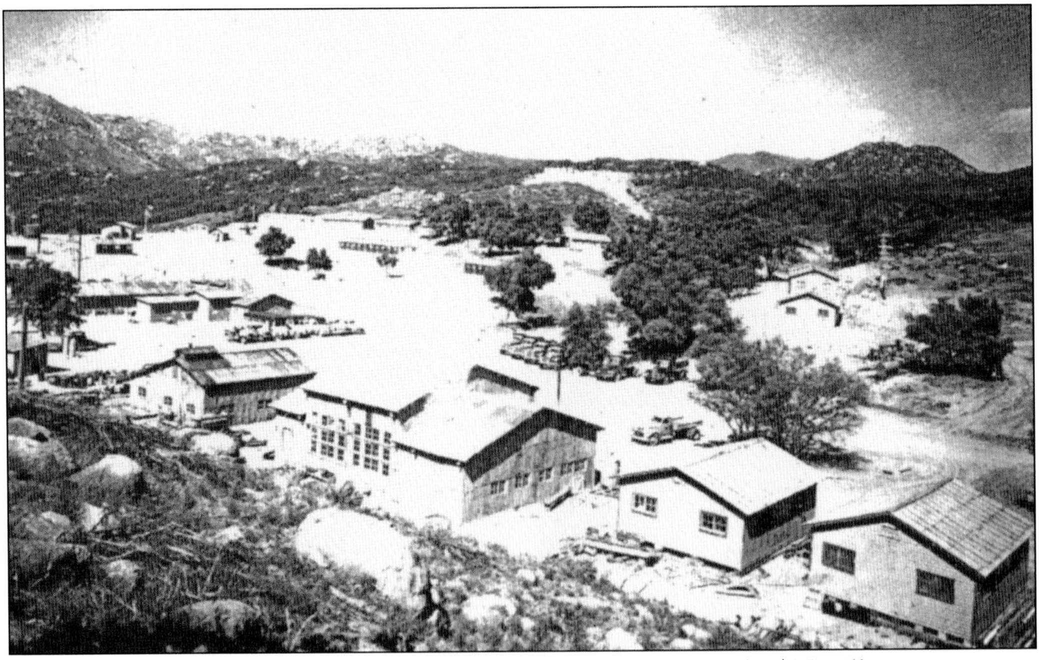

CAMP SIERRA WAY. When the state legislature failed to appropriate the $25 million necessary to create Prison Forestry Camps, the Board of Prison directors fronted construction out of its own pocket rather than miss an innovative opportunity. Called Camp Sierra Way, the California Institution for Men's first structures were completed in the San Bernardino Mountains in 1941. (CIM.)

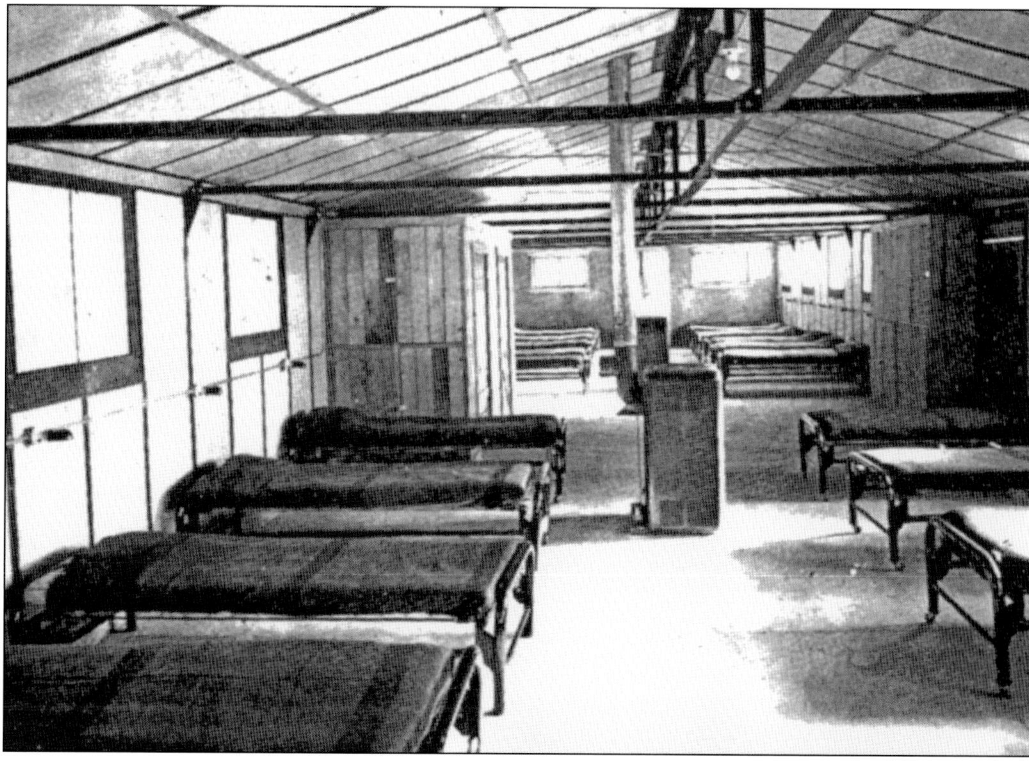

Forestry Camp Barracks. The Sierra Way camp housed 30 convicts who cleared firebreaks, repaired tools, and actually fought fires for the Forestry Service. Added funding from the state in 1943 and the use of barrack buildings donated by the federal government's defunct Civilian Conservation Corps eventually led to 16 Prison Forestry Camps scattered throughout Southern California. (CIM.)

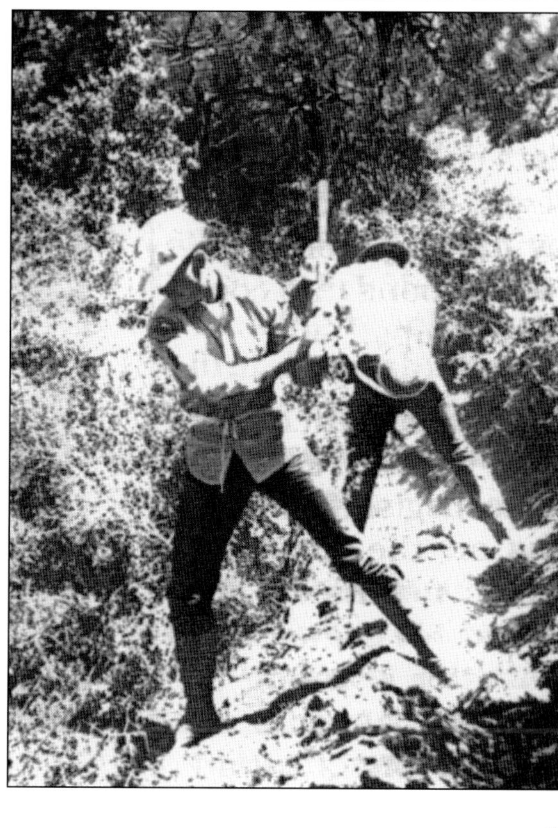

Cutting a Fire Trail. In this photograph, a Division of Forestry foreman is teaching inmates from the California Institution for Men the proper method to create a fire trail. Eventually, three conservation centers were built as staging areas for the existing Prison Forestry Camps: the California Conservation Center at Susanville (1963), the Southern Conservation Center at the California Institution for Men (1963), and the Sierra Conservation Center at Jamestown (1965). (CIM.)

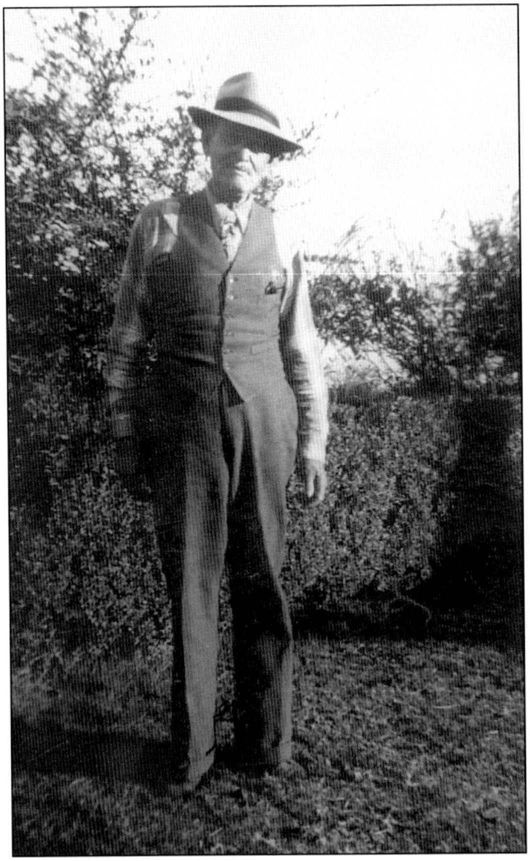

Chino's First Mayor. Charles Elmo (E. C.) Daniels served as Chino's first chairman of the board for 19 years. E. C. Daniels was a descendant of Chief Vann of the Cherokee Nation. His wife, Mary Fears Ansley Daniels, was active in the Thimble Club. She was a descendant of the Earl of Ansley, who received his title from William the Conqueror after the Battle of Hastings in 1066. (VAD.)

13157 Second Street. This is the birthplace of Ruben S. Ayala. In 1900, his grandfather Cesario Ayala, a railroad worker from Mexico, heard about Chino. Getting off the train in Ontario, he asked where Chino was located. Someone pointed southwest. As far as he could see, there were tumbleweeds drifting in the wind. He started walking. After several hours, he finally saw the trees and houses of Chino in the distance. (RSA.)

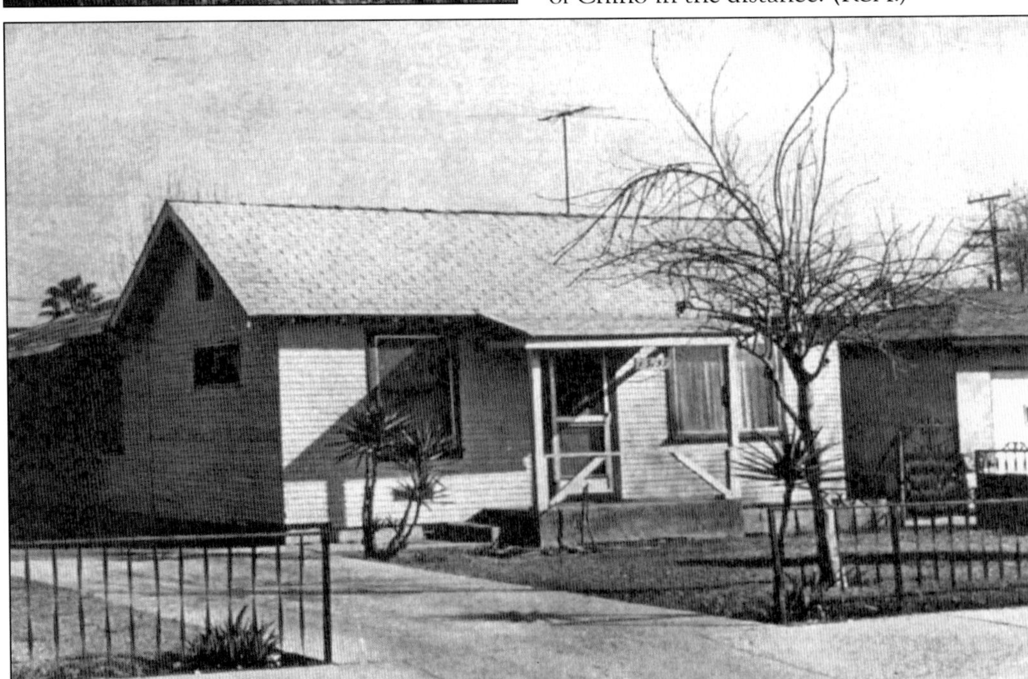

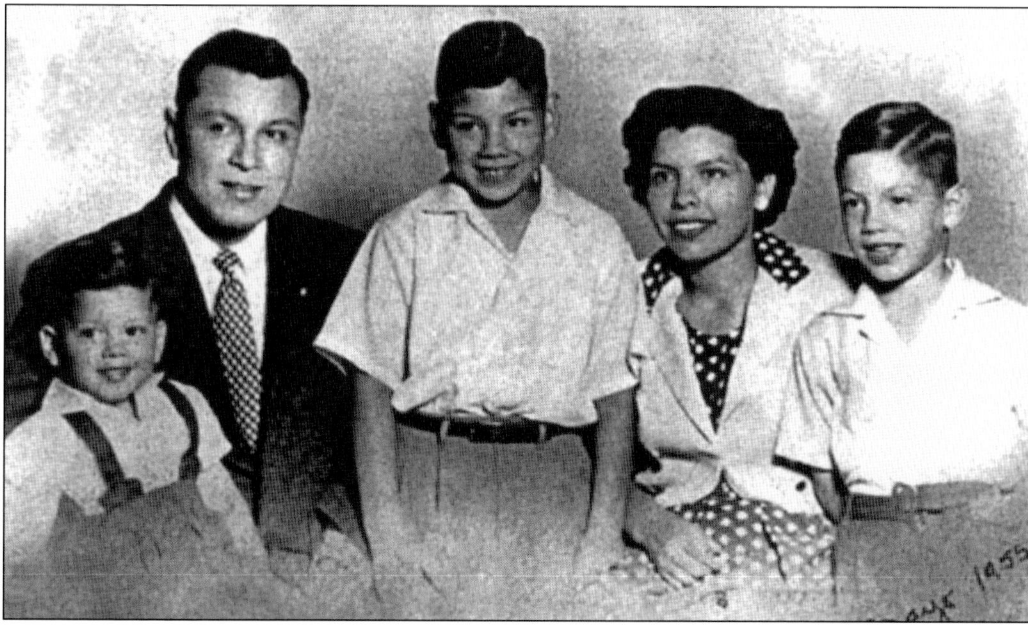

Chino's First Elected Mayor. A record 995 votes were cast in the landmark election of 1955, when Ruben S. Ayala was elected to the school board. This was the photograph that appeared in a newspaper campaign advertisement. Members of the Ayala family are, from left to right, Gary, Ruben, Bud, Irene, and Maurice. Ruben Ayala's political career continued to move forward. In 1963, he became Chino's first elected mayor. (RSA.)

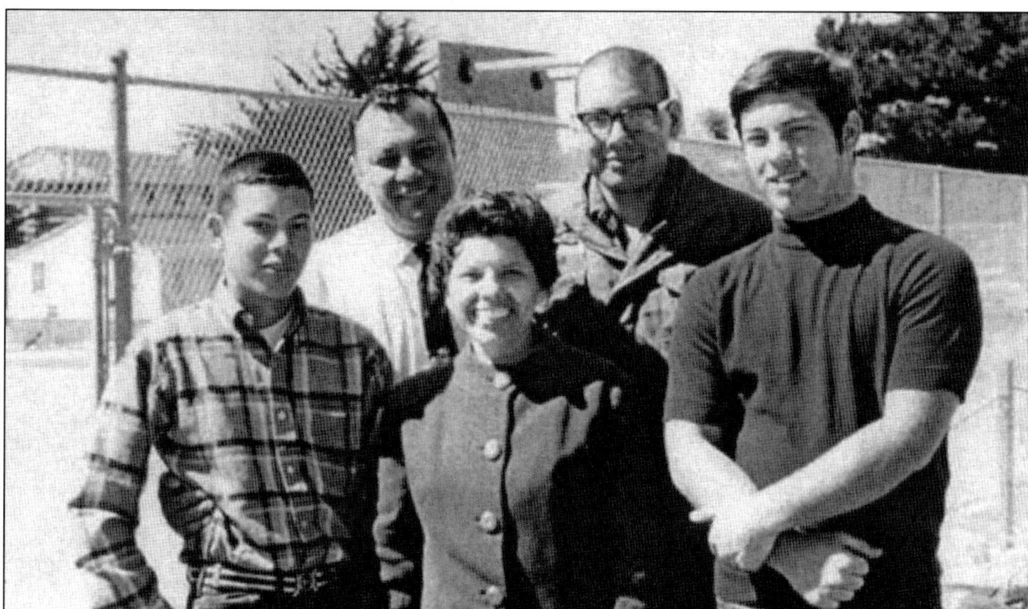

San Bernardino County Seat. Compelled with the conviction that the west end of San Bernardino County needed a voice, Ruben S. Ayala decided to run in the election for the county supervisor seat. In 1966, he became the new county supervisor. Here he is visiting his son Bud during basic training at Fort Ord. Members of his family are, from left to right, Gary, Ruben, Irene, Bud, and Maurice. (RSA.)

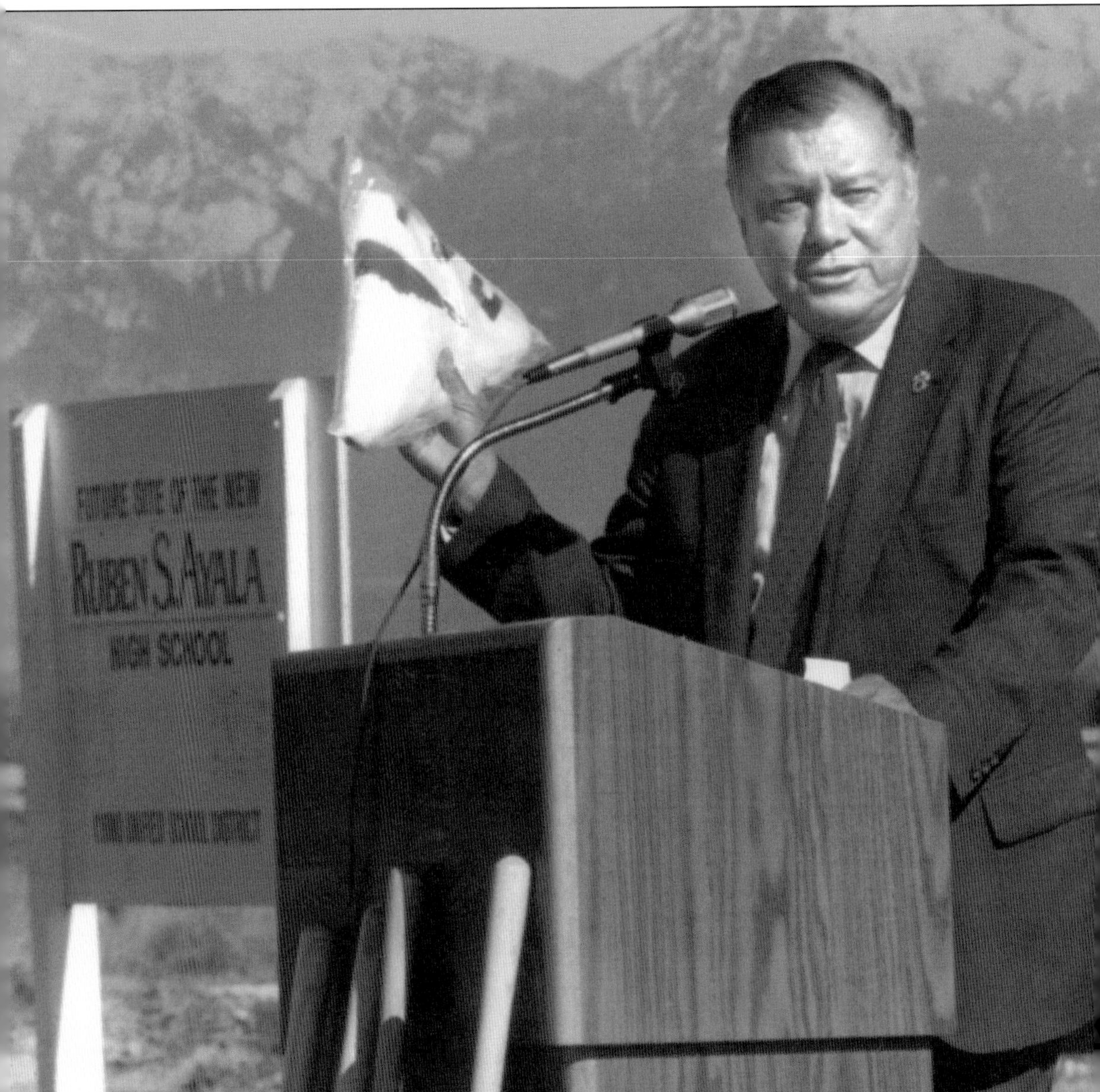

CALIFORNIA SENATOR RUBEN S. AYALA. Born in Chino, Ruben S. Ayala grew up in the Chino Barrio, a segregated area of town where families with Mexican heritage lived. He attended D Street School, the segregated elementary school where children from the barrio were assigned. Graduating from Chino High during the Depression, his small class consisted of less than five graduates. As a youth, he sorted through damaged walnuts behind the warehouse for the Chino Valley Walnut Growers and exchanged the healthy meat he found for bread at Reutgen's Bakery. When a teenager, he worked topping sugar beets with a machete in the American Beet Sugar Company's fields, which were on land where the California Institution for Men now stands. From these humble beginnings, Ruben S. Ayala set his sights and became a California senator, working at the height of political power in his state. Both, the communities of Chino and Chino Hills pay tribute to its native son with accolades that included naming Ruben S. Ayala High School and Ruben S. Ayala Park in his honor. (RSA.)

Six

EDUCATION, FAITH, AND NEWS

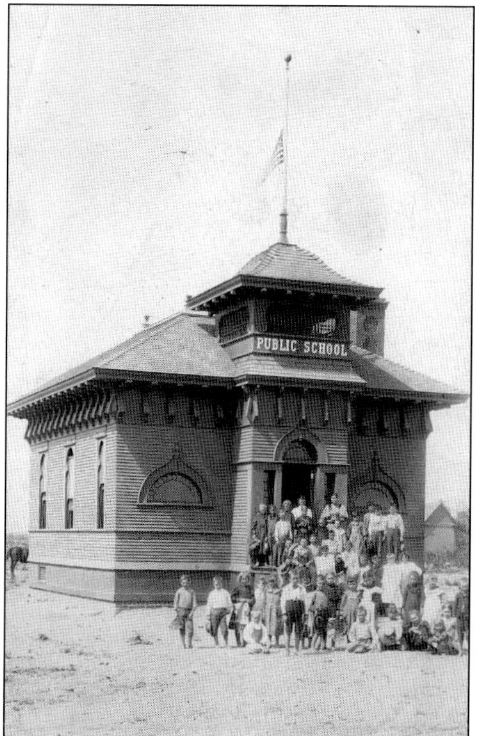

EASTSIDE SCHOOL IN CHINO, 1895. The Eastside School at Edison Avenue and San Antonio consisted of eight grades in two rooms. Joining the classmates were children from the Hispanic farming families. The local sugar beet factory employed these farm workers. Their children arrived at Eastside School each day in a horse and buggy. The school building is now home to a Baptist church. (GB.)

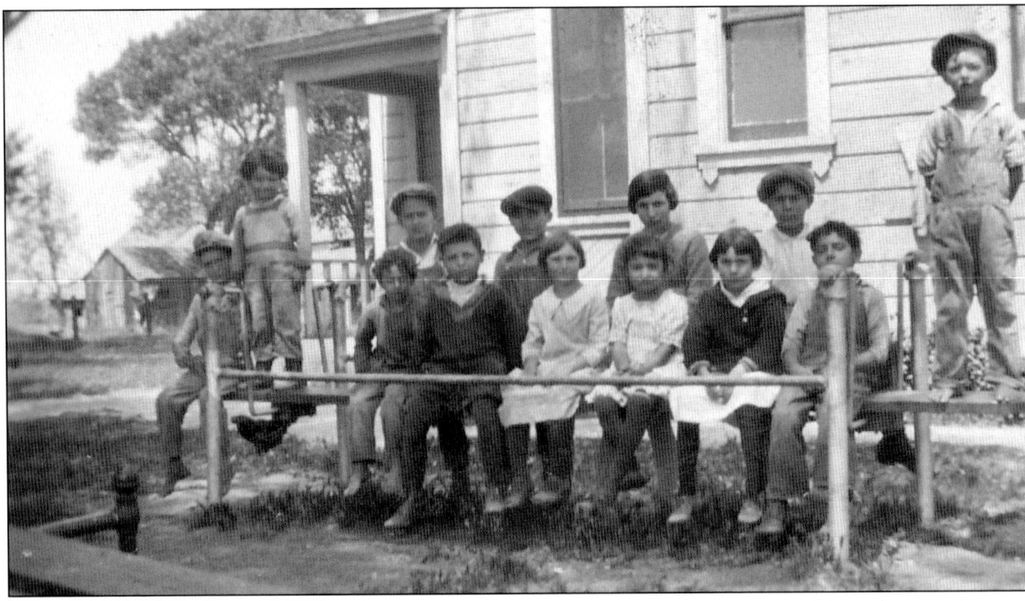

Chino Pioneer School, 1925. Standing with his classmates, at right, is Edward Pine. Born in 1919, Edward Pine married his wife, Barbara, in 1941. Prior to joining the navy, he worked for Lockheed during World War II as a draftsman supervisor. After the war, he was active in the 20-30 Club and the Rotary Club. During the 1960s, he was a member of the Chino School Board and also served as president. (PF.)

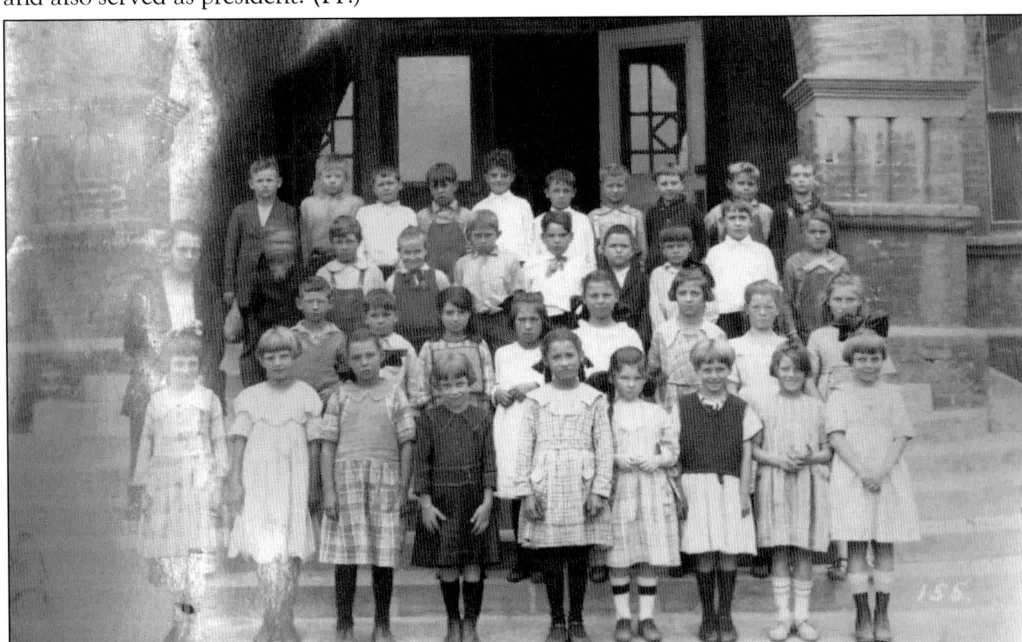

The Big Brick School. The *Chino Champion* reported that Chino schools were closed in 1912 for one week due to scarlet fever. In 1919, teachers were given a $10-to-$25-per-month raise, increasing their monthly salaries to $100. The Big Brick School was condemned after the Long Beach earthquake of 1933, when all brick buildings were condemned. The bricks were then used to construct the Community Building. (GB.)

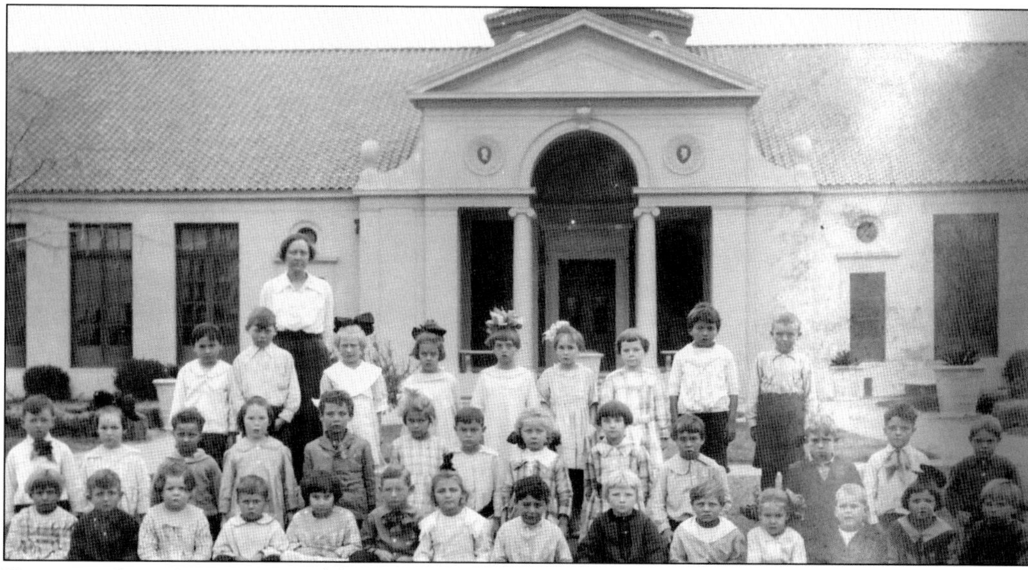

Richard Gird School. Gerald Brown and classmates stand in front of the Richard Gird School. In 1920, Chino School District abandoned the country schools and established a bus system. Jesner Sholander built their 20-passenger bus on a Rio truck chassis. There was a stepladder that the older boys pulled out at each bus stop. The children called it a "cheese" wagon. (GB.)

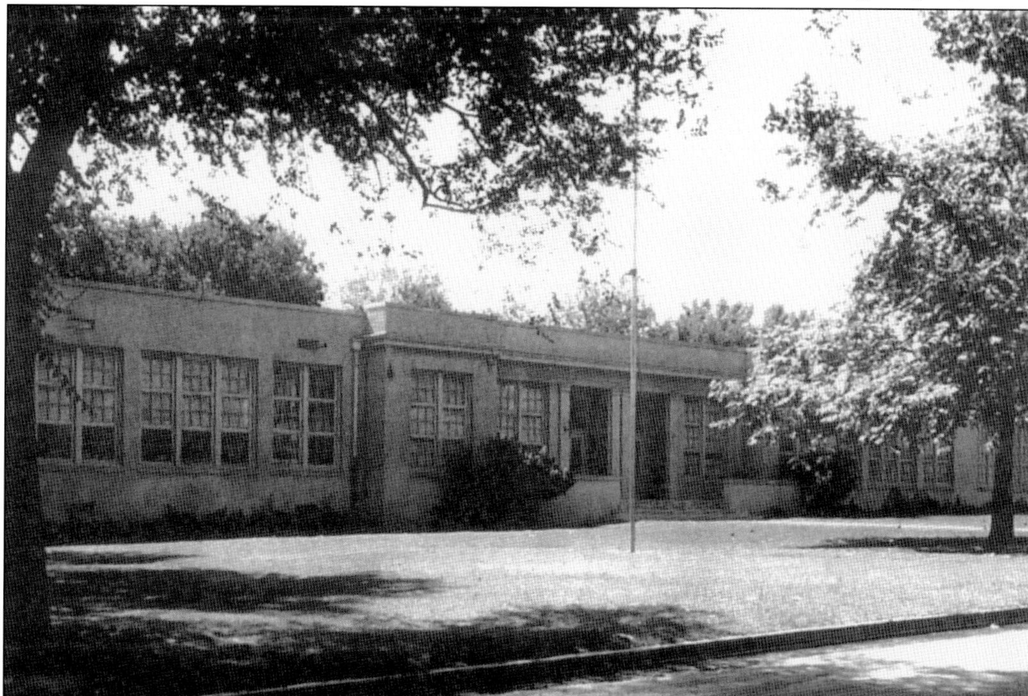

D Street School. This school once stood where Monte Vista Park is now located in Chino. Many families in the neighborhood were originally from Mexico, and their children attended this school. During the summer of 1934, the Chino Recreation Association enrolled 425 children and adults in a projected program that included a supervised playground at this school, as well as other recreational activities. (CN.)

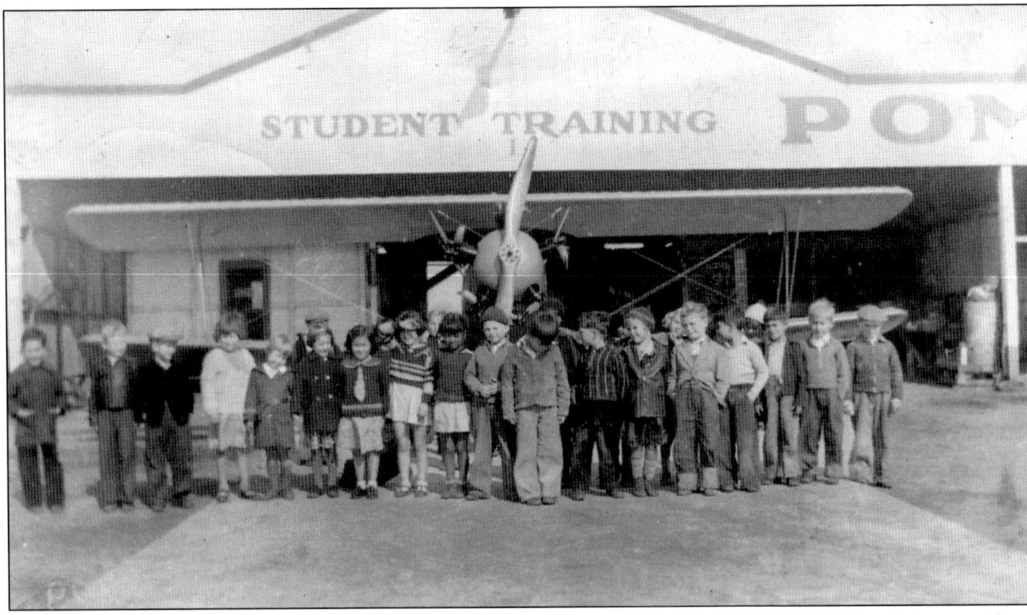

Gird Elementary School Field Trip, c. 1938. David George and his classmates at Gird Elementary School took a field trip to see the Pomona airport on Garey Avenue. Earlier, in 1935, the school district had decided to reopen a kindergarten program. They had dropped that grade level due to budget costs in 1932. (DG.)

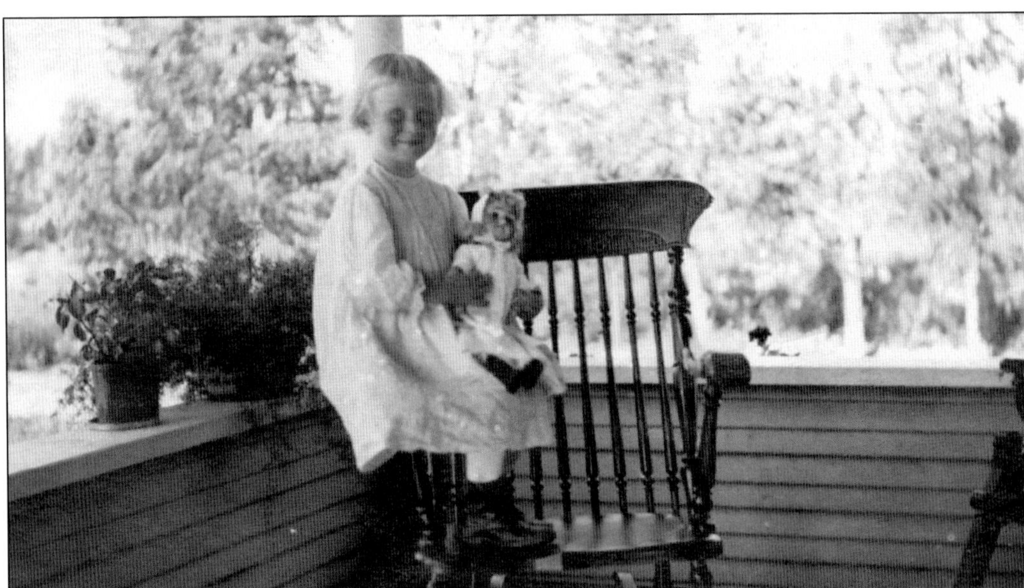

Margaret Perry Arnold. Margaret Perry Arnold grew up to be the head of the cafeteria at Chino Unified School District. She worked from about 1940 to 1970. Not only did the Chino School District provide quality education for children living within its boundaries, but also over the years, it has provided employment and livelihood for numerous Chino citizens. (FW.)

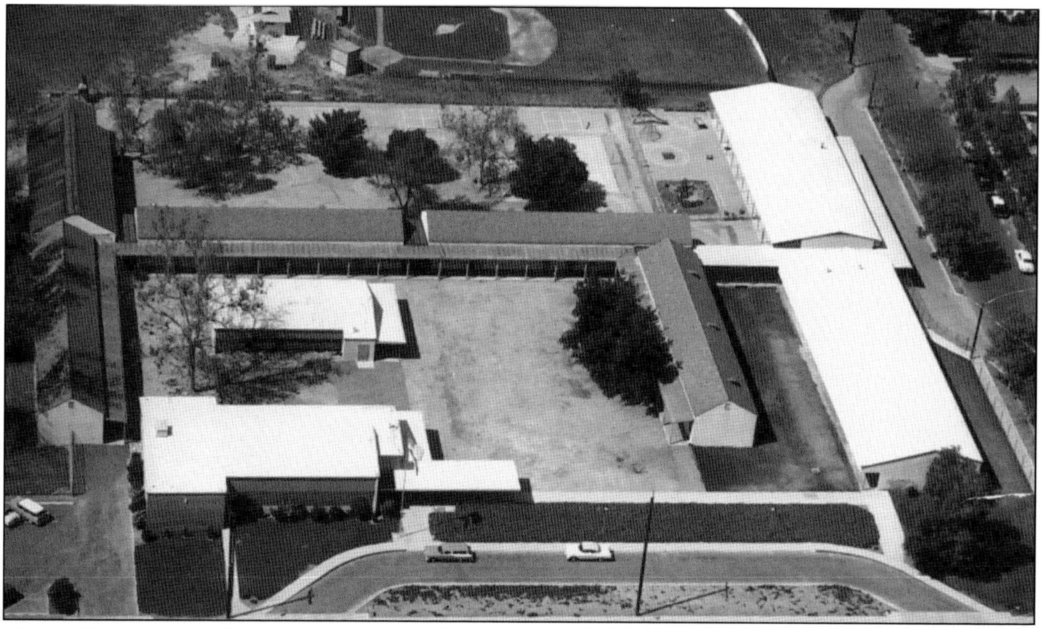

Chino Elementary Schools, c. 1956. The above aerial photograph was taken of the Gird Primary School. A number of schools have been named after the city's founder, Richard Gird. He and his wife, Nellie Gird, played an important role in establishing a system of education for students in Chino. Nellie Gird traveled back to Chino in 1914. She had an October 5, 1894, *Champion* article describing the souvenirs that were placed in a container when the cornerstone for the Chino Grammar School was built. Items included coins, students' names, class colors, a photograph of the Girds, and a jar of sugar from the Chino Valley Beet Sugar Company. Pictured below is the Newman Elementary School, named after the O. J. Newman family. (Both, CN.)

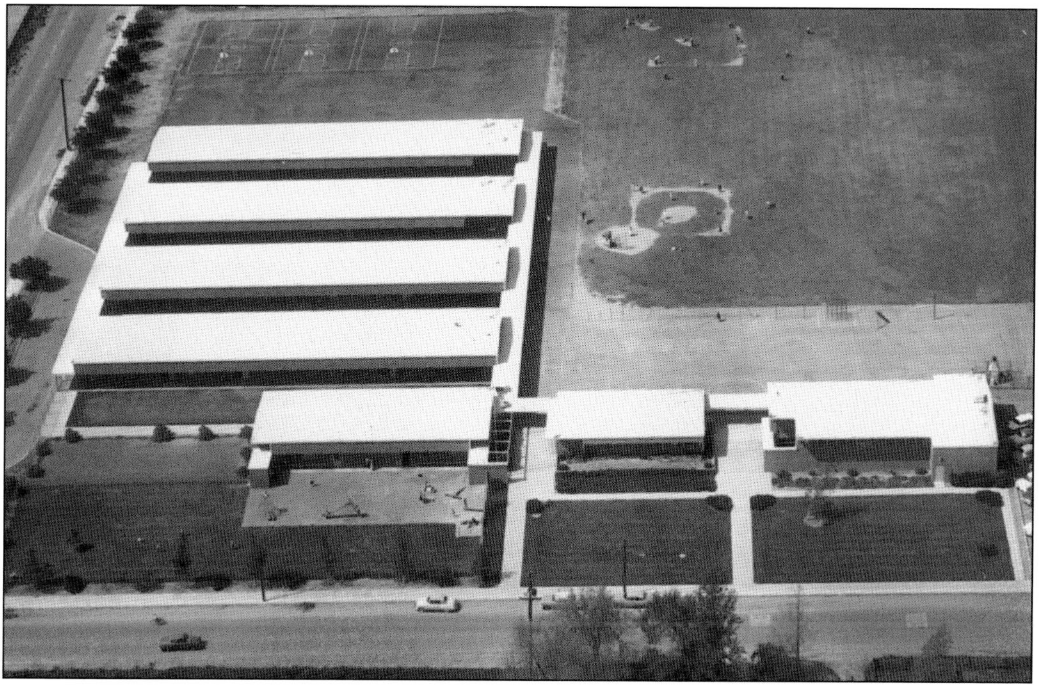

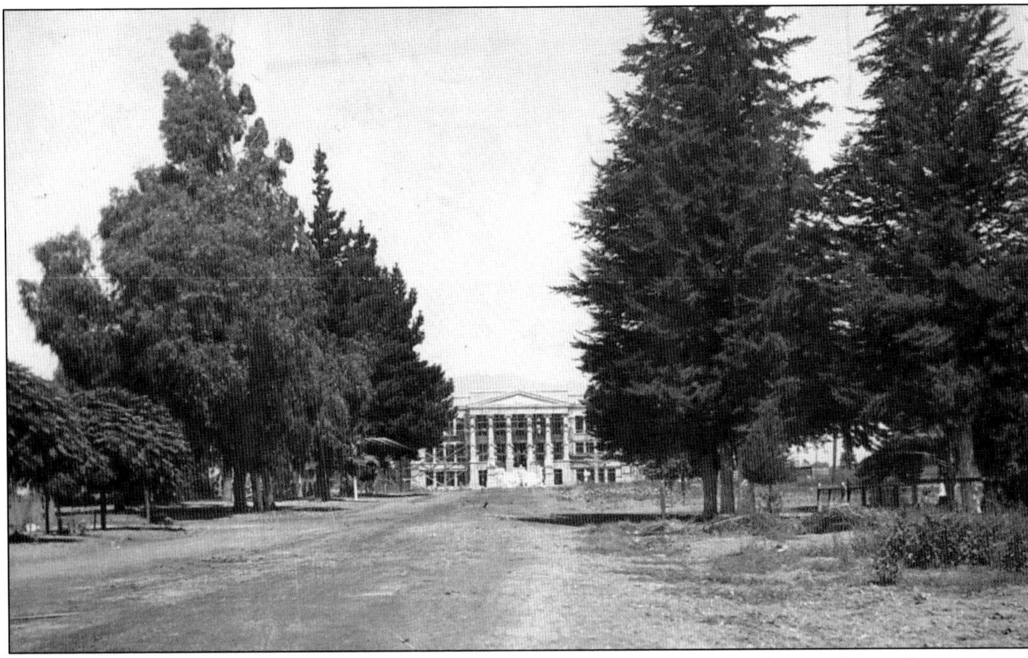

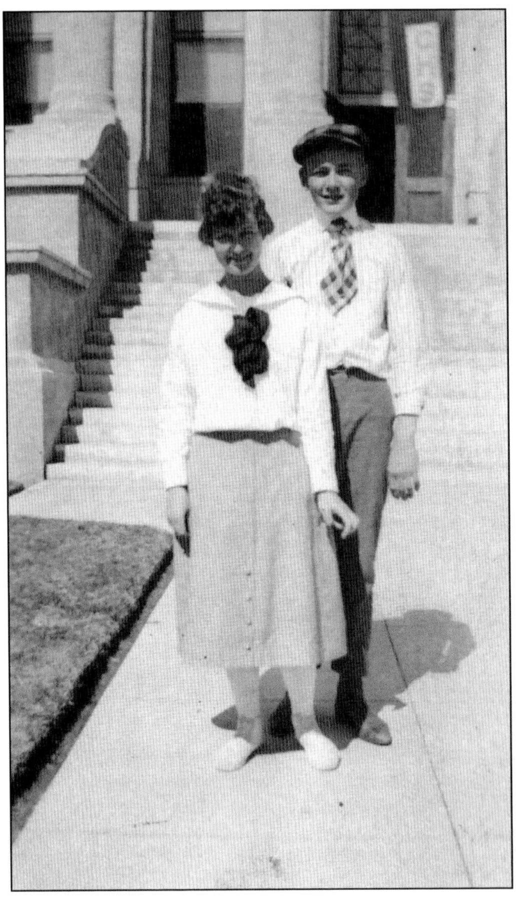

CONSTRUCTION OF CHINO HIGH SCHOOL, 1910. As seen in this photograph, construction was nearly finished on Chino's magnificent new high school building. Once the construction of the high school was complete, its auditorium became the cultural center of town. Prior to that, the opera house on Seventh and D Streets, which Richard and Nellie Gird also helped build, filled that need for the community. (CN.)

ELSIE KEARNS AND RUSSELL WALTERS, 1921. Standing in front of Chino High School, this photograph was taken before Elsie Kearns and Russell (Joe) Walters were married. The young couple were both probably juniors and were dating at the time. By 1928, Chino High School boasted a graduating class of 56 students. (FW.)

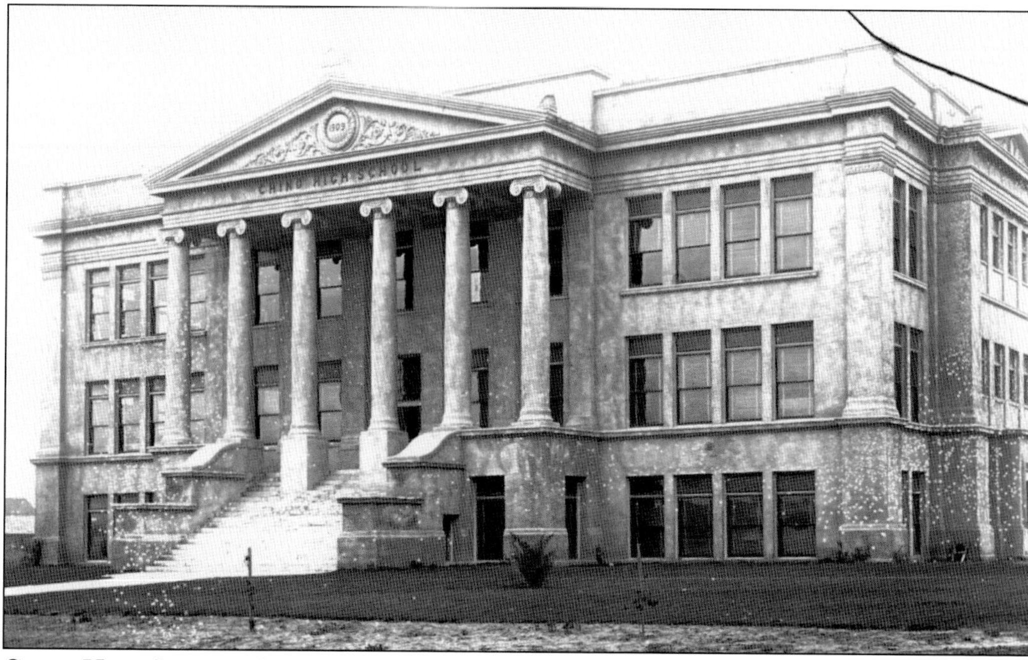

CHINO HIGH SCHOOL, GLASS NEGATIVE. The high school stands proudly as a symbol of progress where Chino's future leaders of the next generation could receive their education. According to the *Chino Champion*, its new auditorium, completed in 1923, cost $84,000 and housed the administration offices, library, cafeteria, two classrooms, dressing rooms, and a wardrobe room. (CN.)

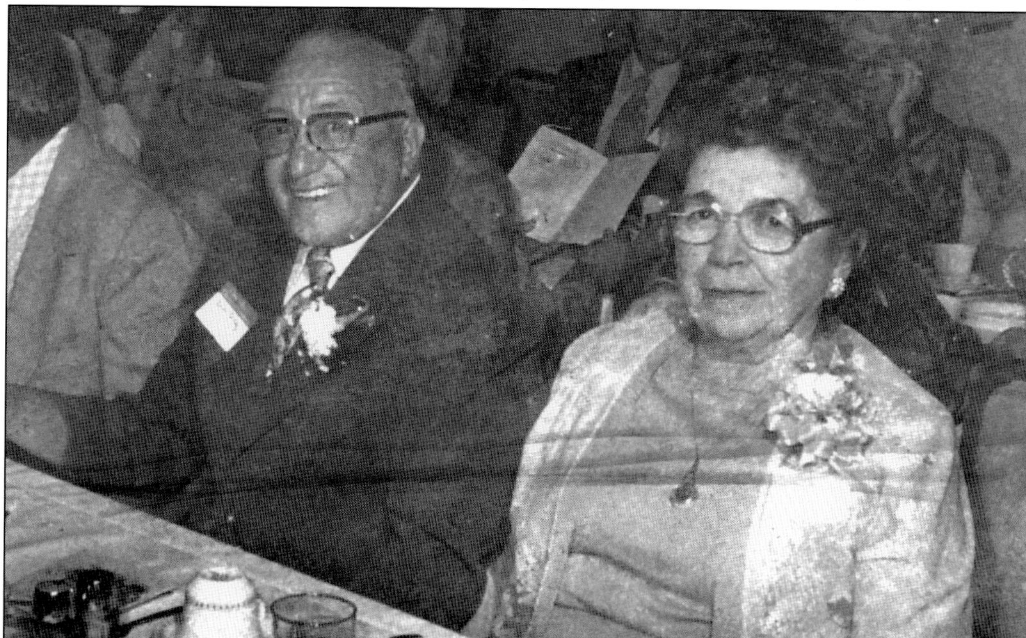

ZEKE AND ALICIA CORTEZ. Zeke Cortez was mayor of Chino in the 1960s. His wife, Alicia Cortez, was a teacher who was also involved with many programs aiding Mexican Americans in the community. In honor of her work in education, as well as her commitment to serve as treasurer for numerous Chino organizations, Alicia Cortez Elementary School was named after her. (CN.)

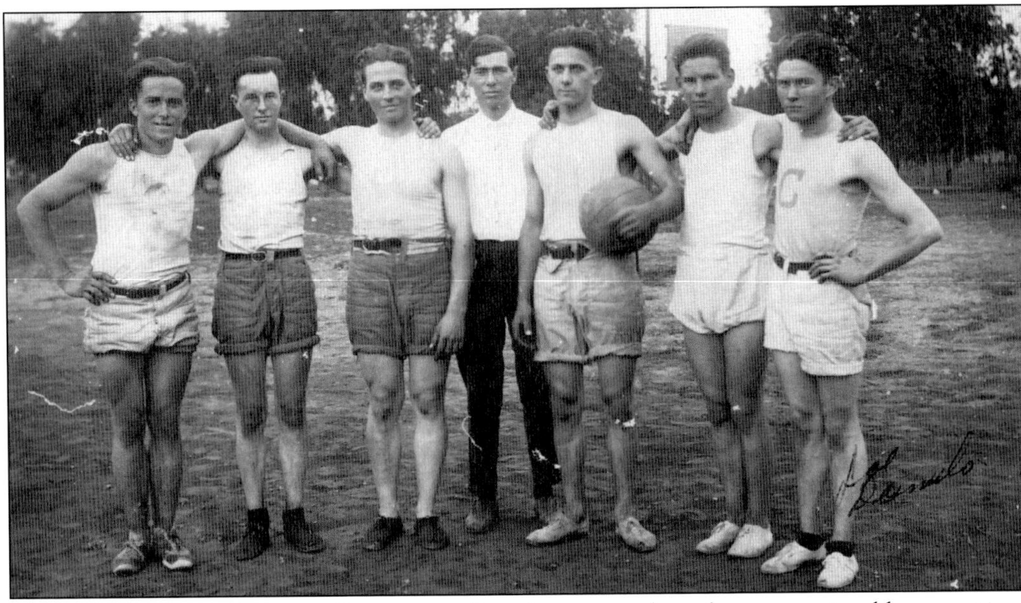

Sports, a Favorite Pastime. Since its earliest days, sports have been an enjoyable recreational activity for many families living in Chino. Above, teammates pose for this 1915 photograph. The members of Chino High's basketball team include, from left to right, Clarence Butterfield, Sears Hazen, Howard Coke, Coach Thomas, Charles York (holding the basketball), Charles Gemmil, and Joseph (Joe) Daniels. Seen below in the 1927 photograph is an early baseball team, the Chino All Stars. Members included J. Martines, Octavio ?, Elins Stavio, Tex Holton, Al Reina, Robert Frady, Louie Lobo, and J. C. Hernandez. In 1953, the city was granted a Little League franchise, so Chino youth could play organized ball. (Above, VAD; below, CN.)

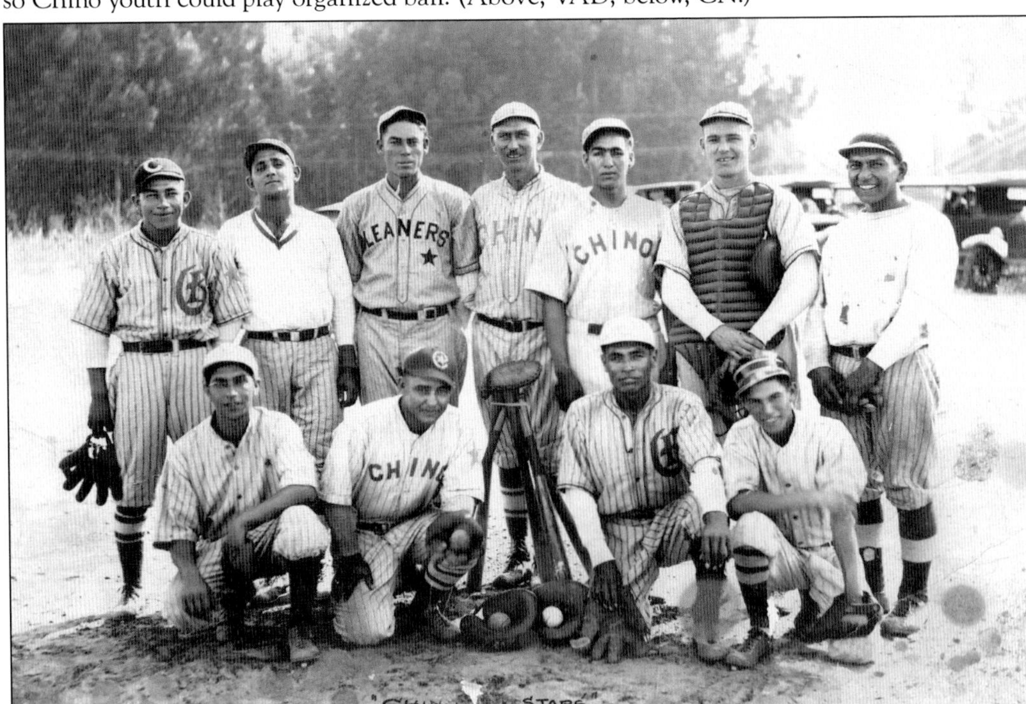

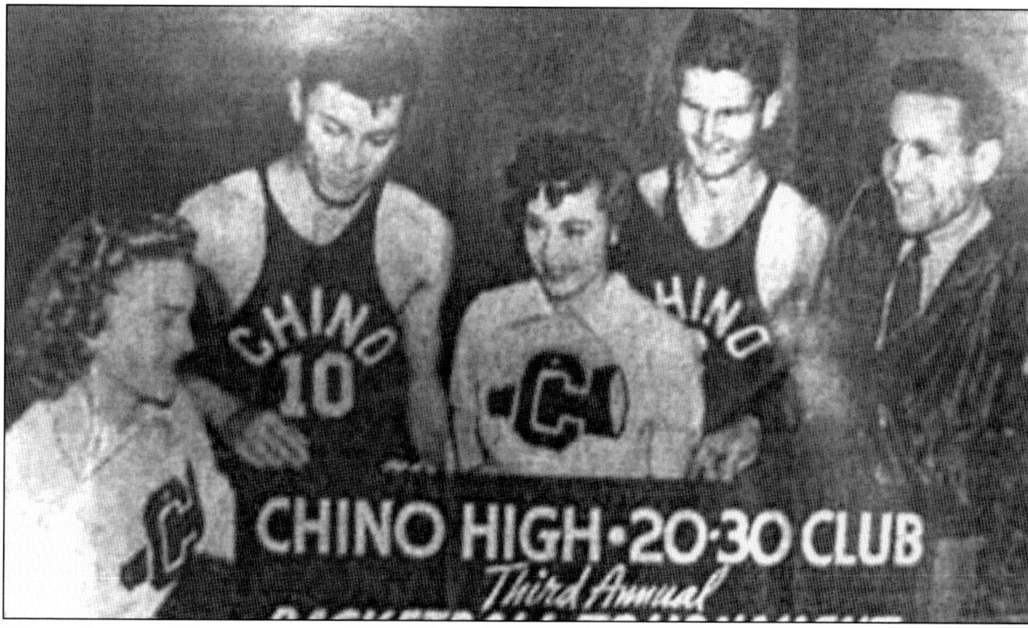

THIRD ANNUAL TOURNAMENT, 1940. Chino High students are, from left to right, Barbara Miears; Ruben Ayala, team captain; Marcia McConnell; Paul Bernard; and Coach Levi Dickey. In his autobiography, Ruben Ayala credits Levi Dickey for the desegregation of Chino's elementary schools. Levi Dickey was vice principal of Chino High School before becoming superintendent of the school district. The Levi H. Dickey Elementary School was named in his honor. (RSA.)

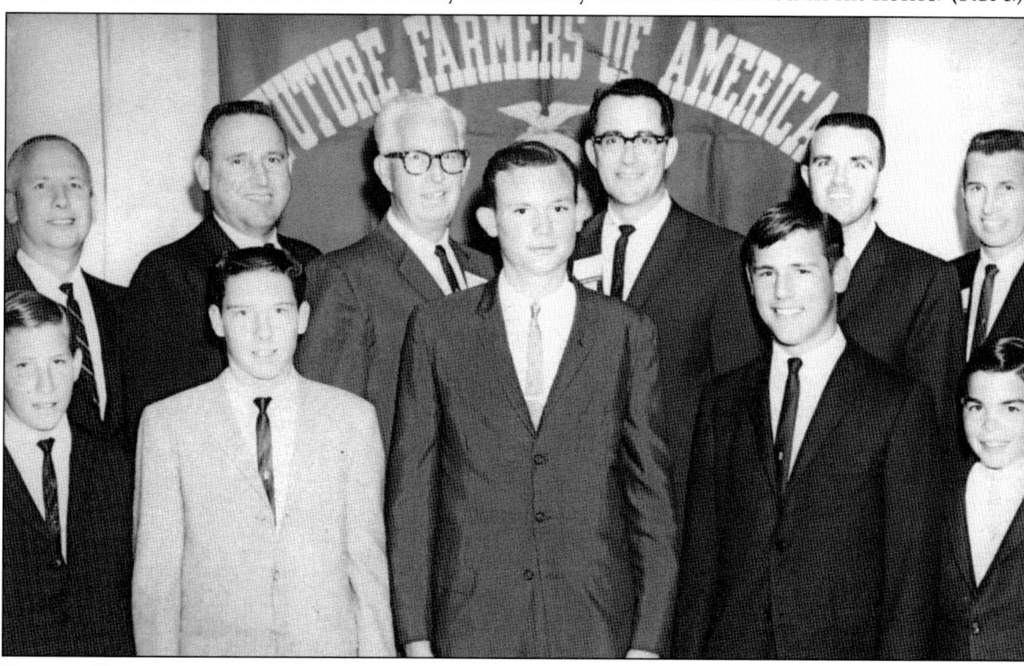

FUTURE FARMERS OF AMERICA, 1964. Many youth from Chino participated in the organization of Future Farmers of America. A highlight each year for local high school students has been participation in the Chino Fair. The fair has been held annually since the mid-1940s, located at the Chino Fairgrounds on the corner of Central and Edison Avenues. (CN.)

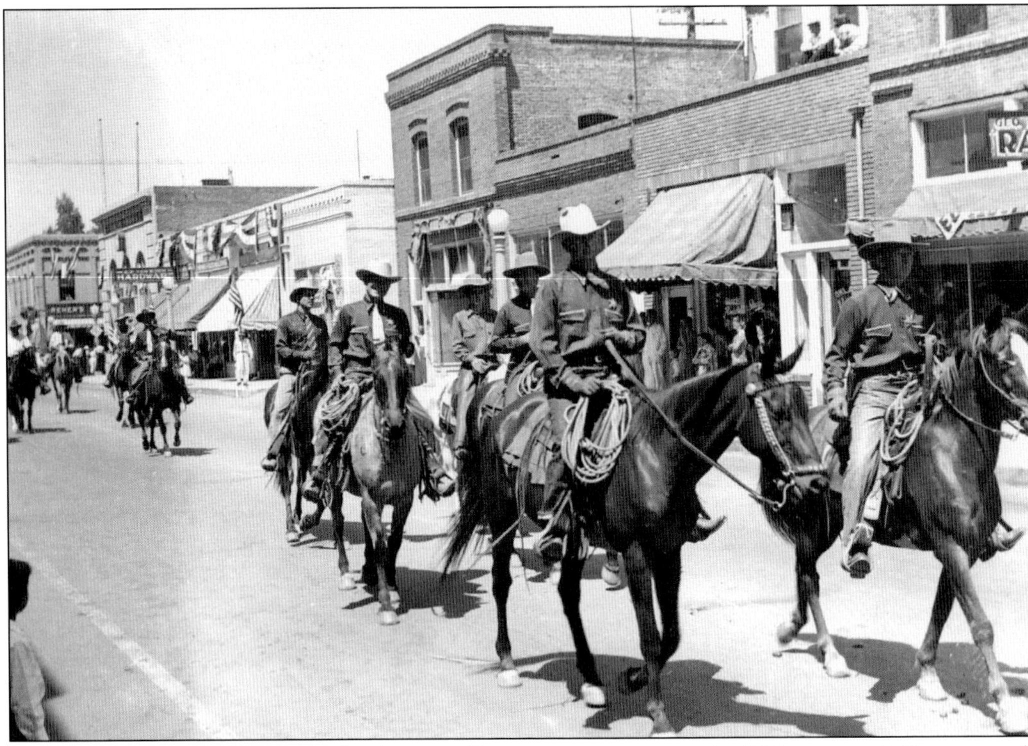

Horsemen Join the Parade. Cowboys and horses were common in Chino, especially on parade day. One of Chino's notable horse ranchers was Revel English, whose stock ranch was located where Don Lugo High School now stands. His other ranch was located on present-day English Road, and his award-winning thoroughbreds earned a high number of prizes in local, city, and state fairs. (CN.)

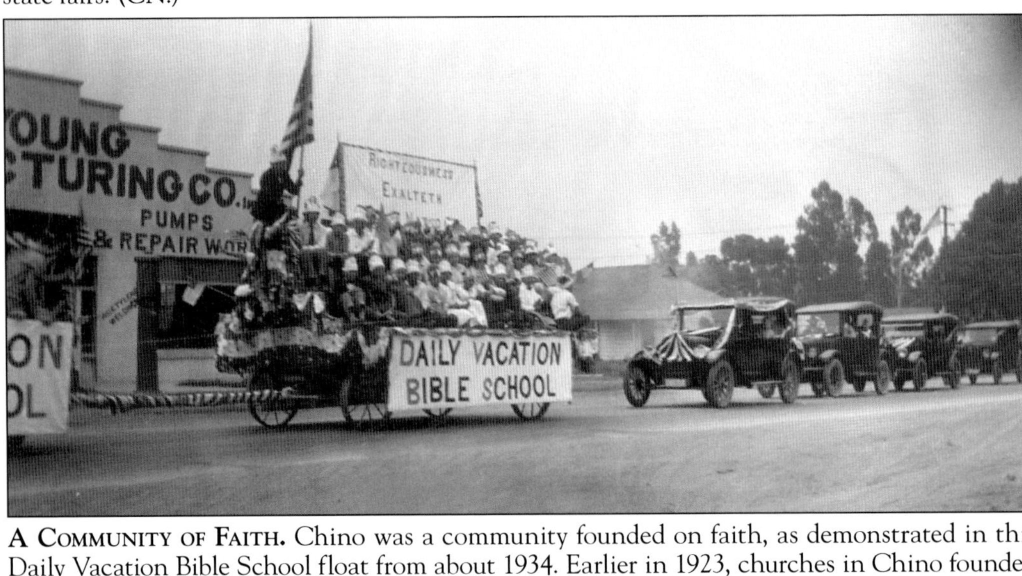

A Community of Faith. Chino was a community founded on faith, as demonstrated in this Daily Vacation Bible School float from about 1934. Earlier in 1923, churches in Chino founded the Ministerial Association with membership including the Baptist, Methodist, Free Methodist, Holiness, and Episcopal churches. A glimpse into Chino's earliest churches can be found in the Chino Rotary Club's 2005 reprint of the book *Chino Valley: Where Everything Grows.* (CN.)

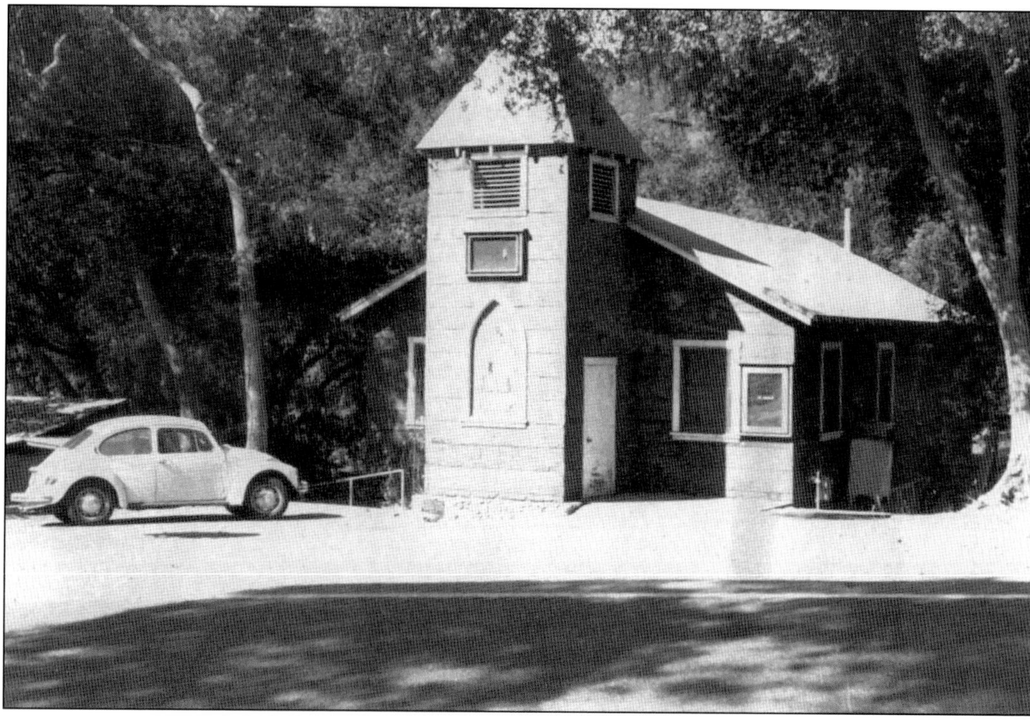

Churches of Chino. Pictured above is a photograph of Carbon Canyon Church. This church was part of the Carbon Canyon and Sleepy Hollow community. Cleve and Elizabeth Purington were instrumental in the development of this small community, located in a canyon near Chino that is now part of Chino Hills. The photograph below is of the Chino United Methodist Church. Dedication services at this first church were held on April 22, 1906. It was built on Sixth Street on the southeast corner, between C and D Streets. Prior to this, members had met in the old opera house on Seventh and D Streets, in the old schoolhouse located on Fifth Street (where the East Side Thimble Club met in 1944), and in the Knights of Pythias Building. (Above, CN; below, UMC.)

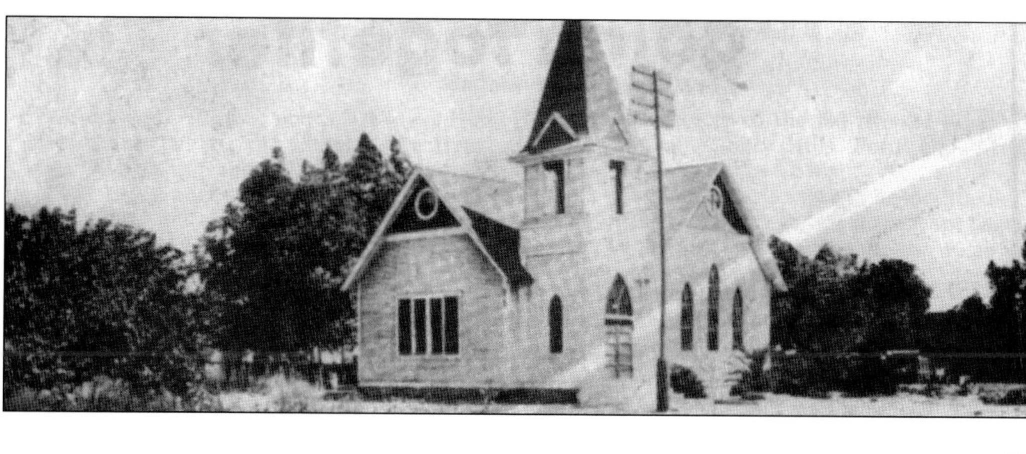

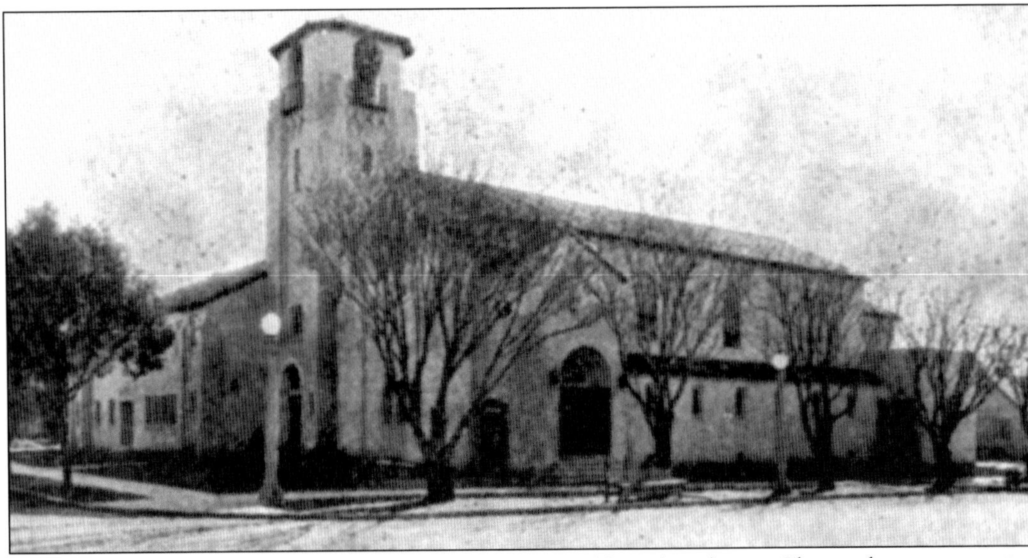

New Building for United Methodists. One of the oldest churches in Chino, the congregation of the United Methodist Church first met in the David E. Moore home. On September 11, 1895, the 18 charter members met at a conference with Rev. Harry White to officially organize. This meeting was held in the Swedish Baptist Church of Chino. This is the congregation's second church building. The original was moved to the back of the new property on Sixth Street at Riverside Drive. (UMC.)

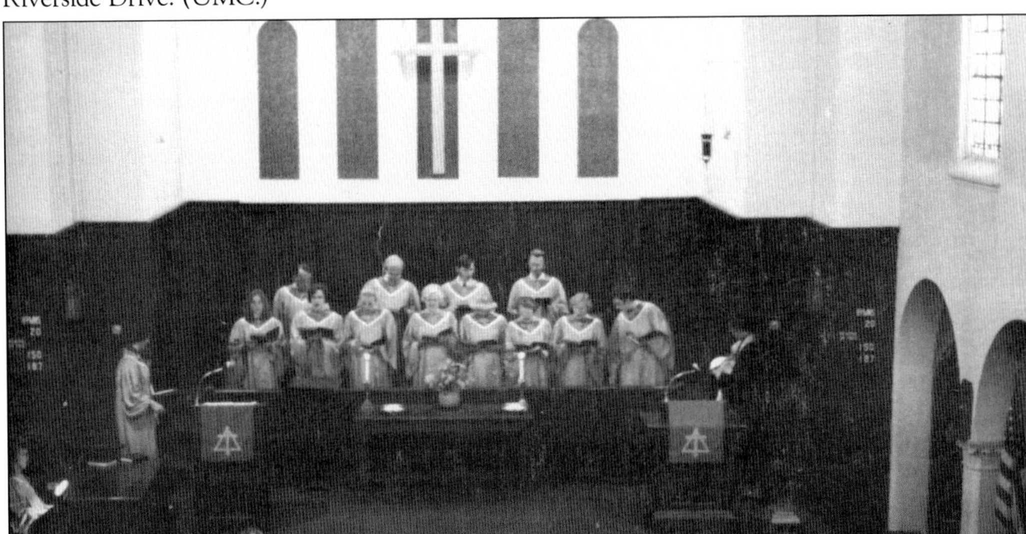

Singing in the Choir, 1980. Over the years, the congregation of the Chino United Methodist Church has been active both within its church body as well as throughout the community. The Epworth League, formerly a Christian Endeavor Society, was organized in 1899. In 1911, Mrs. W. A. Dickey served as president for the newly organized Women's Home Missionary Society. (UMC.)

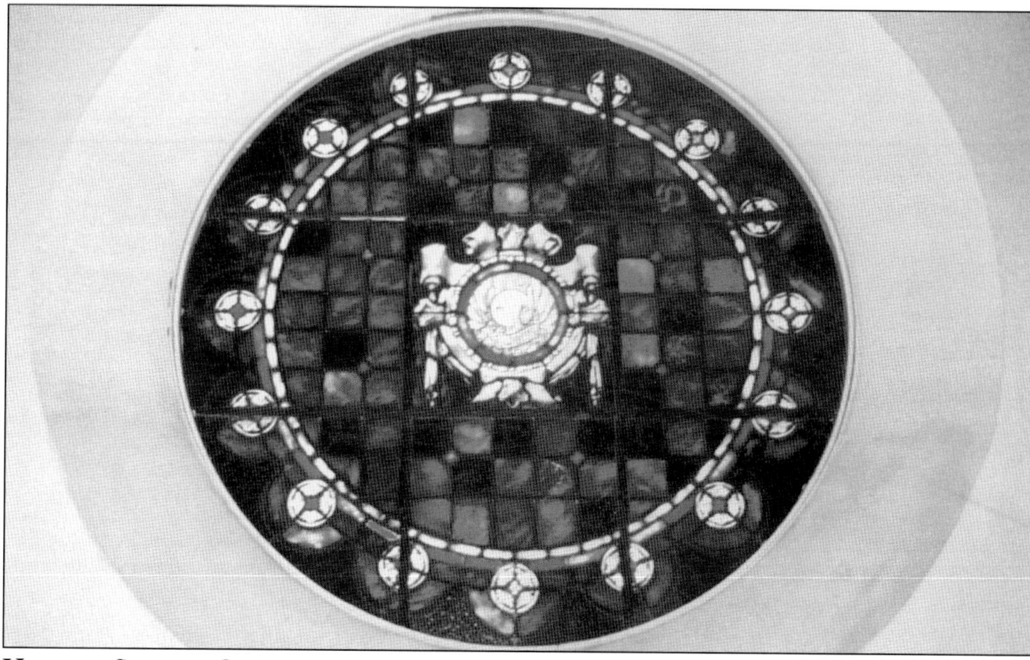

HISTORIC STAINED-GLASS WINDOW. On January 18, 1931, dedication services were held for the second building for the First Methodist Episcopal Church in Chino, which eventually became the Chino United Methodist Church. Bishop Charles Wesley Burns led the celebration. Built according to the style of a Spanish Gothic sanctuary, this beautiful stained-glass window overlooked the seating area where over 300 members could worship together. (UMC.)

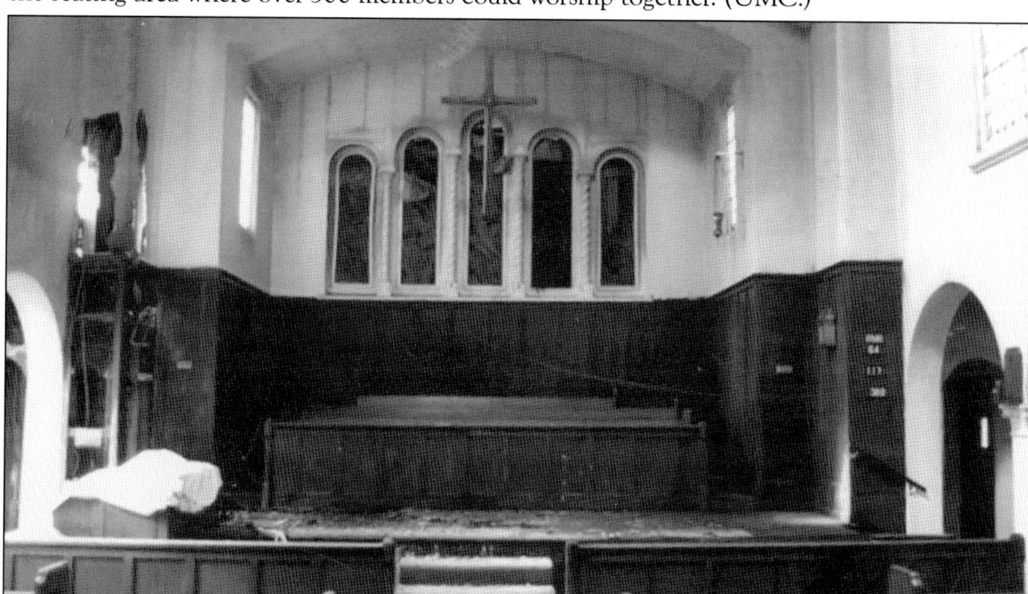

AFTER THE SANCTUARY FIRE. In August 2007, the sanctuary was set on fire by suspected arson. Not suffering any damage, however, was the beautiful cross that can be seen still hanging in this photograph in the midst of the wreckage. This cross was handcrafted by world-famous designer and woodworker Samuel Solomon Maloof in memory of his nephew Tye George, a member of the church. The church was rebuilt and restored. (UMC.)

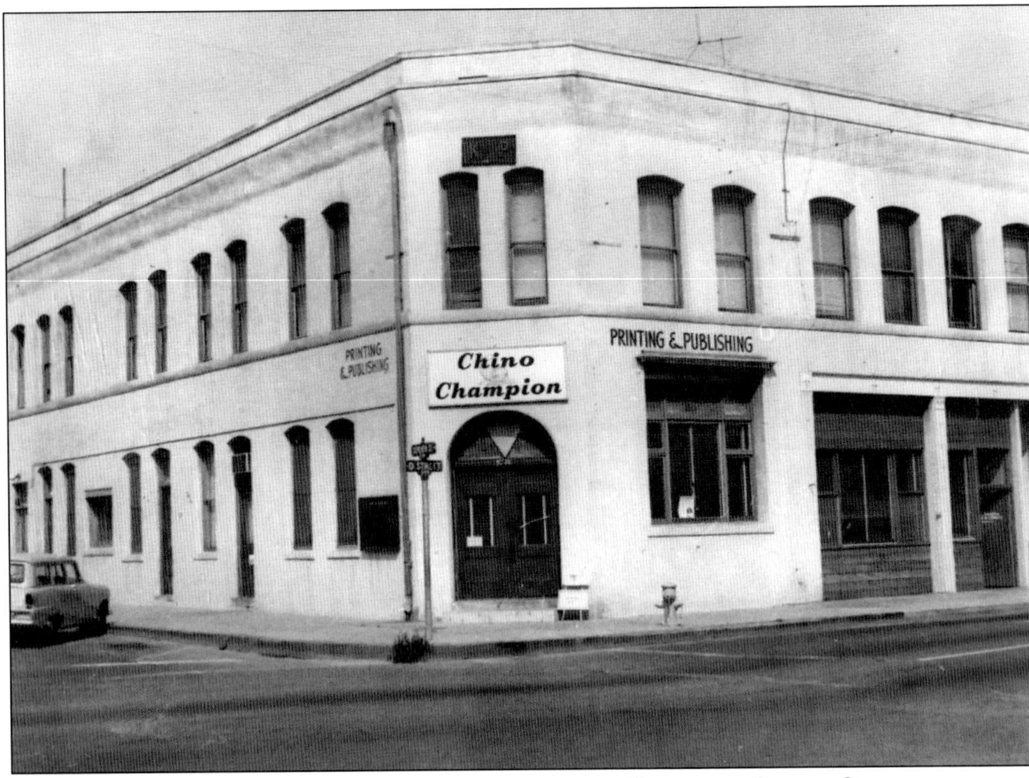

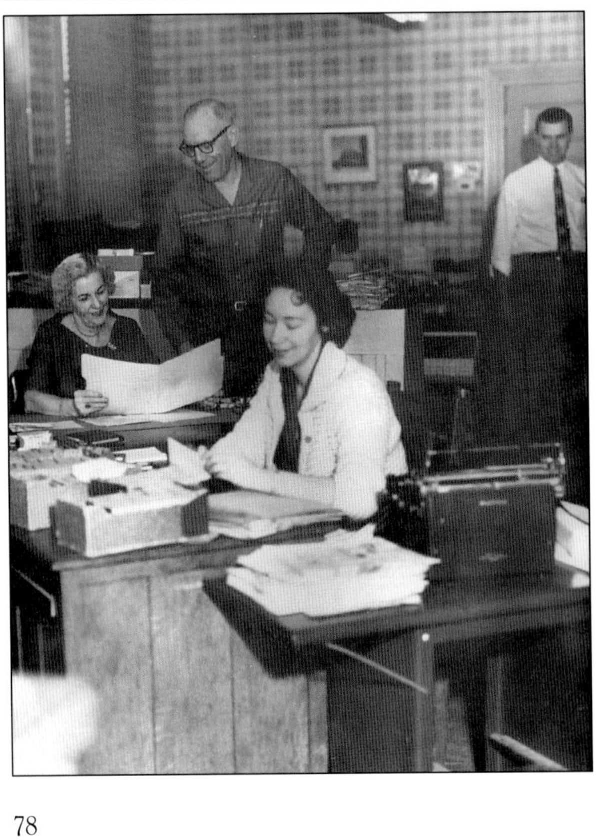

CHAMPION OFFICE, SEVENTH AND D STREETS. On November 11, 1887, in the same month Richard Gird founded the town of Chino, he published the premier issue of the *Chino Valley Champion*. Today the *Chino Champion* is the oldest newspaper in San Bernardino County under the same banner. This photograph shows when it was located in the building that once housed Chino's first city hall and fire station. (CN.)

UNDER NEW OWNERSHIP. In this late 1950s photograph of the front office of the *Chino Champion*, former publisher Robert Frady stands in the center. To the far right can be seen the new publisher, Allen P. McCombs. Gladys Sutherland, left, and Lolita Reina are sitting at their desks, hard at work. (CN.)

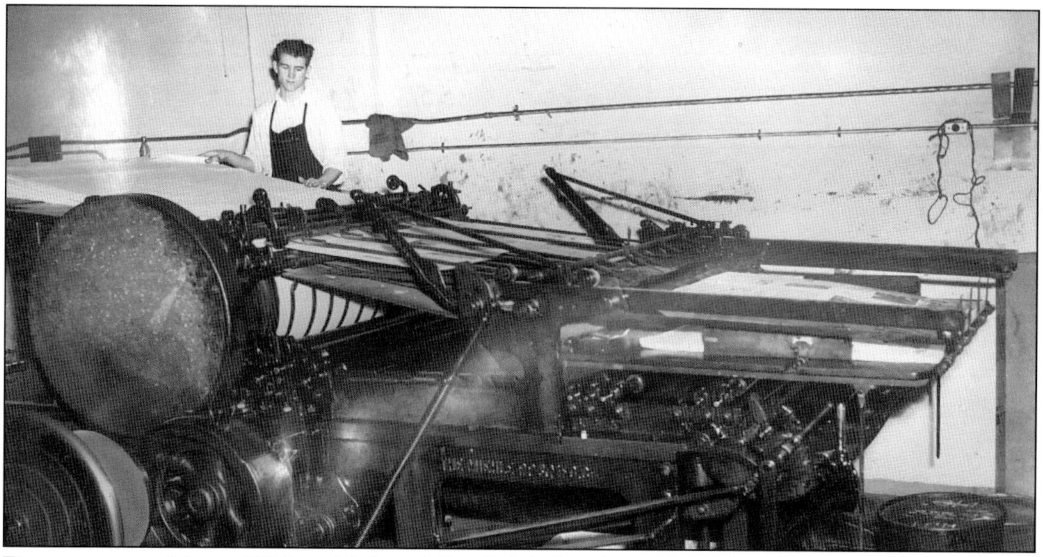

Printing the News. With publisher Allen P. McCombs at the helm, the printing press stayed busy, keeping Chino current with community news and world affairs. With a journalism bachelor's degree from Stanford University and a master's degree from Harvard, McCombs purchased the *Champion* when he was 27 years old. Even though fresh out of graduate school, he had years of experience under his belt, having covered news ranging from General McArthur's homecoming to the Conference for Conclusion and Signature of Treaty of Peace with Japan. He covered the international peace conference in San Francisco on his way from a reporting job with the *Honolulu Advertiser* to graduate school. Shown above, operating the old sheet-fed No. 1 Miehle Press used during the 1950s is Don Underwood, a student from Chino High. Below is the roll-fed Duplex press, which replaced the old sheet-fed. (Both, CN.)

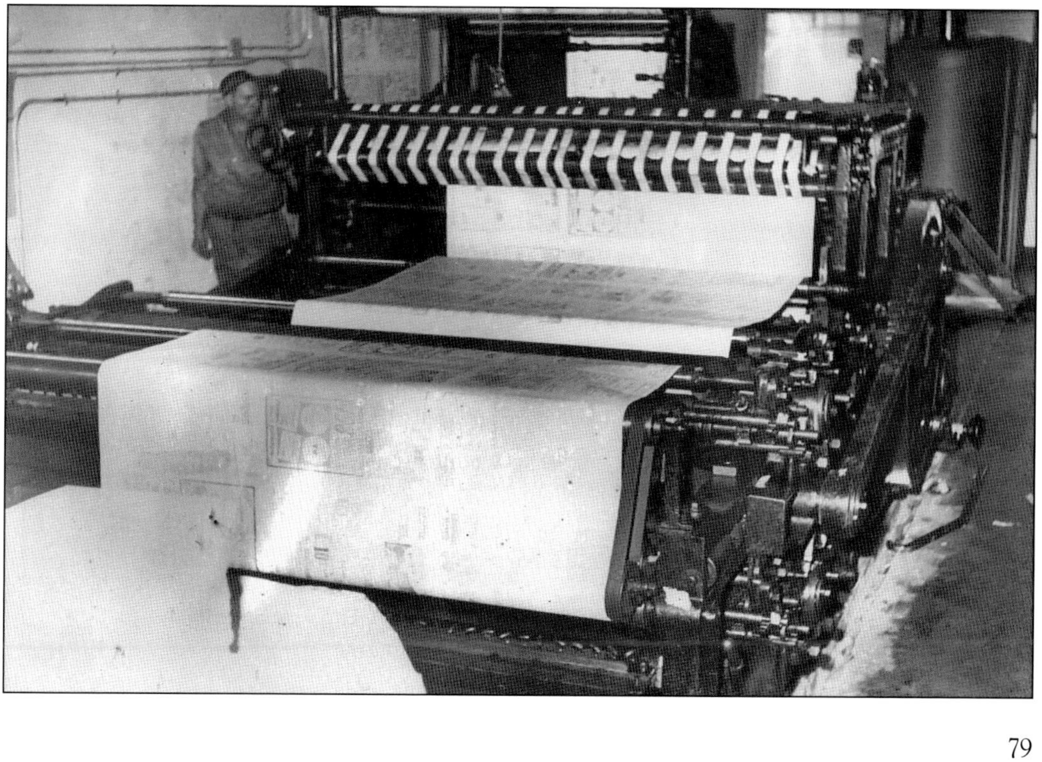

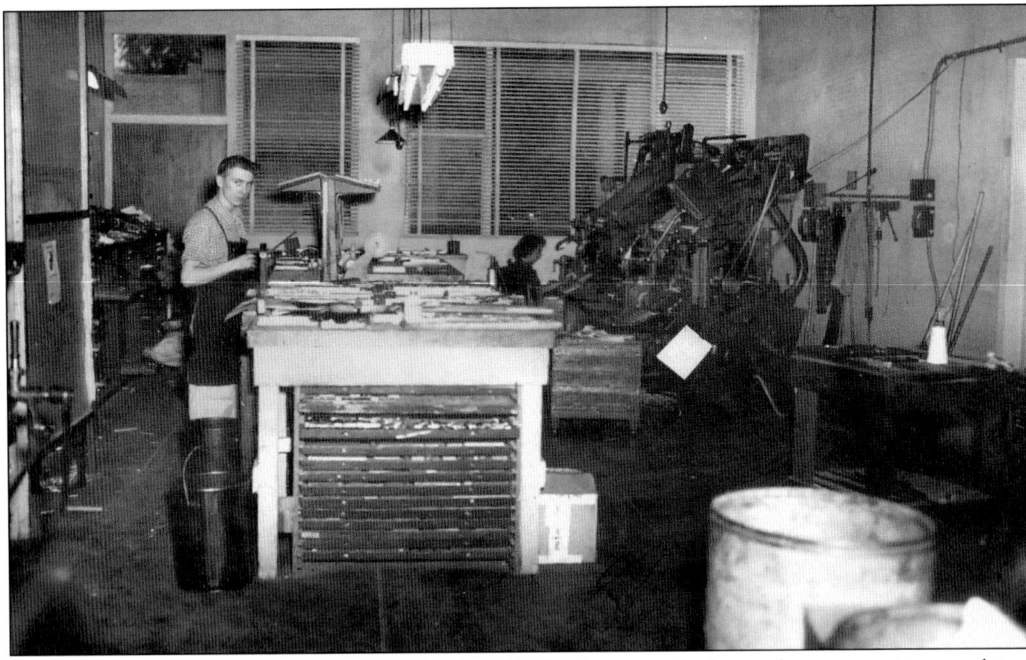

SHOP WITH TYPESETTING MACHINES. This late 1950s photograph shows the typesetting machines at the *Champion* while it was still in its offices at Seventh and D Streets. Under the ownership of Gretchen and Allen P. McCombs, Champion Publications also published the *Chino Valley News*, *South Ontario News*, and the *Mountain Courier News* in Crestline during the late 1900s. (CN.)

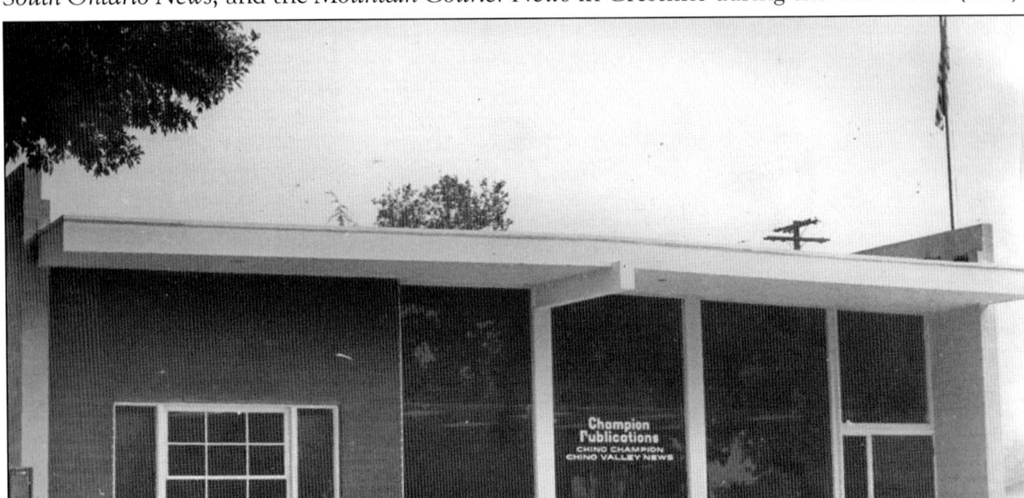

CHAMPION PUBLICATIONS IN NEW BUILDING. In 1970, the *Champion* moved from its location on Seventh and D Streets (the building formerly housing Chino's first city hall) two blocks east into the building that was previously home to Chino's post office. The new offices on Ninth and D Streets were remodeled to meet the expanding needs of the newspaper for its growing community. (CN.)

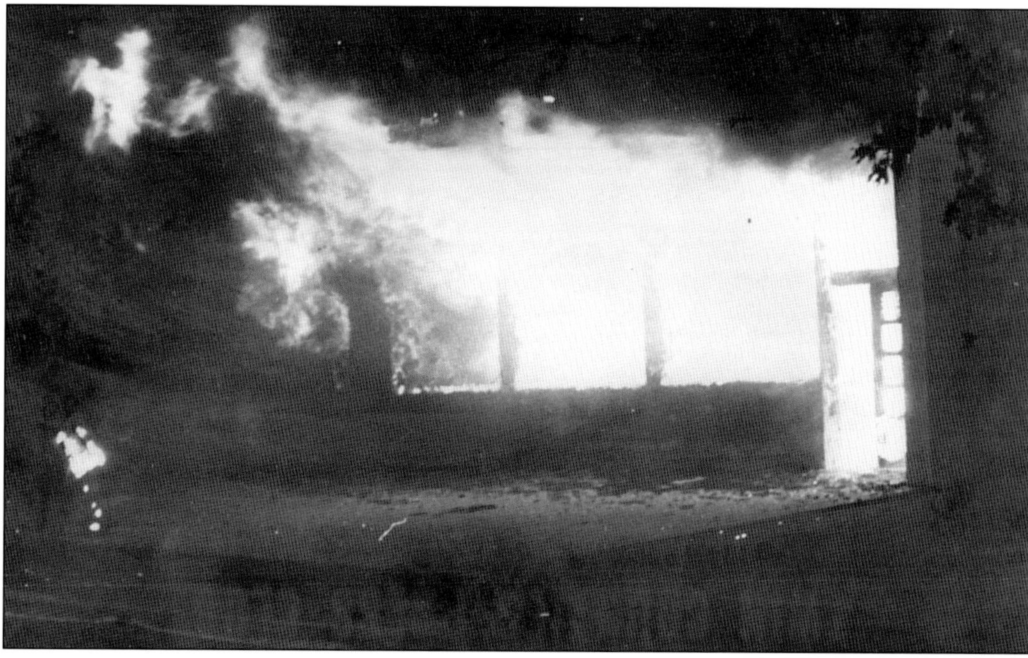

Arsonists Start Fire. In May 1971, *Champion* publisher and school board member Allen P. McCombs was attending a school board meeting regarding the expulsion of a Mexican American student from Chino High. Racial tensions were high as crowds packed the room and overflowed outside. Suddenly, police chief Frank Meehan caught the attention of McCombs, who then left the meeting only to hear the *Champion*'s office as well as fellow board member John T. Tomlinson Jr.'s attorney office had been the victims of firebombings. Racing to the scene, McCombs was relieved to find the workers of the *Champion*'s mailing crew all safely outside. Firefighters fought the blaze, but much of the building was gutted. (Both, CN.)

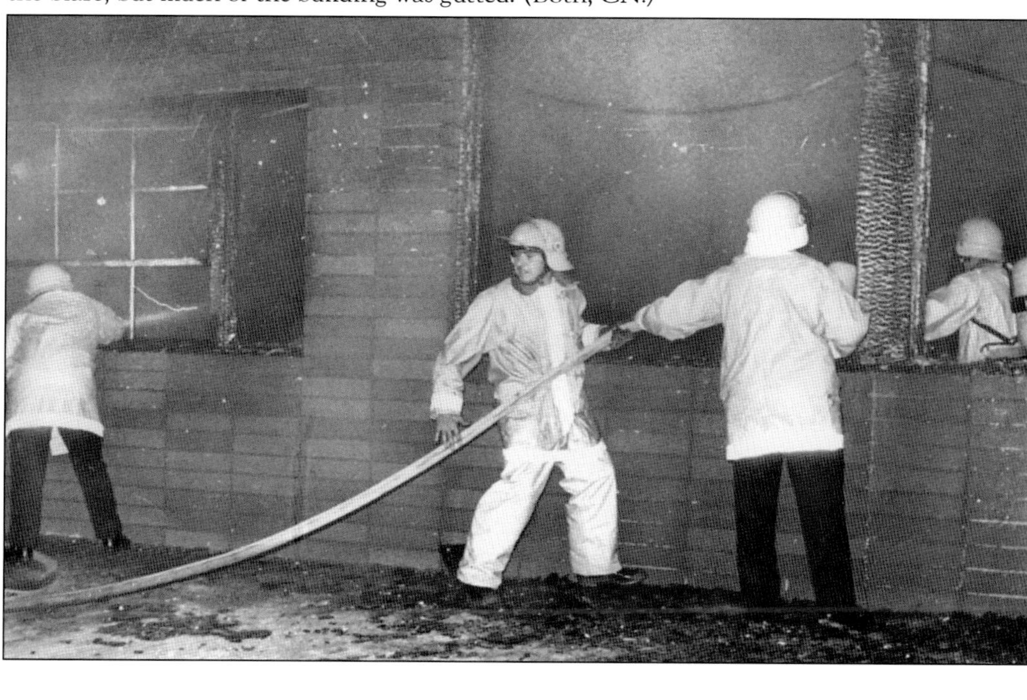

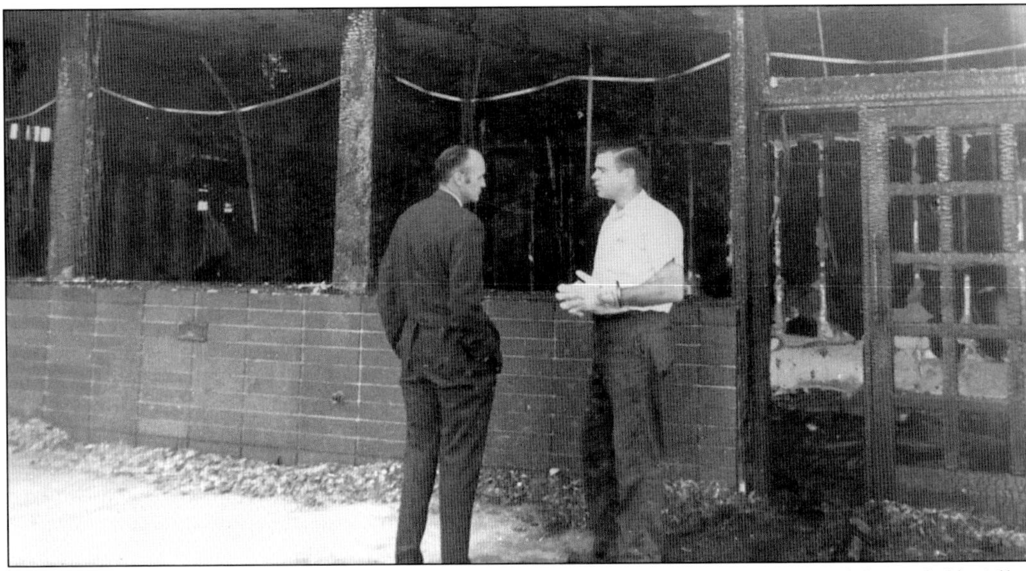

Publisher Inspects Damage. Along with superintendent of school Royce Lapp (above, left), Allen P. McCombs inspects the damages. The following week the newspaper was produced in rented facilities with community members volunteering to help. In his editorial regarding the tragedy, McCombs encouraged Chino to move forward toward healing. As a newspaper publisher, he believed in community involvement. He has served in a variety of capacities, including membership in the Rotary Club, appointment to the city planning commission, and president of the chamber of commerce and United Way. He also served as president of the California Press Association, as well as the California Newspaper Publishers Association (CNPA) in 1982. His wife, Gretchen, served the CNPA as women's chairperson in 1983. She was also instrumental in the founding of the Chino Valley Community Chorus and sponsoring the Seventh Street Theater. (Both, CN.)

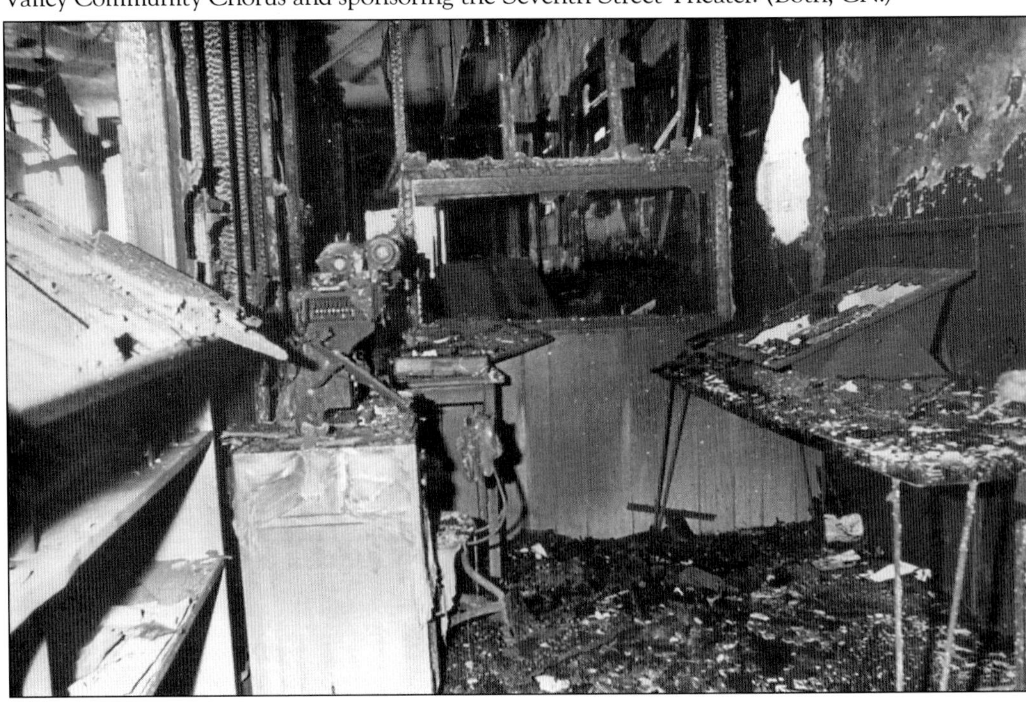

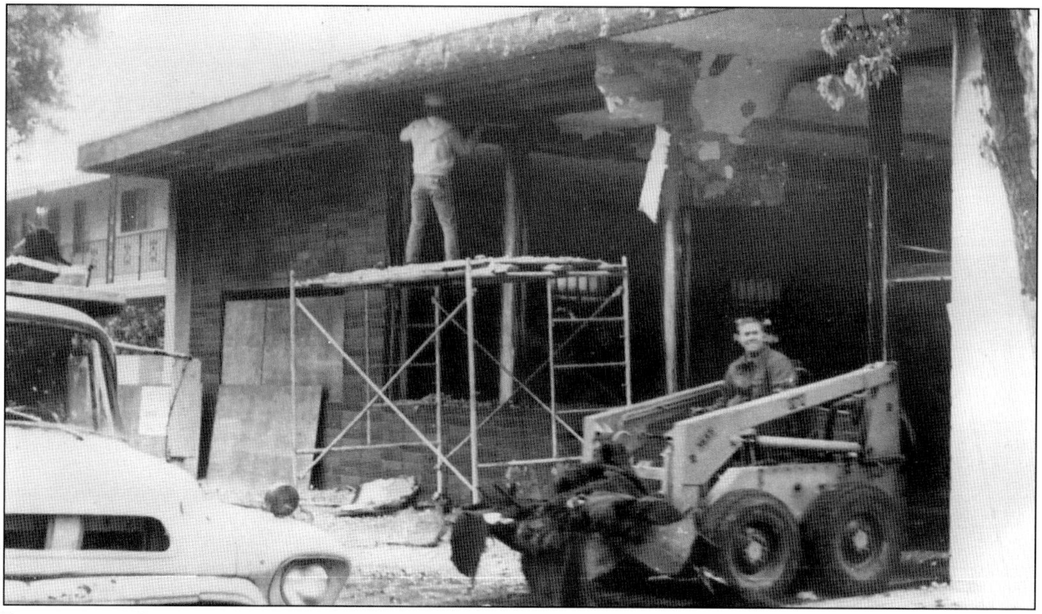

REBUILDING CHAMPION PUBLICATIONS. Construction to repair fire damage began immediately, which demonstrated Allen P. McCombs's commitment to his community and its newspaper. He and his wife had originally settled in Chino mostly because of his family's interest in the newspaper field. After Harvard, he had enlisted in the U.S. Navy and served as an officer for three years. When his military stint was finished, he knew he wanted to return to his roots in journalism that began as a 10-year-old boy publishing a neighborhood newspaper, the *Hilltop News,* with his friend in his hometown of Berkeley, California. Checking into the newspaper business, he discovered the *Chino Valley Champion* offered an opportunity in the late 1950s with a community of 8,000 residents, a readership of 1,800, and income of $75,000 gross. He never looked back. (Both, CN.)

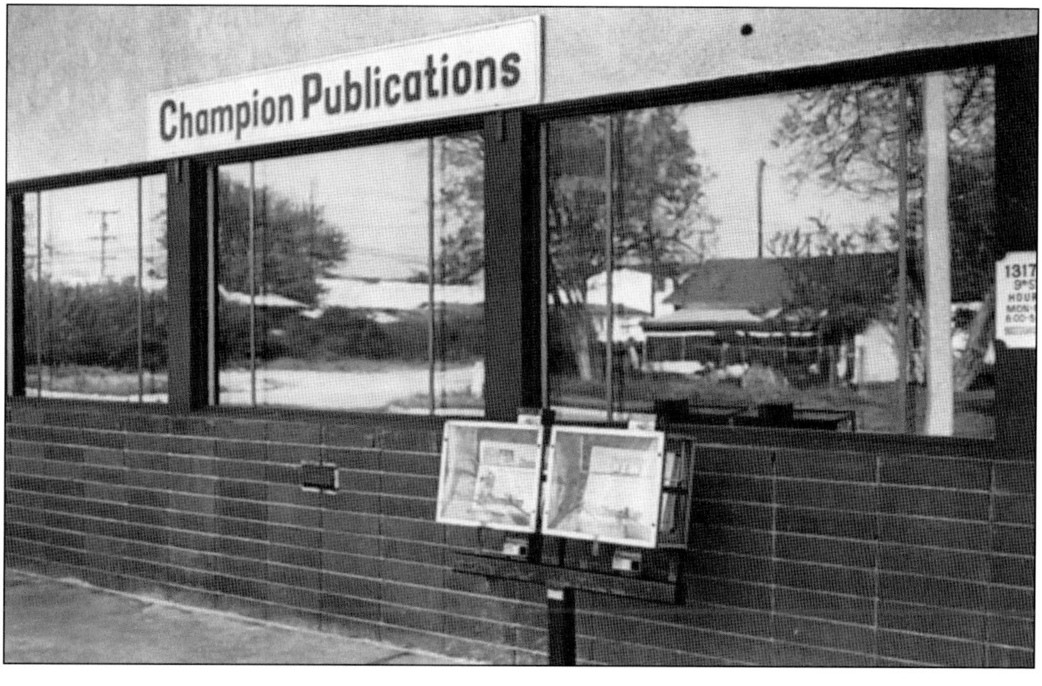

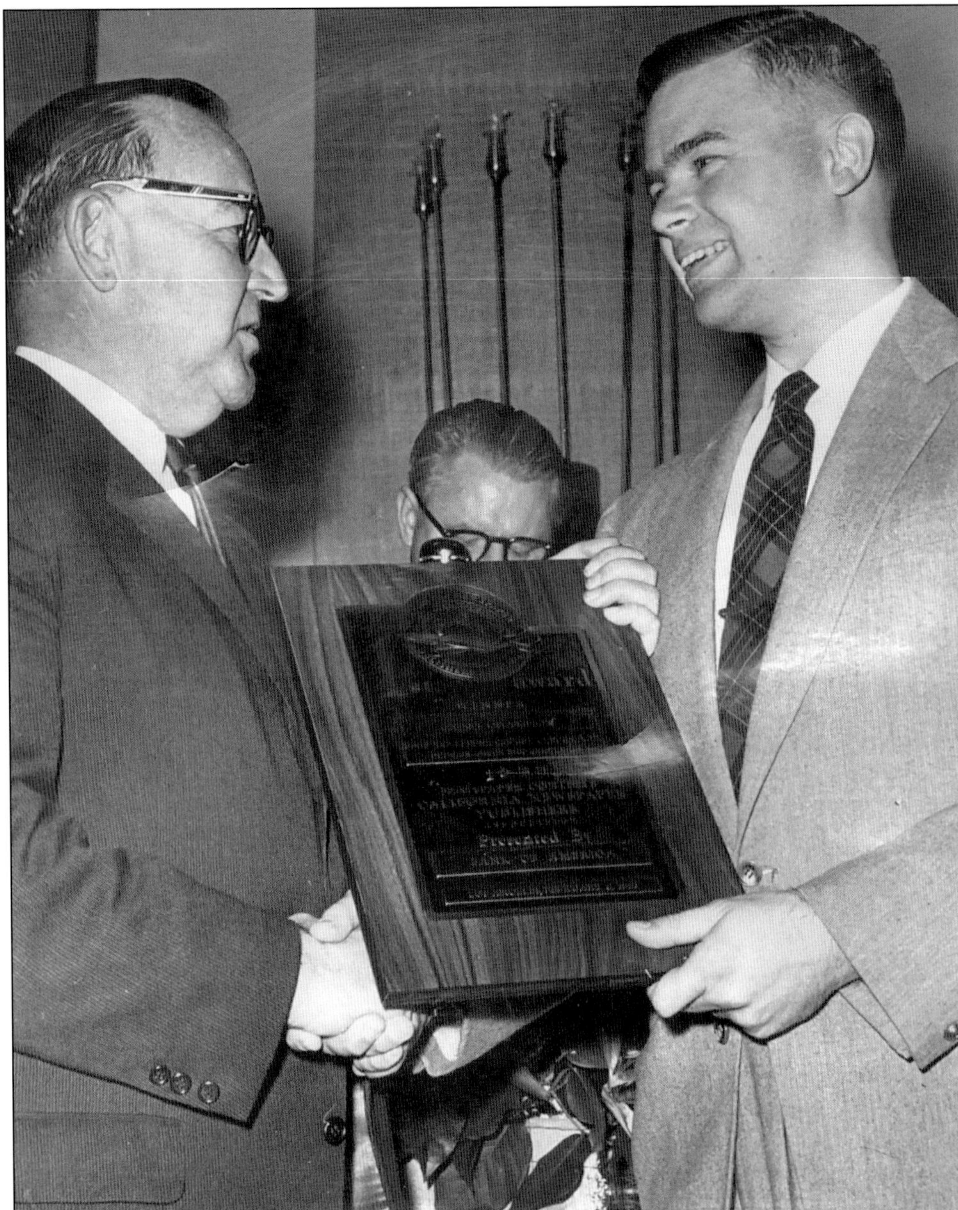

Publisher Receives Award. Gov. Edmund G. (Pat) Brown Sr. presents *Chino Champion* publisher and editor Allen P. McCombs with the 1961 award for Best Youth Interest Coverage from the California Newspaper Publishers Association. Over the years spanning his memorable and influential career, McCombs has received various awards and accolades, including the honor of contact with Presidents Nixon, Reagan, George H. W. Bush, and Clinton, two of which were at the White House. On August 17, 2010, the chamber of commerce awarded McCombs with a lifetime achievement award, the first of its kind, given out by this organization. Respected as a true historian for the city of Chino and its surrounding communities and grateful for his willingness to share his knowledge with others, the chamber honored Allen McCombs for his association with the oldest business in its membership. They also recognized him for his years of service to the chamber, including his leadership position as board president in 1959. (CN.)

Seven

The World at War

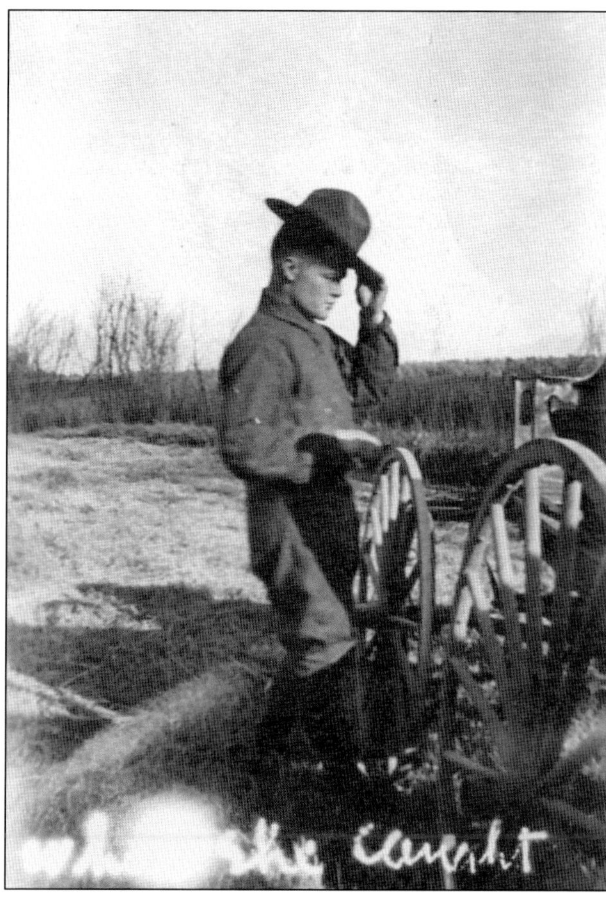

Shipping out to France, 1917. Many of Chino's men served in World War I, including John A. Daniels. Daniels is shown dressed in uniform, just before he shipped out to France. When Chino held a war rally at city hall, John A. Daniels had been one of the first to enlist. He is the son of Chino's first mayor, E. C. Daniels. (VAD.)

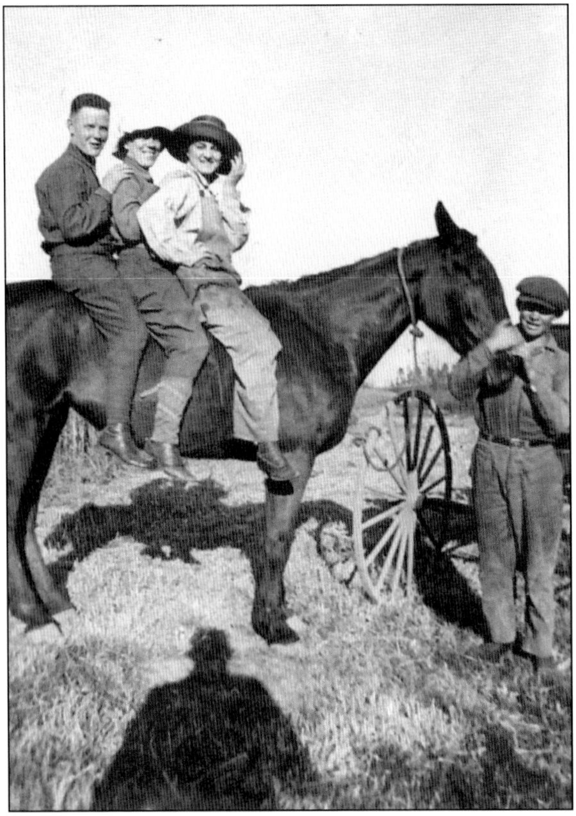

World War I, Ready to Leave. Enjoying a last-minute get together before saying goodbye to their soldier are, from left to right, enlisted man John A. Daniels, August Ann Austin, Ferneena Austin, and Joe Daniels. When John A. Daniels returned after the war, he married Ferneena Austin. Joe Daniels (John's brother) married August Austin, Ferneena's sister. (VAD.)

Serving in France, World War I. Ready for battle are John A. Daniels (left) and an unidentified soldier. Back at home in Chino in 1917, military registration clerks were appointed for the draft. Many of the city's men stepped forward to register to defend the cause of freedom, adding up to the surprising total of 437 enlistments. (VAD.)

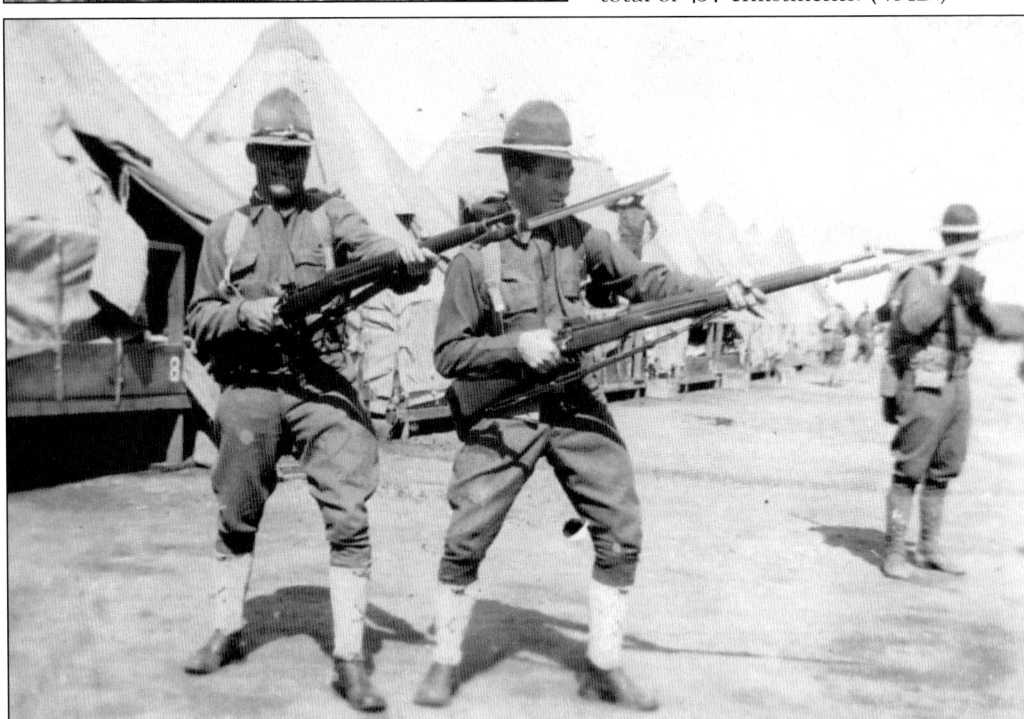

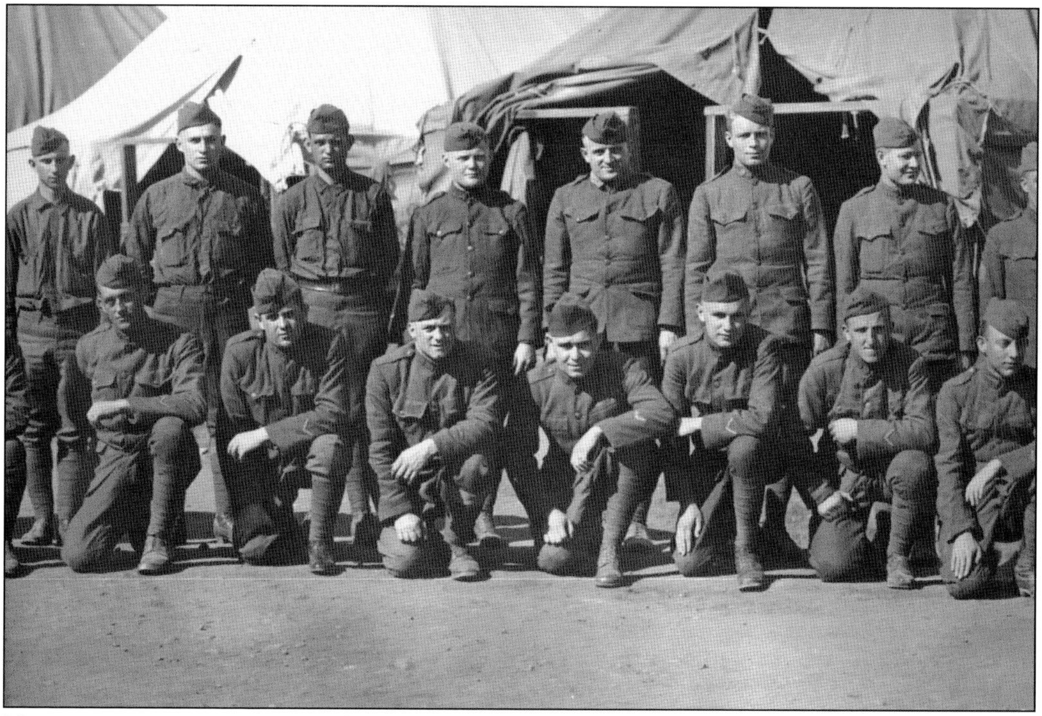

Veterans of World War I. John A. Daniels poses with his Company B, 160th Infantry, in this photograph taken while serving in France. His hometown newspaper, the *Champion*, supported the war effort by printing articles asking citizens to purchase $50 war bonds. Enough Liberty Bonds were sold to Chino residents to raise $22,000. The *Champion* also printed many letters written by soldiers expressing their gratitude to the countless friends, neighbors, and family members who took the time to write to them and send them fresh-baked goods from home. In the photograph below of veterans from World War I, John A. Daniels is standing second from the right in a white shirt. (Both, VAD.)

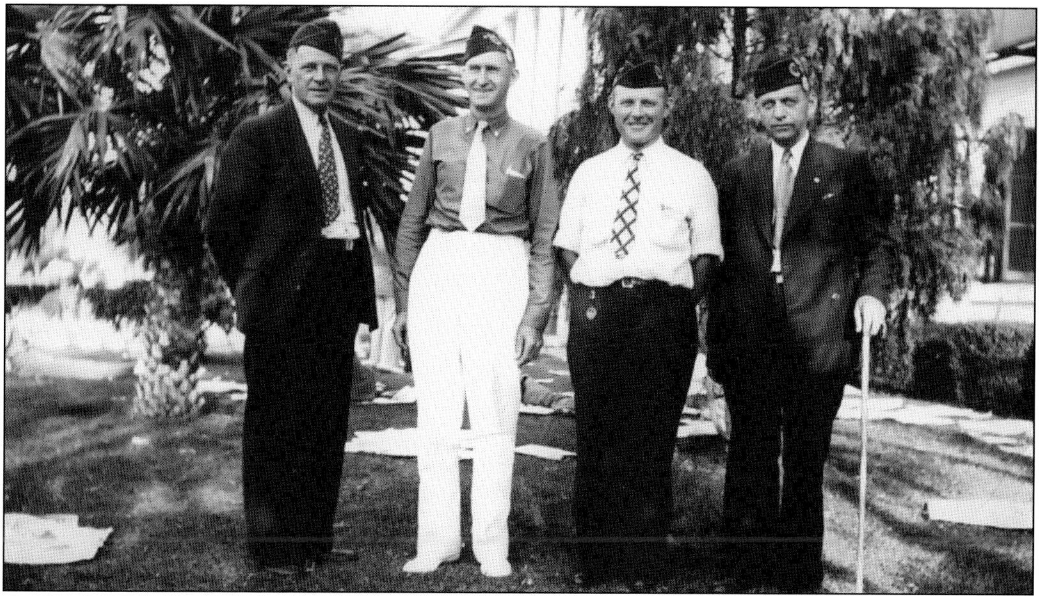

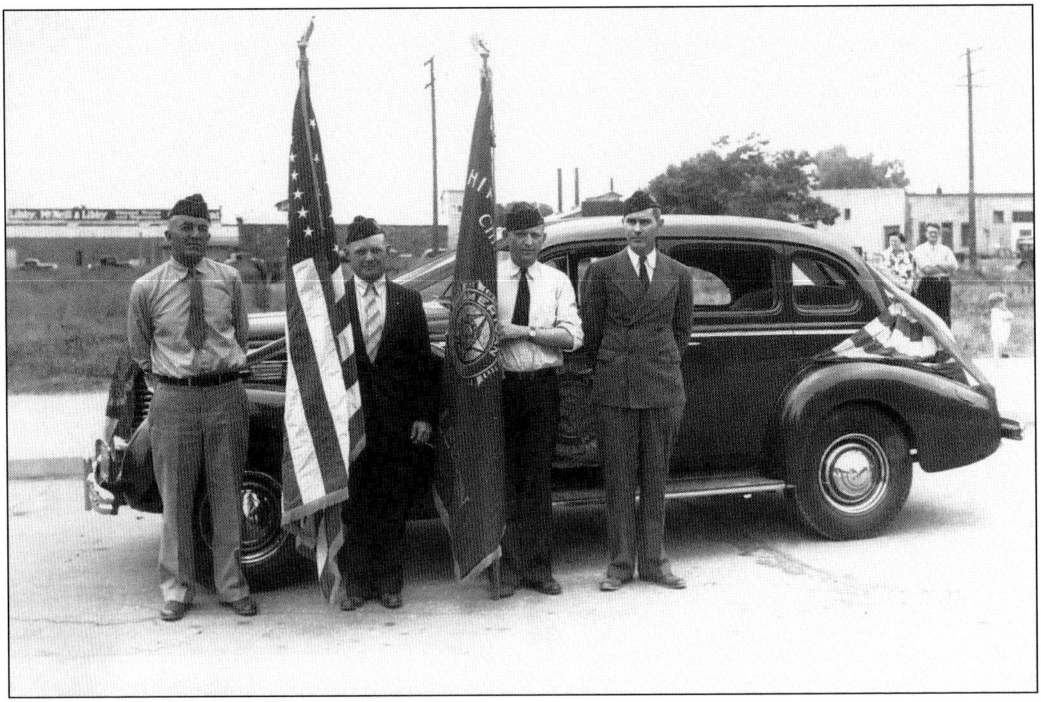

Honoring Servicemen. Carrying the American flag is World War I veteran John A. Daniels. Often working behind the scenes, women were also active in support of the war. The *Chino Champion* reported how Margaret Fowler visited France in 1918 on behalf of the YWCA war effort. She was the founder of what is currently known as the Boys Republic. (VAD.)

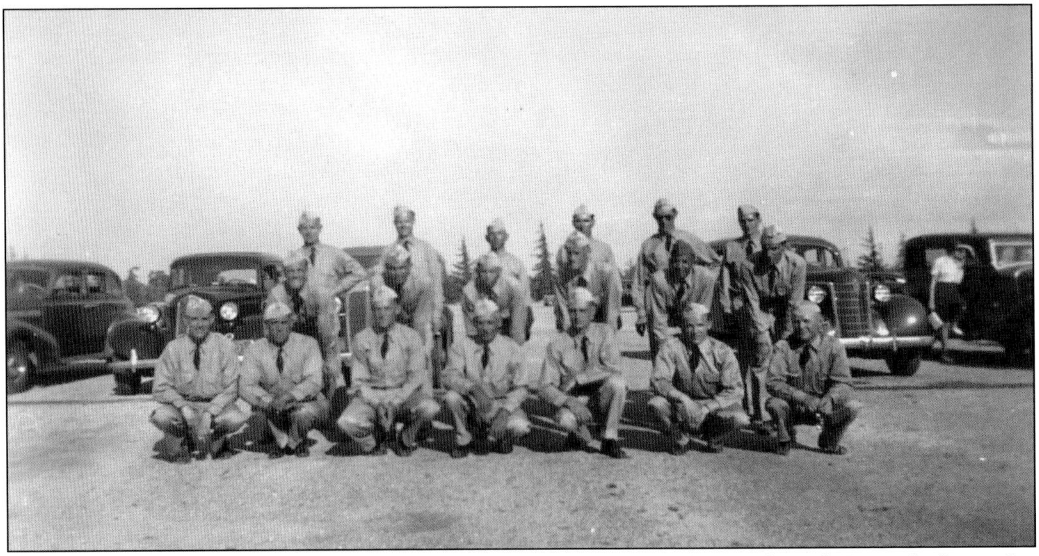

Chino National Guard. During the World War II era, John A. (J. A.) Daniels formed a National Guard in Chino. Drills were held on his field. Over at the Chino Fairgrounds, a camp was constructed to house German prisoners of war. These men labored on local farms, filling in for the absence of many Chino men and helping with the food supply during shortages caused by the war. (VAD.)

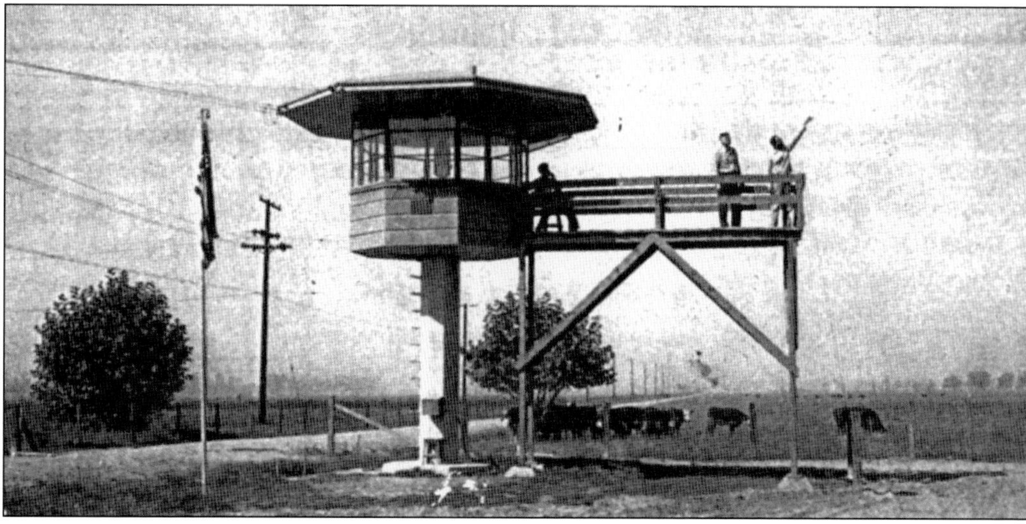

Guard Towers, c. 1942. When Kenyon Scudder became superintendent of the Chino Institution for Men in 1941, he stopped construction of a 25-foot-high wall, which included seven gun towers, on the ground of it being too oppressive. The completed portion of the wall was turned into a handball court, and the unused towers were converted to World War II observation posts, which were used against the threat of a Japanese air attack. The inmates manned these lookout towers. (CIM.)

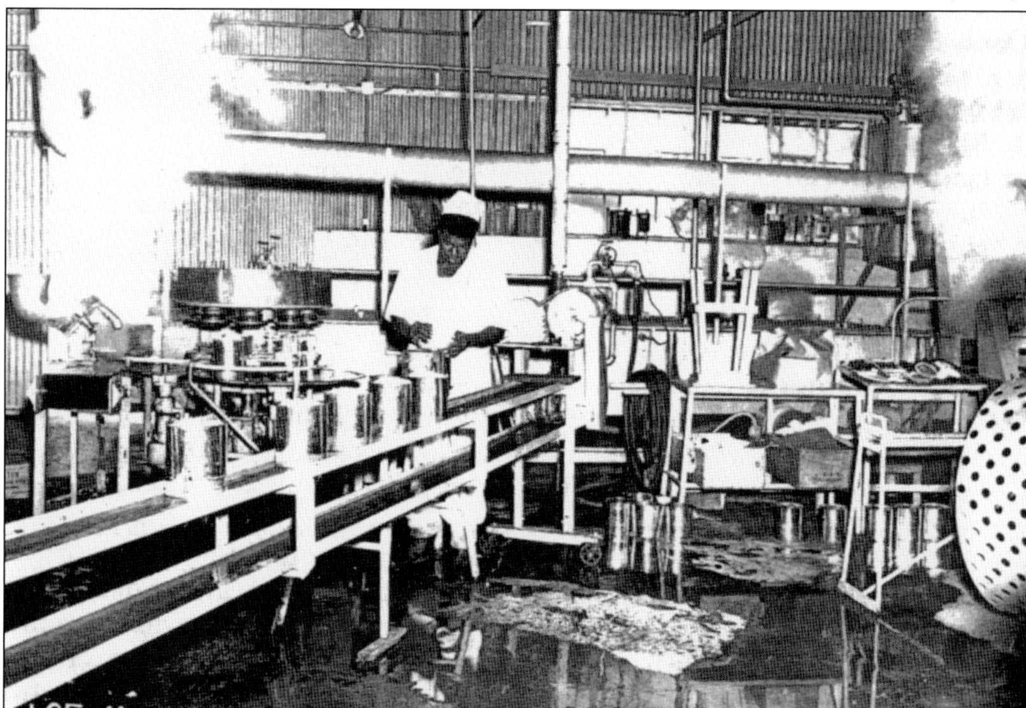

Cannery Supports War Effort, c. 1943. When a local cannery failed, Supt. Kenyon Scudder purchased the equipment and had it rebuilt on the grounds of the California Institution for Men. Landing a federal contract to provide canned corned beef hash and beef stew to American troops in the Pacific theater, the cannery delivered 36,000 cans of food in its first production phase for the war effort. (CIM.)

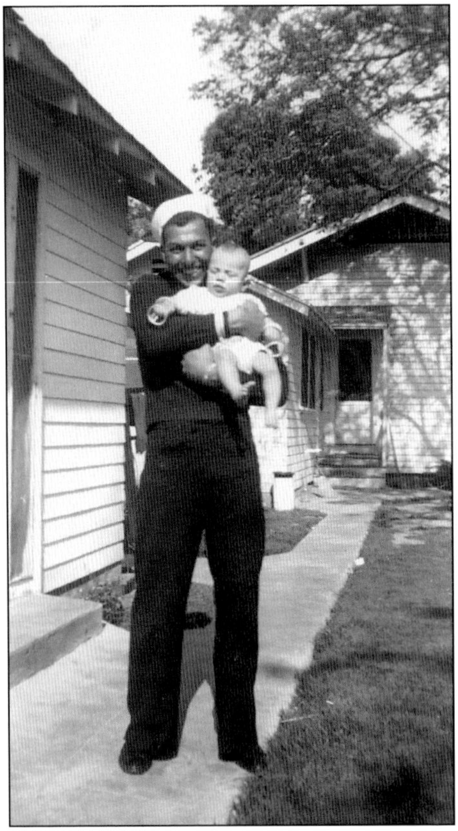

Richard George, World War II. On April 16, 1944, Richard (Dick) George posed for the photograph holding infant Sid (Butch) Hopkins Jr. A sailor, Richard George also flew aircraft. He married Esther Ebeling, daughter of Chino barber Henry Ebeling. Henry's shop was at 5210 D Street, which is where Owen's Bistro is now. Sid Hopkins became a doctor and married Janet Cattle, daughter of Chino mayor Howard Cattle. (DG.)

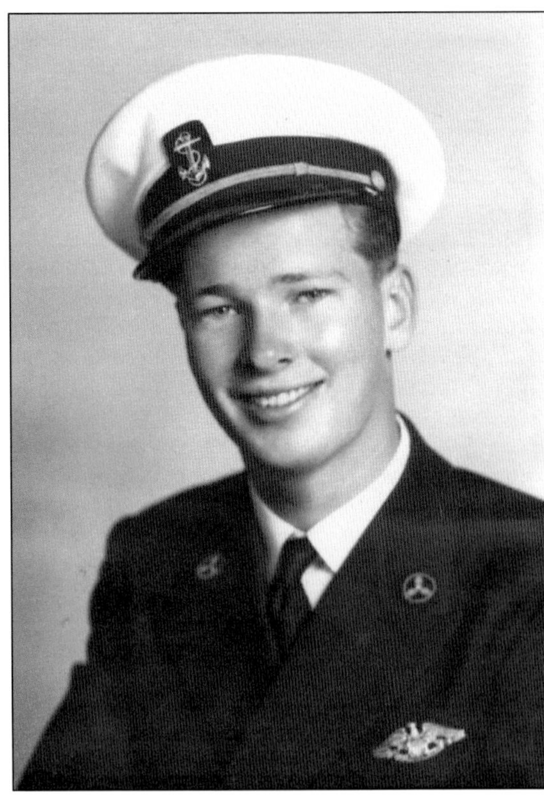

James Walters Serves, 1941. Russell (Joe) and Elsie Kearns Walters were proud to see their son James Walters serve in World War II. As a result of the war, in 1942, the *Champion* featured front-page news from the U.S. Office of Civilian Defense with detailed information on action each family should take if the air raid siren sounded. (FW.)

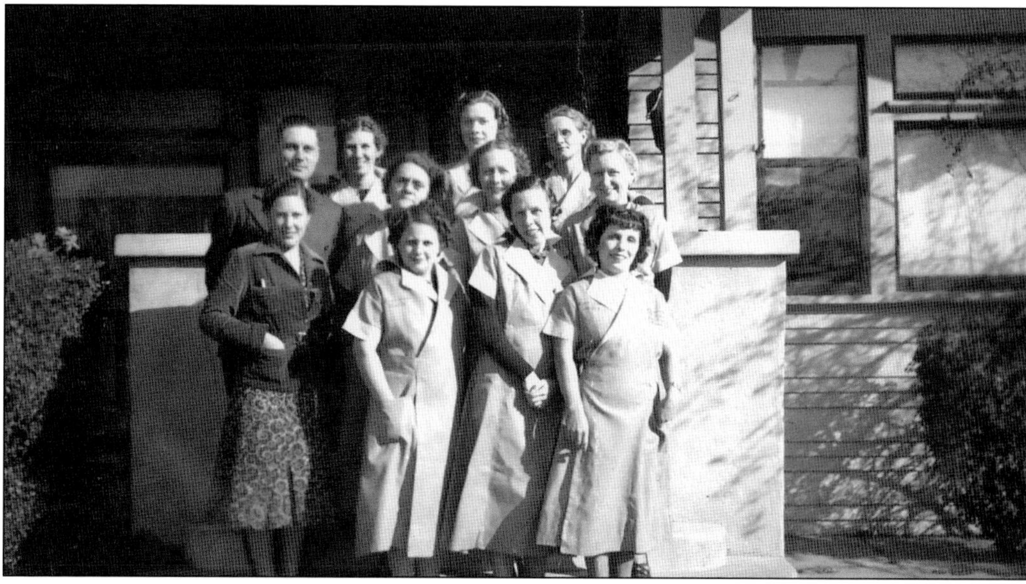

ACTIVE ON THE HOME FRONT. Women in Chino were not idle during World War II but stayed active in a variety of capacities. Margaret Pine worked in the aviation industry in Bakersfield to support the war effort. Here in this *c. 1941* photograph, Evelyn Walters Bennett joins other women probably to demonstrate Watkins products. (FW.)

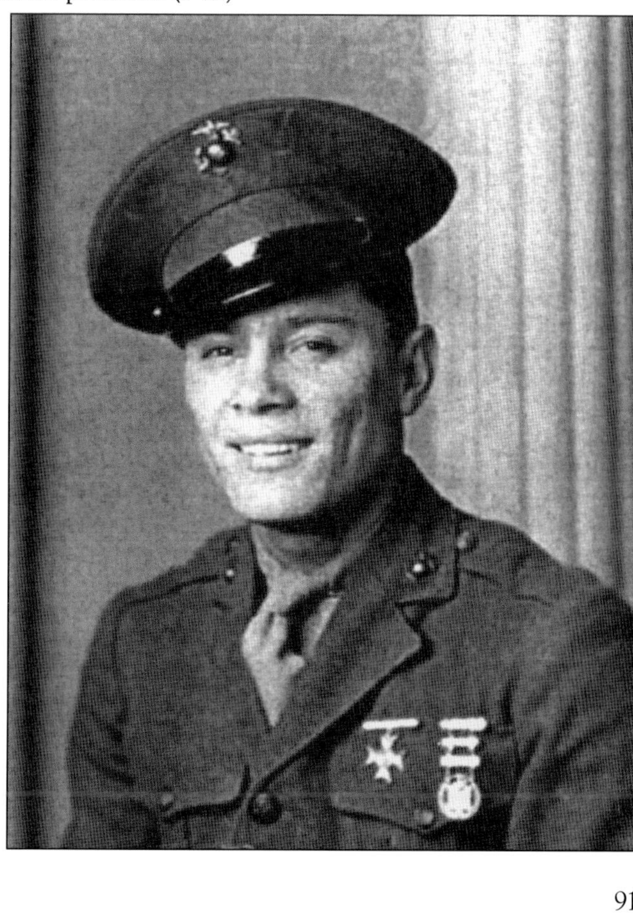

U.S. MARINE CORPS, 1942. Ruben S. Ayala enlisted and served a four-year tour of duty with the First Marine Division and saw action in the South Pacific. He recalled that his friends who also enlisted included Wes Shulz and James Rappatoni (U.S. Navy), Sef Diaz and John Cummins (Marines), Roy Marabella (Army Air Corps), and Leo Fletcher (U.S. Army). Sadly, his friend John Esparza became Chino's first casualty of the war. (RSA.)

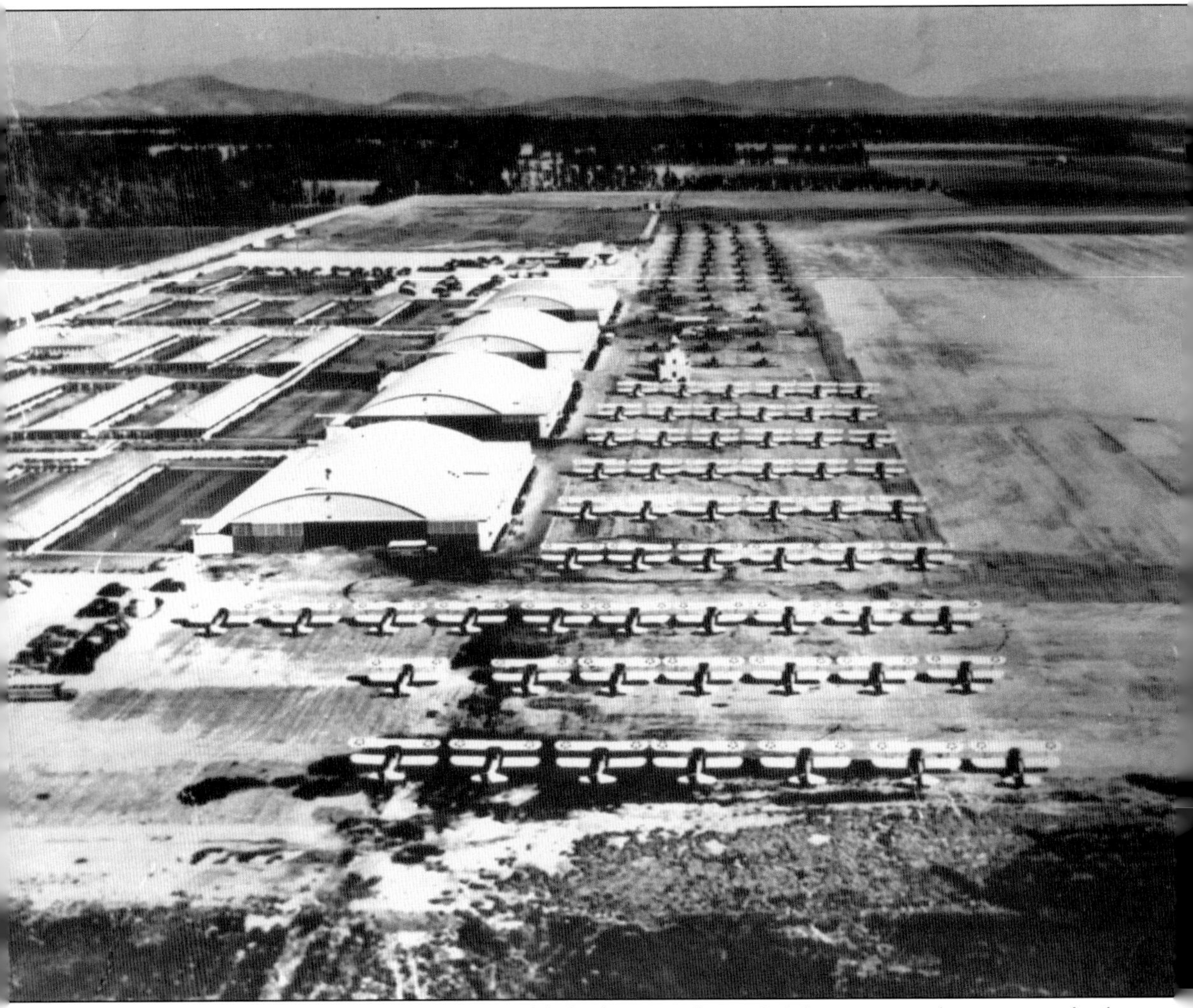

Cal Aero Field. This airport was established in Southern California as a pilot training facility during World War II. Constructed by Maj. C. C. Moseley in 1940, Cal Aero Academy was one of over 40 civilian-owned flying schools dedicated to help with the war effort by training 30,000 pilots each year. It provided 10 weeks of primary training to army cadets and 10 weeks of basic training. Graduates of Cal Aero then transferred to an army-operated flying school for their last 10 weeks of advanced training. After the war, thousands of World War II aircraft were brought to Cal Aero's storage and reclamation facility. It became known as the war bird restoration capitol of the United States. Originally located in what was zoned as the city of Ontario, Cal Aero Field has since become part of the city of Chino and has transitioned into what is now known as Chino Airport. (CN.)

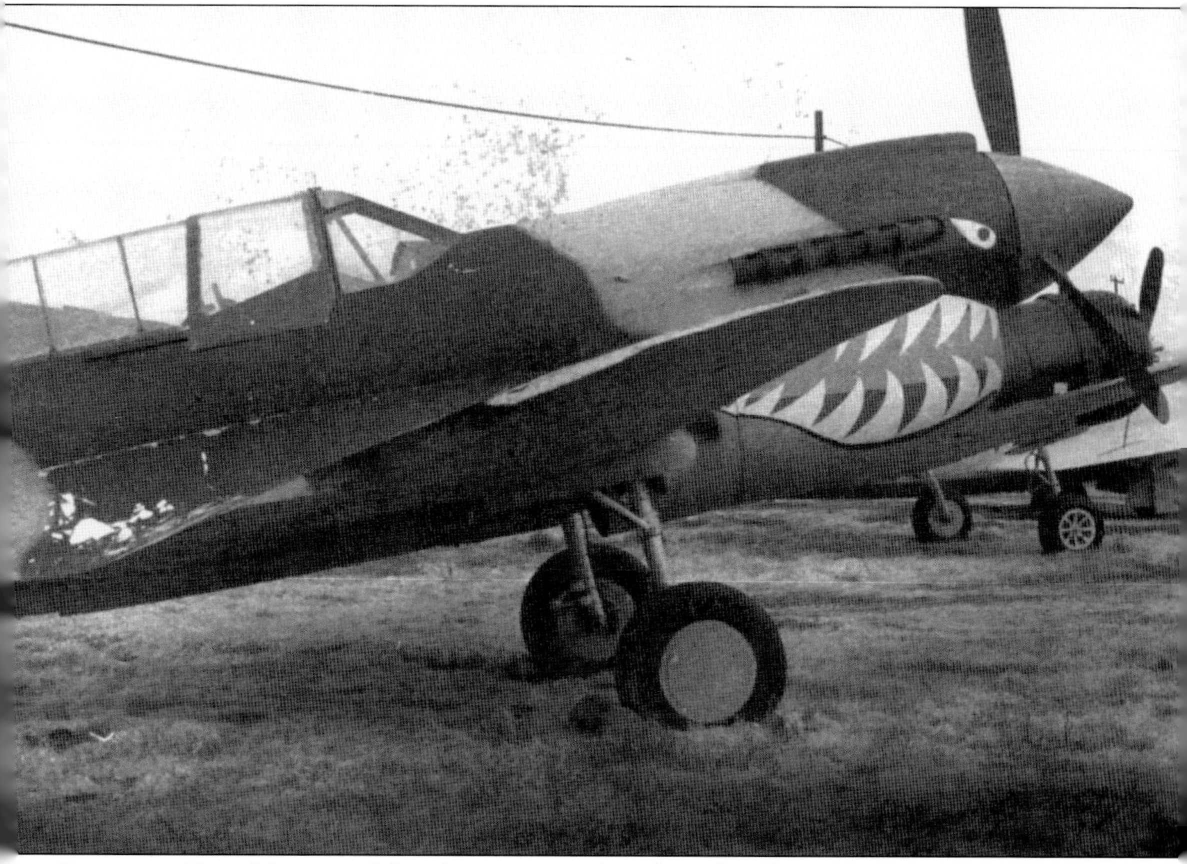

Planes of Fame Museum. After the war, aircraft such as this Flying Tiger were brought to Cal Aero and scrapped for the price of their aluminum to be recycled into common household products and other items. It broke Ed Maloney's heart to see such beautiful and historical planes quickly destroyed, and so the idea for a museum was born. Originally opening his museum in nearby Claremont in 1957, the museum's collection included 10 aircraft. Since that time, Planes of Fame has moved to Chino Airport, boasting a collection of over 150 aircraft with more than 50 that can still be flown. Maloney pioneered the concept of a flying air museum, and each May the skies overhead buzz with the drone of World War II and historic aircraft in their annual Planes of Fame Chino Air Show. Over 40,000 spectators viewed the amazing aerial feats in the 2010 air show. (CN.)

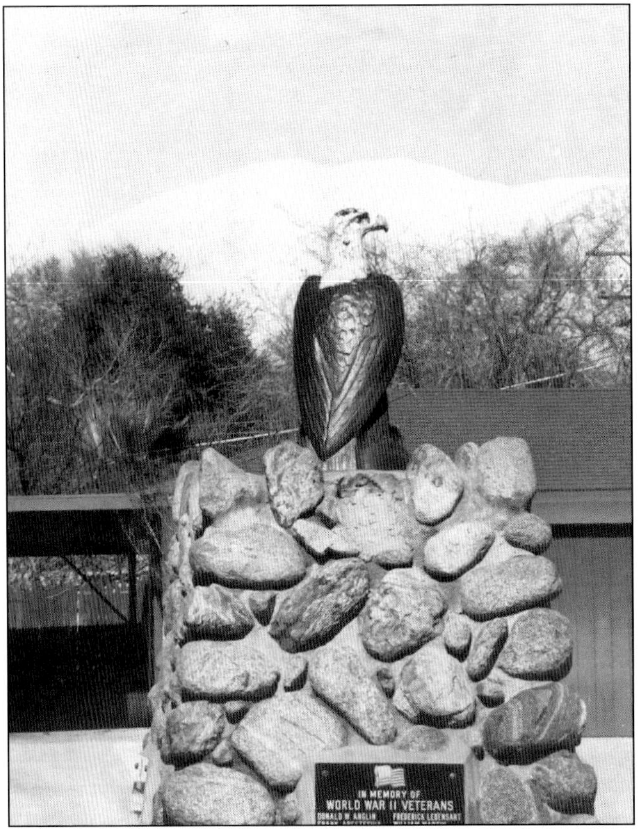

American Legion Eagle Monument. Now located in front of the Community Building on Tenth and B Streets, this monument honors Chino's finest who have sacrificed their lives in the cause for freedom. The families of Chino have been proud to serve in many wars. The *Chino Champion* reported that in a three-day draft sign-up in 1942, a total of 419 men enlisted, with 290 of those having been born in Chino. (CN.)

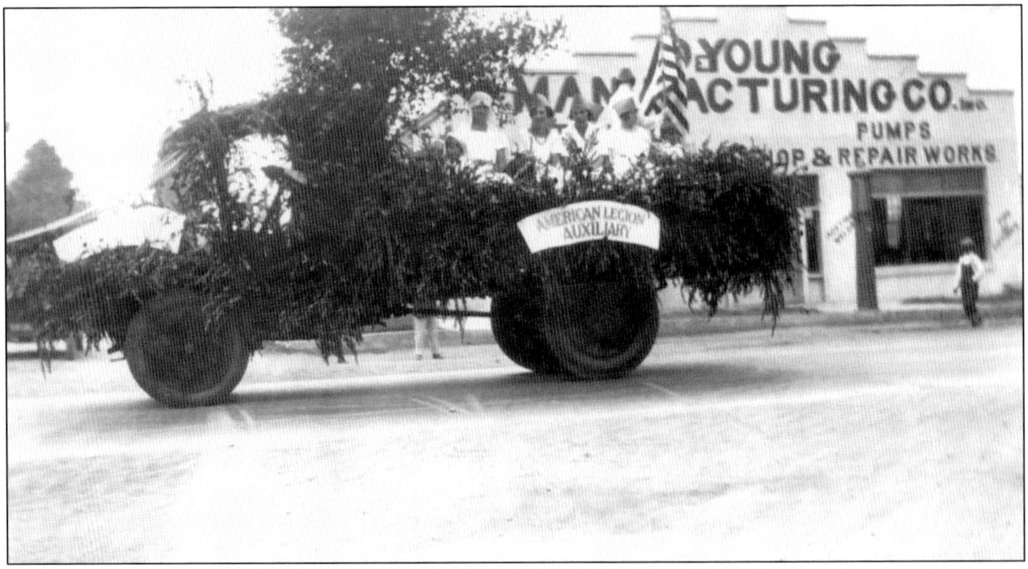

American Legion Auxiliary. Veterans were honored with a float during this parade. Many Chino families served in World War II, such as the children of Roy and Ruth Pine. Daughter Lillian joined the U.S. Navy. Frank and Walter flew as pilots. Edward joined the U.S. Navy as a B-29 engine mechanic. He was on Iwo Jima from 10 days after the initial landing until the end of the war. (CN.)

Eight

A Community that Cares

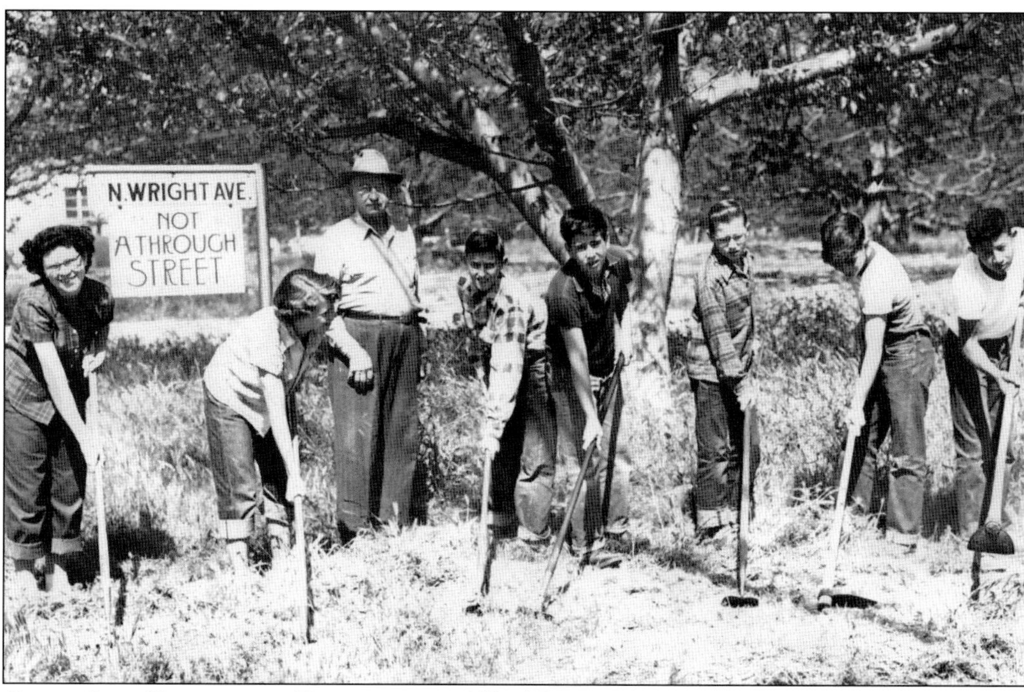

Chino Busy Farmer and Farmerettes. Alfred Brown, State Farm Insurance agent, took this group of hardworking youngsters out in May 1952 to clean up blind intersections in Chino. Busy at work are, from left to right, Eilene Wilson, Dorothy Anderson, Alfred Brown, Jim Imbach, Ken Matlin, Michael Brown, John Yzurdiaga, and Jesse Moreno. (GB.)

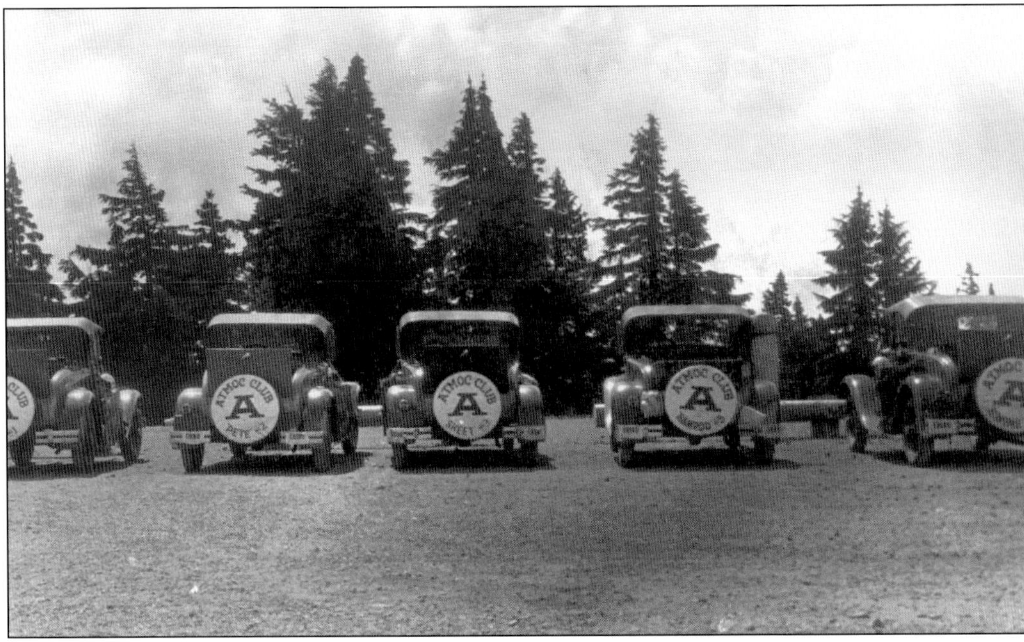

Chino's ATMOC Club. Community spirit and neighborliness have always been essential ingredients in the everyday life of Chino. When youths were seen hanging around on city streets, local businessmen led by Art Wagner decided to create Chino's own social club for boys, All True Men of Chino (ATMOC). The intent was to give Chino's future generation of leaders activities to increase community awareness, provide a network of support with positive role models, and host a variety of interesting events to help keep the youth out of trouble. In the above photograph, a caravan of automobiles has assembled, sporting the club's logo, to head off together on one of their trips. In the photograph below, the members of the ATMOC Club are seen visiting the Mariposa Grove of Big Trees at Yosemite National Park. (Both, CN.)

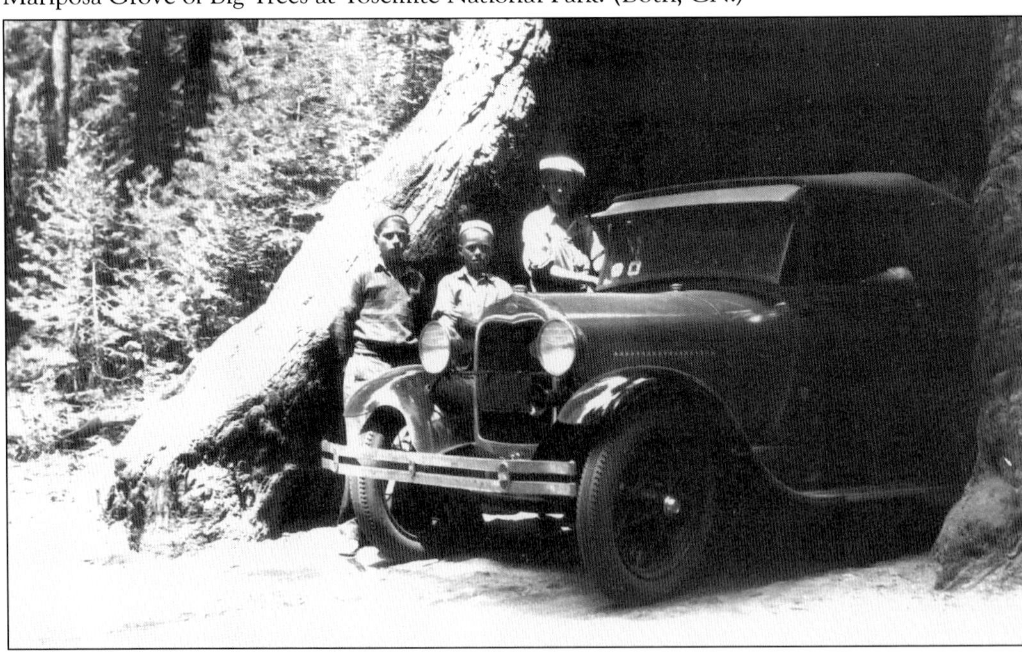

BOYS CLUB AT THE DEN. In 1934 and 1935, the Galbreath Grocery store was rented for $5 a month to form the Den, a place for young men to socialize together. A pool table and snooker table were rented, and each member paid 50¢ a month to belong. Rules for joining the Den were no alcohol or girls allowed. (GB.)

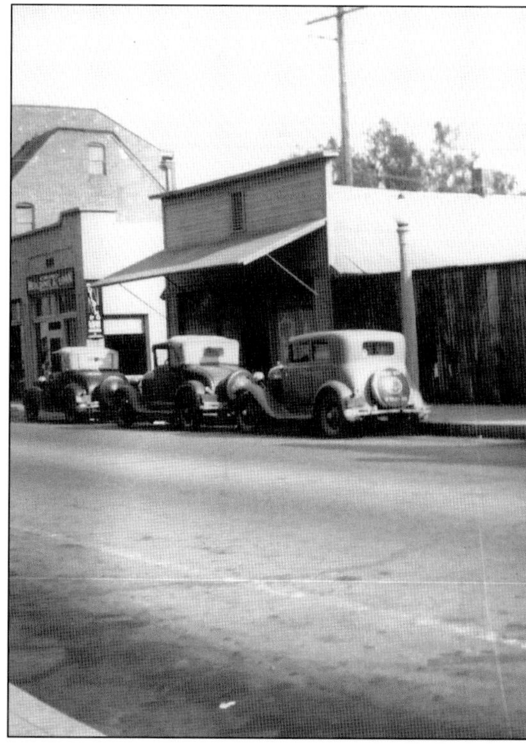

ATMOC REUNION, NOVEMBER 3, 1978. Men who met for the reunion at Art Wagner's included, from left to right, (first row) Ralph Blickenstaff, Ruben Cespedes, Howard Cattle, Bert Birnie, Dale Frady, and Art Wagner; (second row) Elmer Gray, Malcolm Woodhead, Dave Liskey, John Sagouspe, Willard Preston, "Shorty" Howell, Ashton Barnum, and George Marks; (third row) unidentified, Bob Peters, Frank Gregory, Earl Newman, ? Sonke, Earl LaBaw, Gerald Brown, Bill Rehkopf, Harry LaBaw, Gaylord Van Dusen, and Reinhard Karlson; (fourth row) Elgar English and Bill Evans. (GB.)

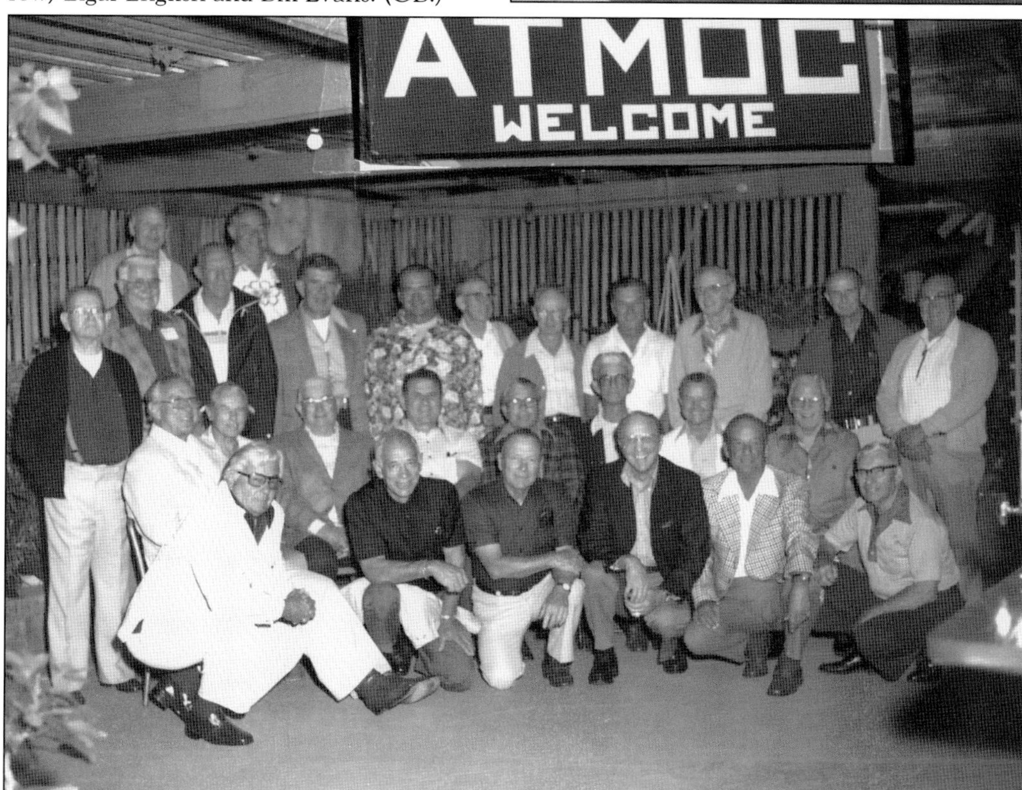

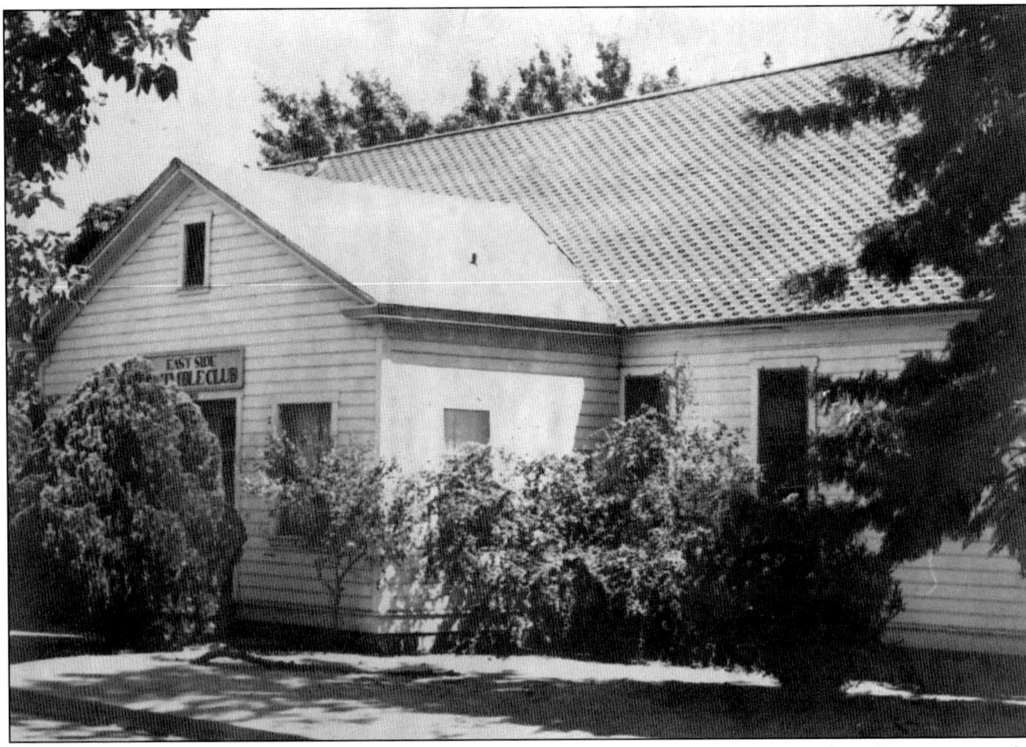

CHINO'S THIMBLE CLUB. The goal of the East Side Thimble Club was "to be of service to the community." In 1920, the Thimble Club purchased Chino's oldest school building as their headquarters. The club was incorporated as a nonprofit organization in 1923. Community functions, church meetings, and social events took place at the Thimble Club, with members organizing and serving the food. The West Side Thimble Club was separated from its sister organization by Central Avenue. Women helped provide clothes and nutrition for local schoolchildren and made quilts during the wars. Known for their tireless fundraising efforts, many organizations in Chino were aided financially. The Thimble Club was disbanded in the early 1970s, and the old schoolhouse building was turned over to the Chino Valley Historical Society, founded in 1970, for its museum. (Both, CN.)

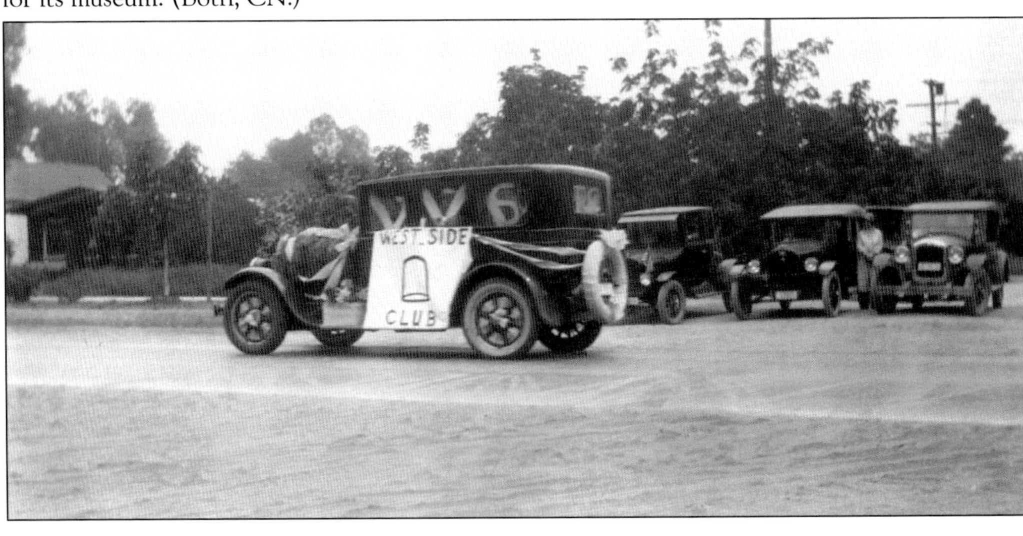

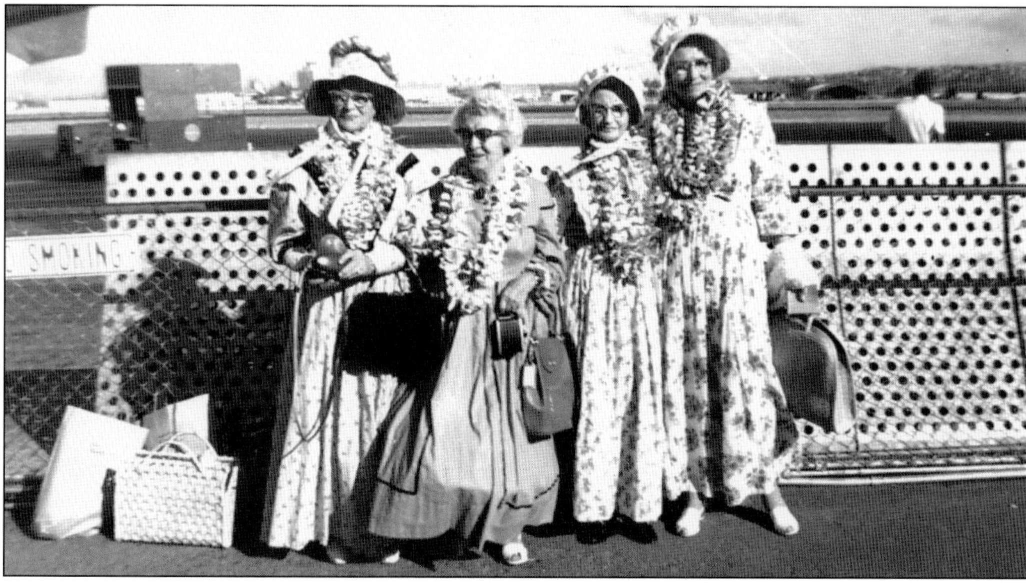

Queens Visit Hawaii, 1962. A pageant was held to help celebrate Chino's Diamond Jubilee. Contestants were members of the East Side Thimble Club, born before 1900. People placed bids for the winner, who would travel to Hawaii. Alice Brown won, but they decided to send all four finalists together. Chino's Diamond Jubilee Queens are, from left to right, Florence Grant, Cora Younkin, Alice Brown, and Bertha Gray. (GB.)

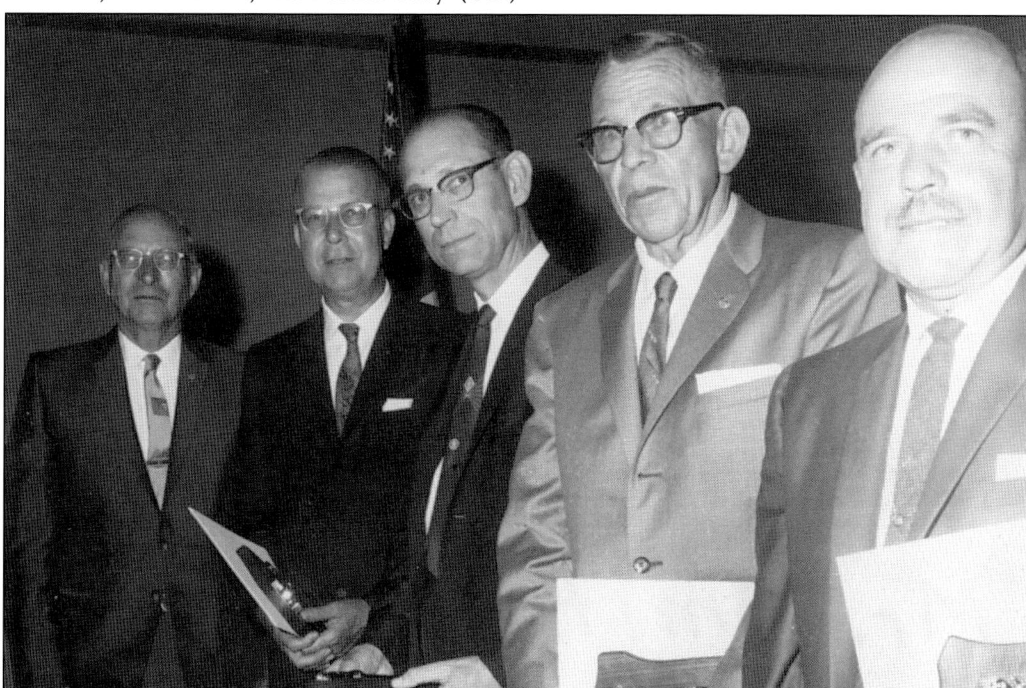

Lions Club Charter Members. Being honored for their community service as Lions Club Charter members are, from left to right, unidentified, Bob Fritz, Glen Patton, Carl Anderson, and ? Smith. First held in the Community Building, the Lions Club annual Corn and Potato Festival has been a much-attended event each year at the Chino Fairgrounds. (CN.)

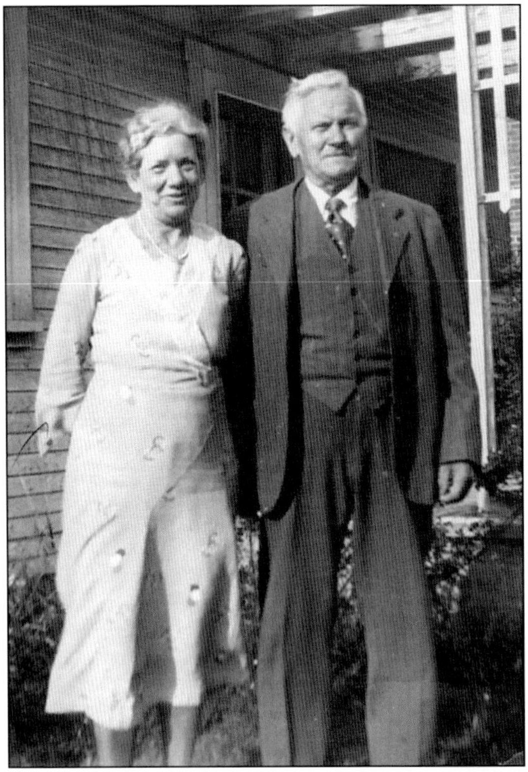

Eva and Fred Walters, c. 1919. This photograph was taken on the Walters' ranch on Riverside Drive, between Oaks and Magnolia Avenues. An engineer with the railroad, Fred Walters drove the local train. Eva Walters was the first matron of Chino in the middle of the first decade of the 20th century. The first matron of Chino served as president of the International Order of Eastern Star, a fraternal Christian organization. Just one month after she was named to this position, Eva Walters delivered twins, Evelyn and Everett. (FW.)

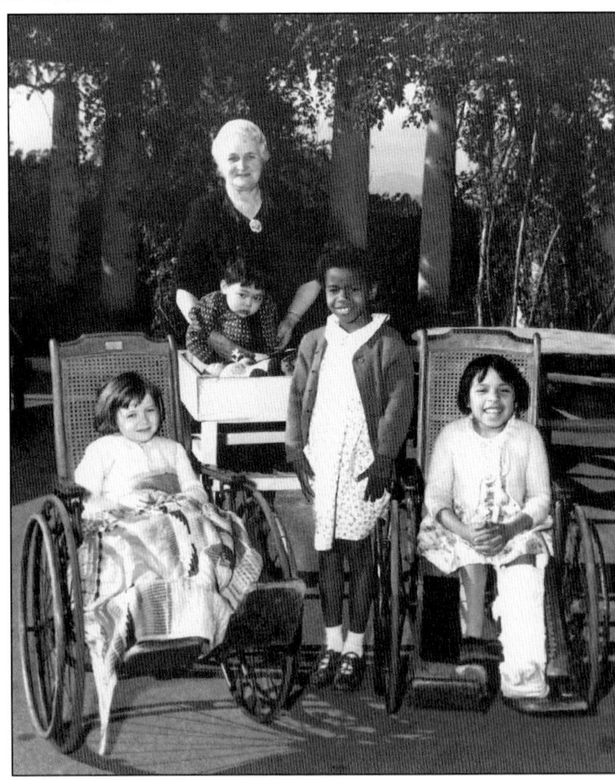

Casa Colina Helps Polio Victims. Frances Eleanor Smith, for her tireless aid to people in need, was given national honor as the Ideal American Mother in 1936. A polio victim when she was 10 years old, Mother Smith regained her health and founded a convalescent home for crippled children on the property of what is now known as the Boys Republic. It was named Casa Colina. (CCC.)

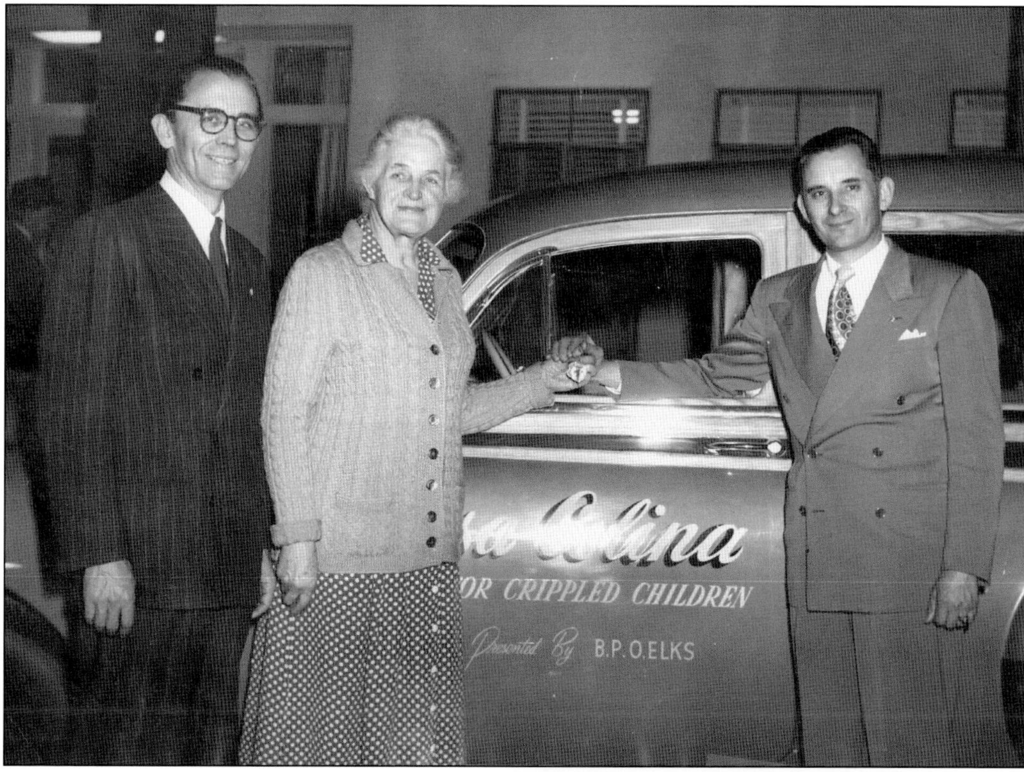

CAR PRESENTED BY ELKS. Mother Smith was a tireless fundraiser. Here in this photograph, the Elks donated a car for use by Casa Colina. When not raising funds, Mother Smith lived up to her name and provided nurturing care for the children at Casa Colina, reading to them and cooking for them. Christmas parties at Casa Colina were always a festive affair because of her contributions and enthusiasm. (CCC.)

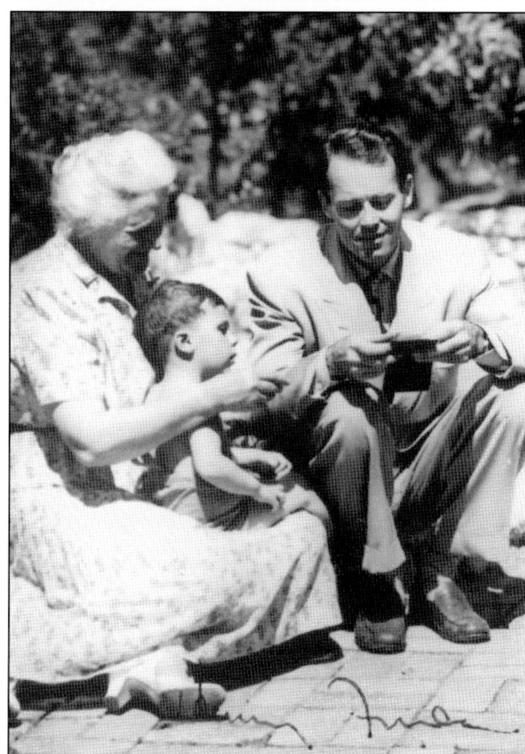

CELEBRITIES GIVE GENEROUS DONATIONS. Many famous celebrities supported Mother Smith's work at Casa Colina through generous donations. She made frequent visits to Hollywood parties as well as county rodeos and fairs to help raise money for modern equipment and therapeutic programs for the children. Here in this photograph, Henry Fonda presents a donation to Mother Smith. (CCC.)

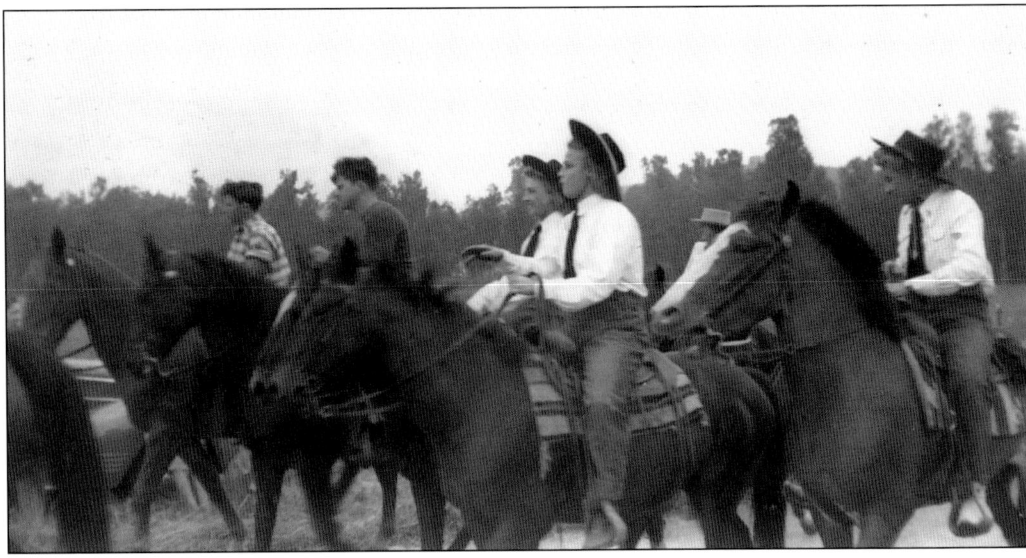

Chino Rancho Ride. Instituted in 1938, Chino Rancho Ride's first annual outing drew 240 horseback riders to the event. A way to celebrate Chino's rich heritage, it was truly a community event. A total of 30 acres, located west of the Aerojet property, was purchased, and horse owners and neighbors camped on an open field, north of Bird Farm Road and Ramona Avenue. The ride headed west on Bird Farm Road around the golf course, then turned south on Pipeline, and then went on to Aerojet for a total ride that was a little over 3 miles. Equestrian events were important to the festival. Some of these events were musical tires (musical chairs on horseback) and the boot race. Edward Pine was the third president of the Association of the Rancho Ride. His son Dennis Pine is currently president of the organization. (Both, GB.)

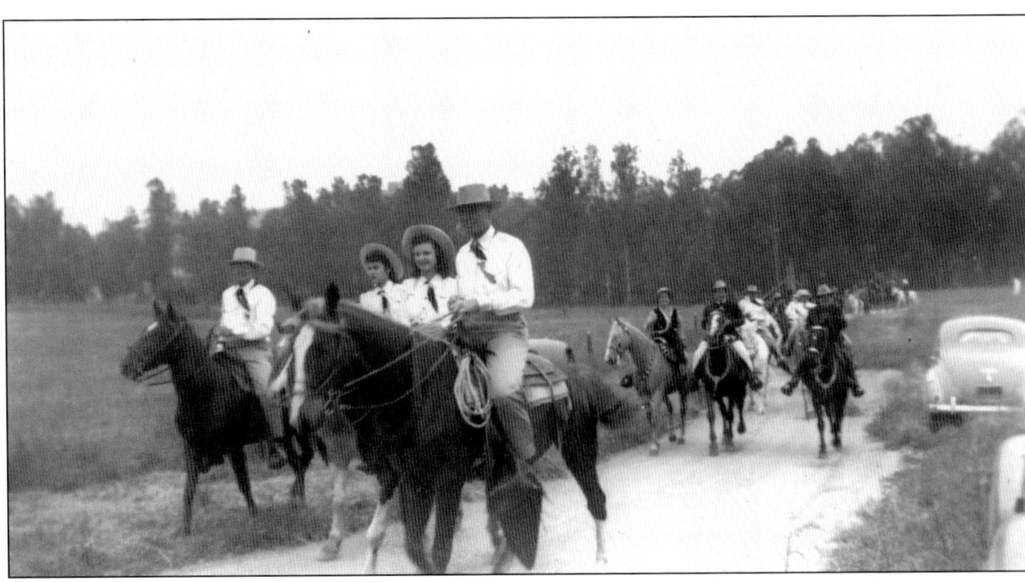

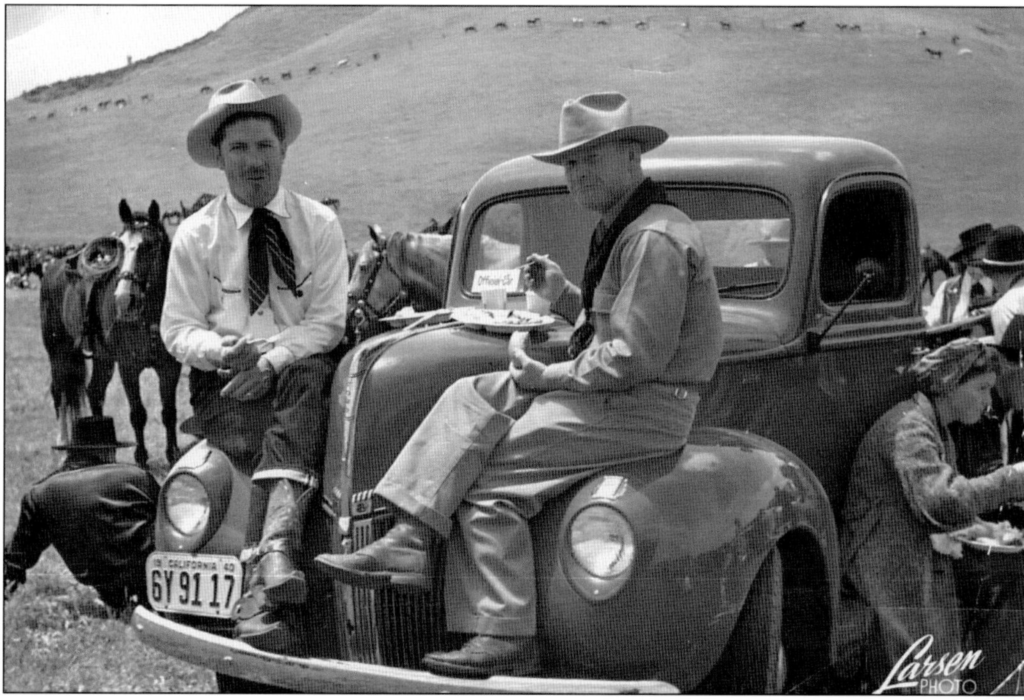

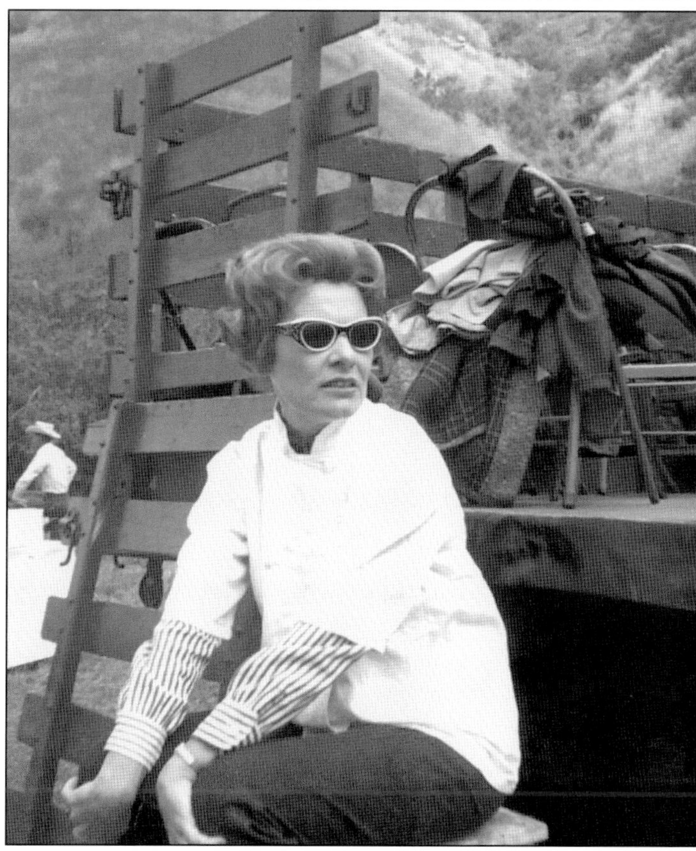

A Fun and Festive Event. In the above photograph, John A. Daniels (right) enjoys a plate of beans at the Chino Rancho Ride around 1940. Georgia Bennett Rudin reminisced how every year during her childhood family and friends rode out by horseback to Soquel Canyon in search of Joaquin Murrieta's hidden treasure. The Rancho Ride took place on the last Saturday of April each year for 40 years. Kiwanis dug a deep pit barbecue. Evelyn Walters Bennett is sitting on the barbecue truck in the photograph at right around 1960. The final ride was held in 1977, with a total of 1,200 people and 1,000 horses. The event came to an end mostly due to property development in the area. (Above, VAD; right, FW.)

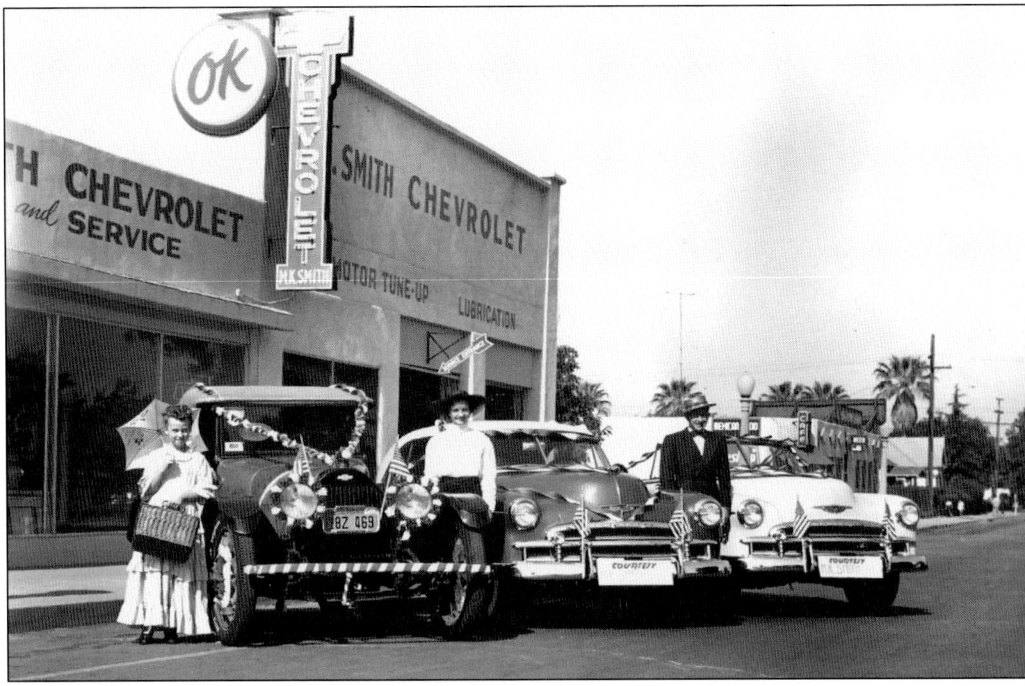

M. K. Smith Joins Parade. All decorated and ready to join the 1940s parade, M. K. Smith Chevrolet sports community spirit. In World War II, Chevrolet made tanks, not cars, so the dealership survived on servicing vehicles while selling tractors and used cars. After M. K. Smith retired, his son Robert (Bob) took over the dealership. Bob and Cheryl Smith's two sons, Marc and Todd, currently run the business. (MKS.)

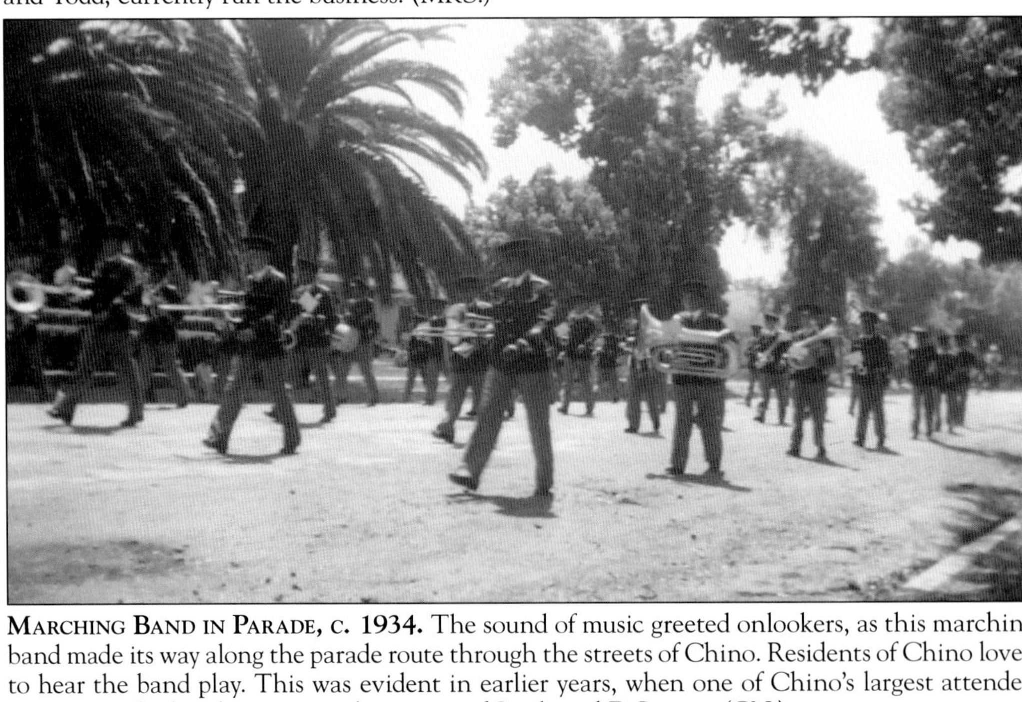

Marching Band in Parade, c. 1934. The sound of music greeted onlookers, as this marching band made its way along the parade route through the streets of Chino. Residents of Chino loved to hear the band play. This was evident in earlier years, when one of Chino's largest attended events was the band concert at the corner of Sixth and D Streets. (CN.)

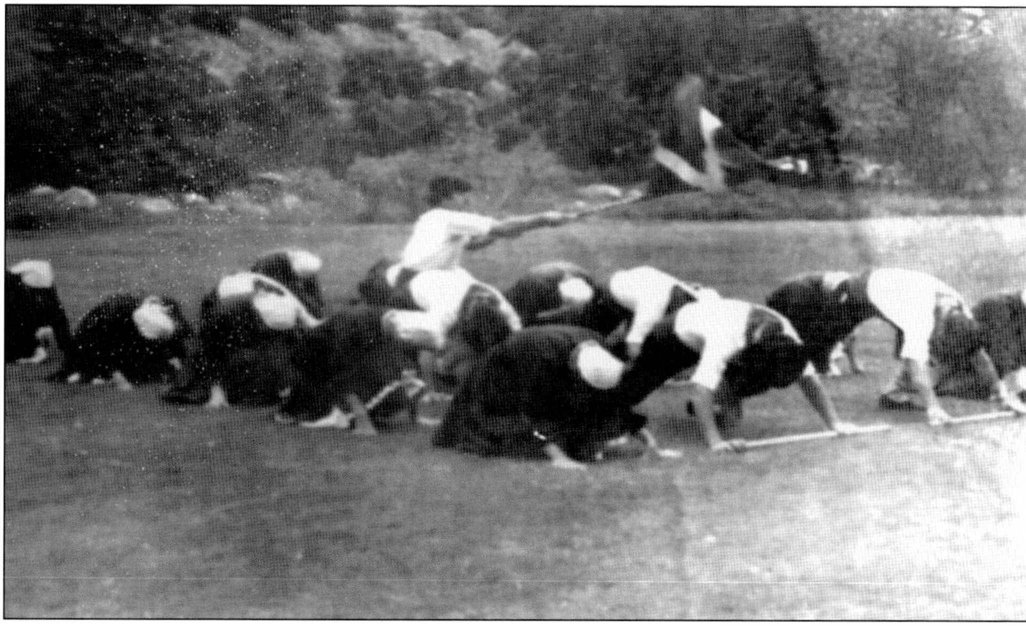

Basque Flag Dance. Called the Ikurrina Dantza, this ceremony is part of the Sunday Basque Labor Day festivities. In the dance, one member of the team carries the Nationalist flag of the seven Basque Provinces. The rest of the dancers perform a salute to the flag and then bend to the ground as the flag is waved over them in symbolic blessing. Jeanne Berterretche is part of this group. (BF.)

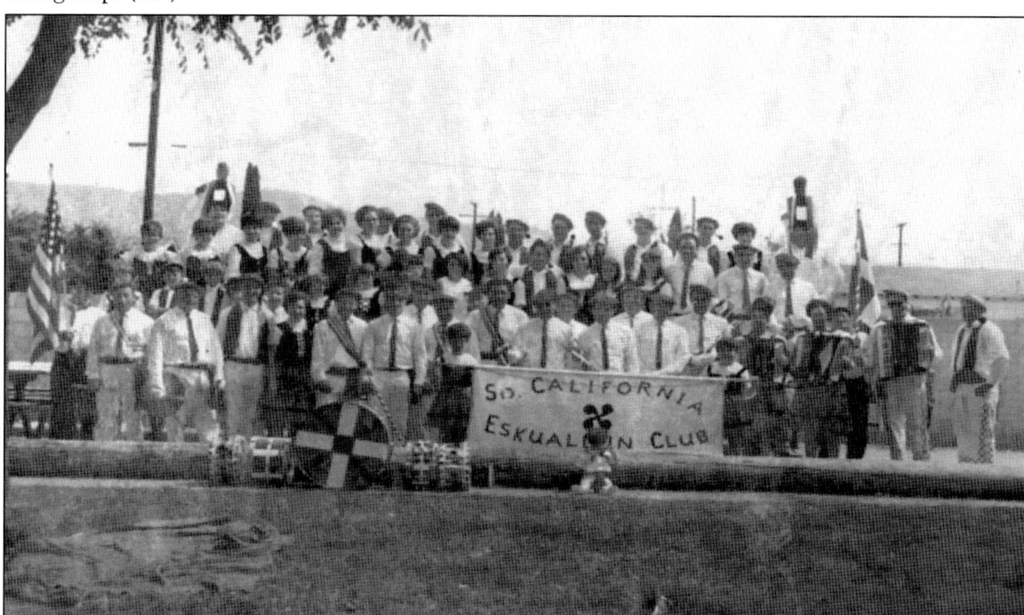

Eskualdun Club at Chino Fairgrounds, c. 1968. The Eskualdun, or Basque, Club is dedicated to perpetuating the traditions of the Basque people. The club performs various functions in the Chino community, including participation in the Labor Day events. Among the club members portrayed here are Jeanne Berterretche (age 9) and Marie Berterretche (age 13), daughters of Monique and Pierre Berterretche. (BF.)

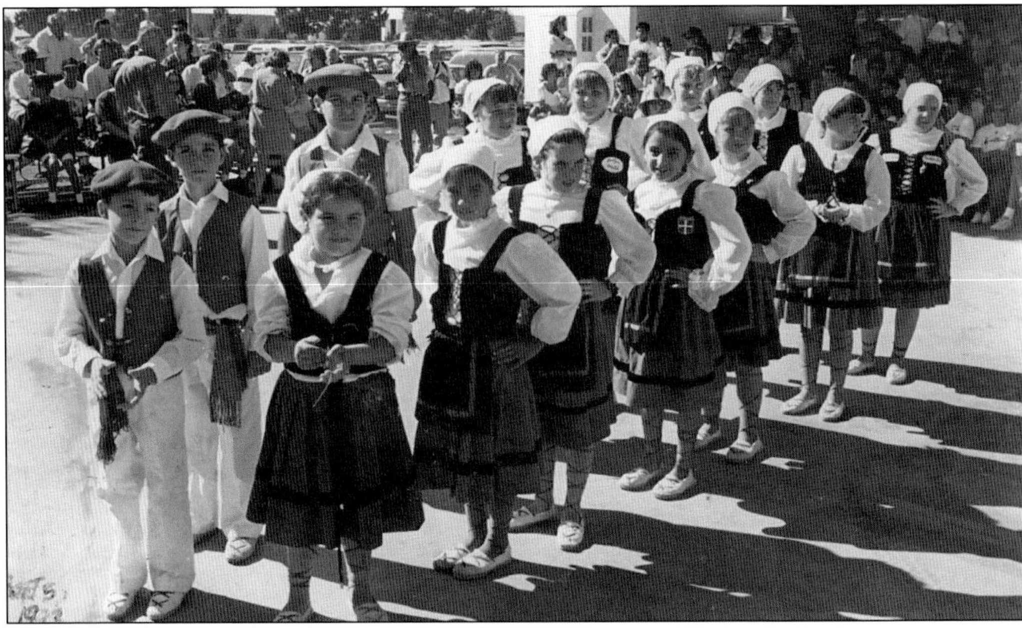

Children at Basque Picnic. Every year, during Labor Day Weekend, the Basque population of Chino gathers for a two-day heritage celebration. The Sunday festivities take place at either Puddingstone or the Chino Fairgrounds and include dances in traditional costumes, as seen above. Michelle Sorarrain is pictured in the first row. (BF.)

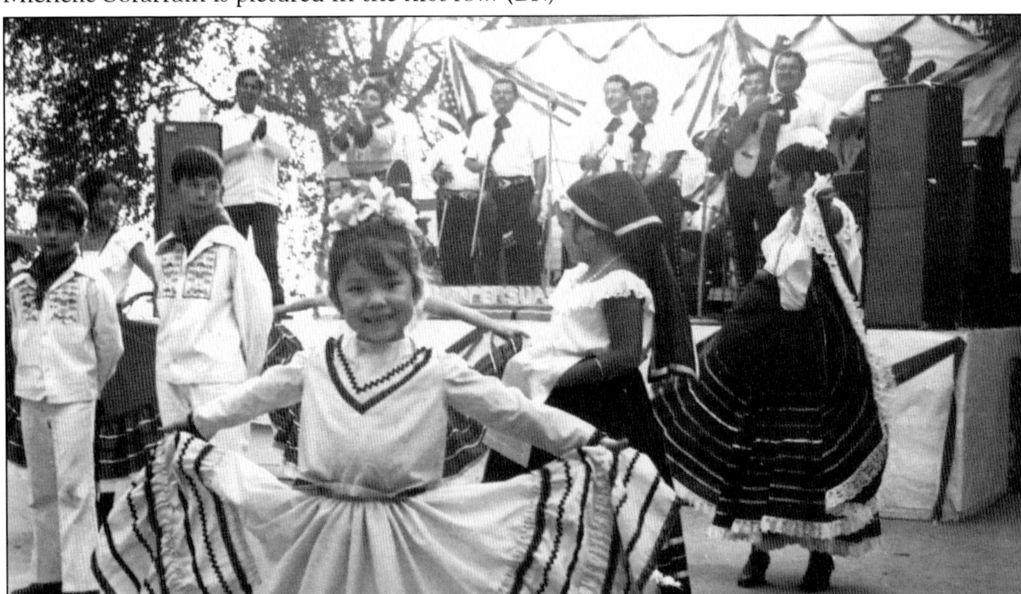

Fiesta in Chino. This photograph shows the Mexican American community celebrating a fiesta. Families such as the Salgados immigrated to the United States and settled in Chino. Martin Salgado was born in the unincorporated area of Chino in 1882. His daughter, Mary Ann Salgado Guillen, was a graduate of Chino High School. At 17 years old, she was fiesta queen for Our Lady of Guadalupe Church. In 2011, the Chino Research Group published the history of the Mexican American community of Chino in the book *The Chino We Remember.* (CN.)

Nine

PIONEER FAMILIES

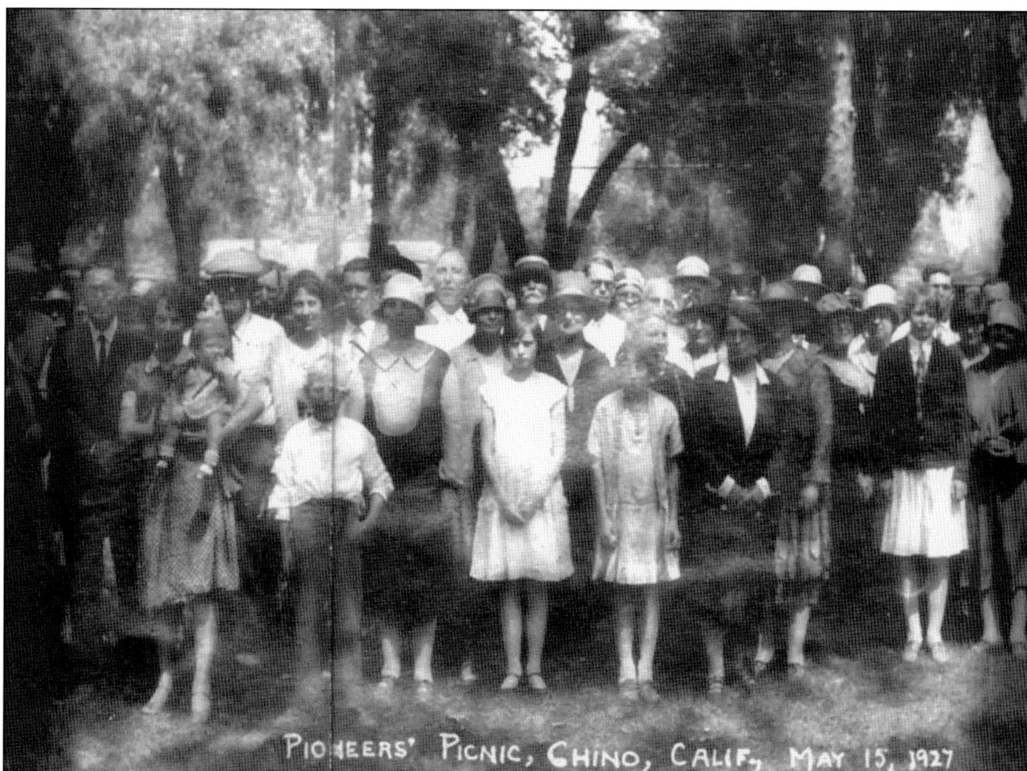

CHINO VALLEY PIONEER PICNIC. According to the *Chino Champion*, the Pioneer Picnic was first held in Orange County and attended by several hundred people. Having moved to Chino the following year, it has been held here ever since, with centennial festivities taking place in the Community Building in 2010. Gerald Brown, whose family contributed this photograph, was honored the previous year as the pioneer who attended the most picnics. (GB.)

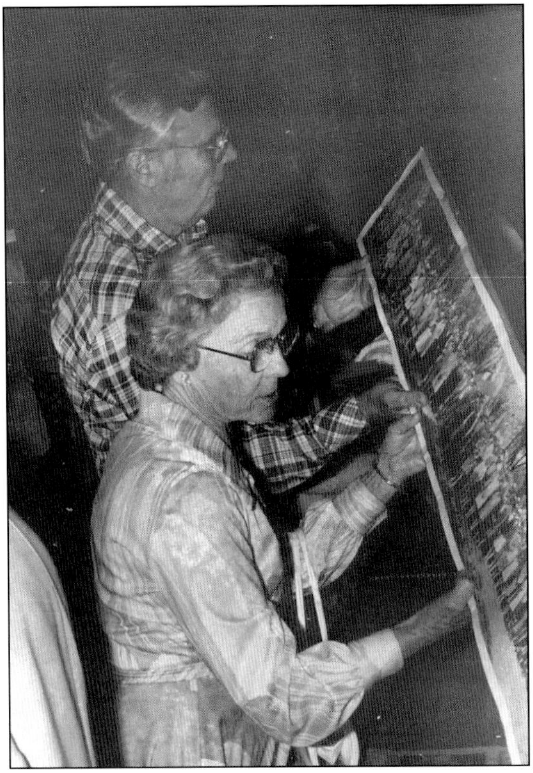

A Panoramic View. Supervisor Robert O. Townsend and Edith Solter McCann examine the photograph of Chino's Pioneer Picnic held on May 15, 1927 (see previous page). Edith McCann was a 1918 graduate of Chino High School. The Robert O. Townsend Junior High School in Chino Hills is named after Supervisor Townsend. (CN.)

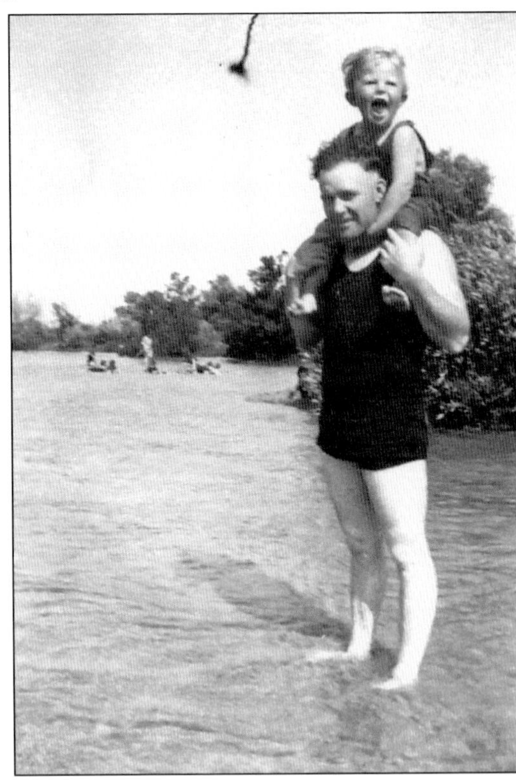

Swimming on a Summer's Day. On a hot summer day in the Chino Valley, John A. Daniels (standing) enjoys a refreshing swim, probably in the Santa Ana River. Typical of most rivers during the summer months of Southern California, the water level only reached up to most people's ankles. During the rainy season in the winter months, however, water levels could rise quickly with flood warnings in effect. (VAD.)

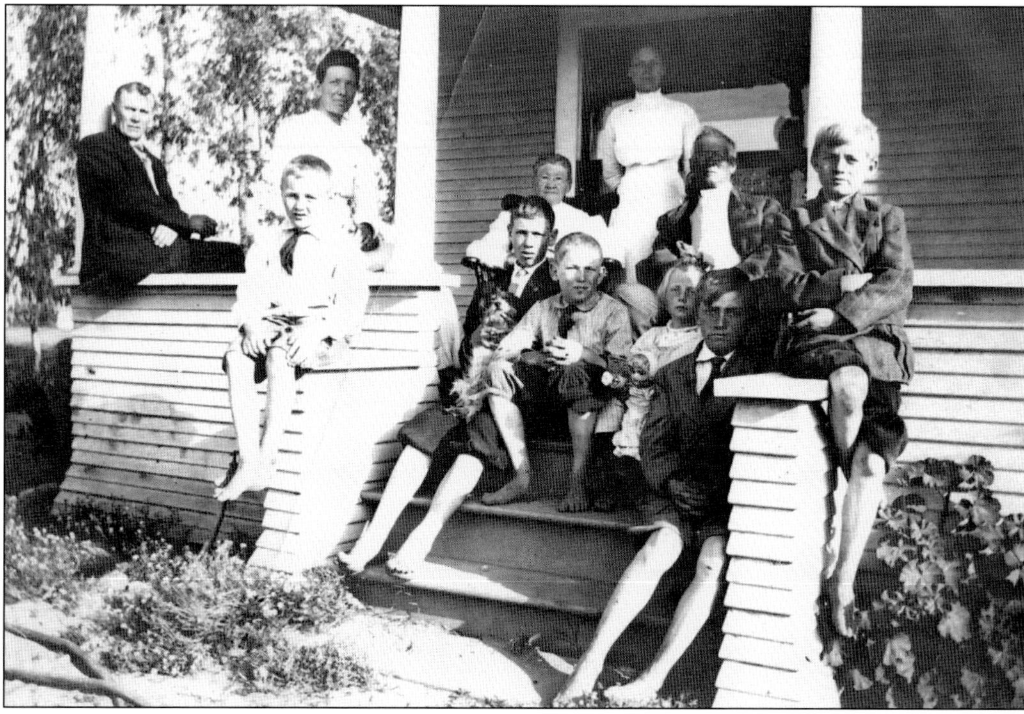

THE BIG W RANCH. Harriet Weber and her family owned an elite property on Riverside Drive, near Benson, known in the community as the Big W Ranch. Part of the building still stands where Flo's No. 2 restaurant serves home-style cooking on 5650 Riverside Drive. Flo's No. 2 is a sister restaurant to Flo's Airport Café. (FW.)

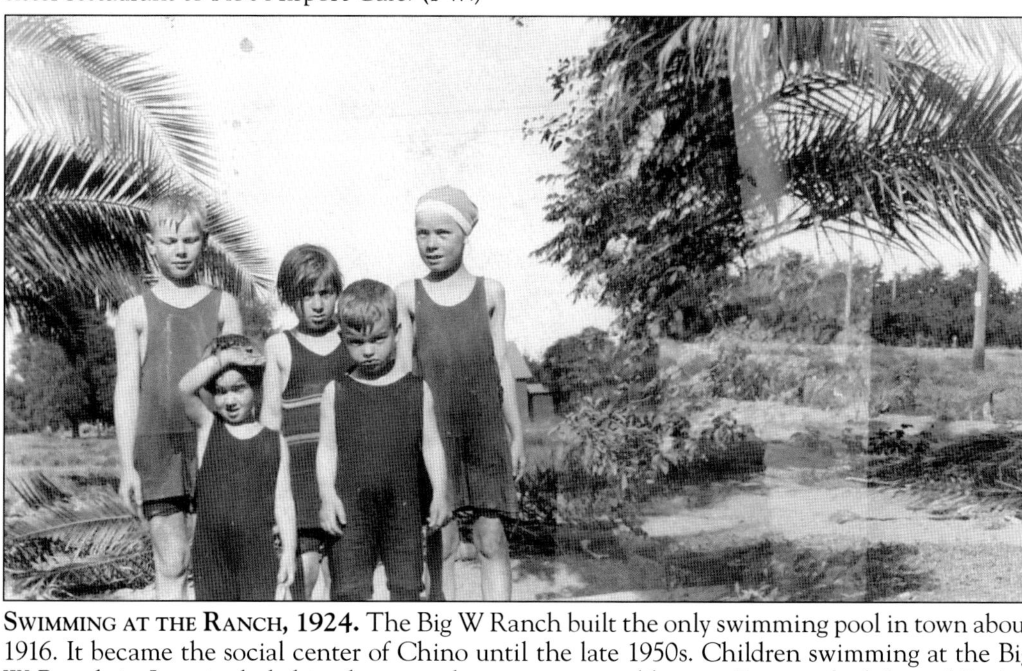

SWIMMING AT THE RANCH, 1924. The Big W Ranch built the only swimming pool in town about 1916. It became the social center of Chino until the late 1950s. Children swimming at the Big W Ranch in June included in the second row nine-year-old twins Everett, far left, and Evelyn Walters, far right. (FW.)

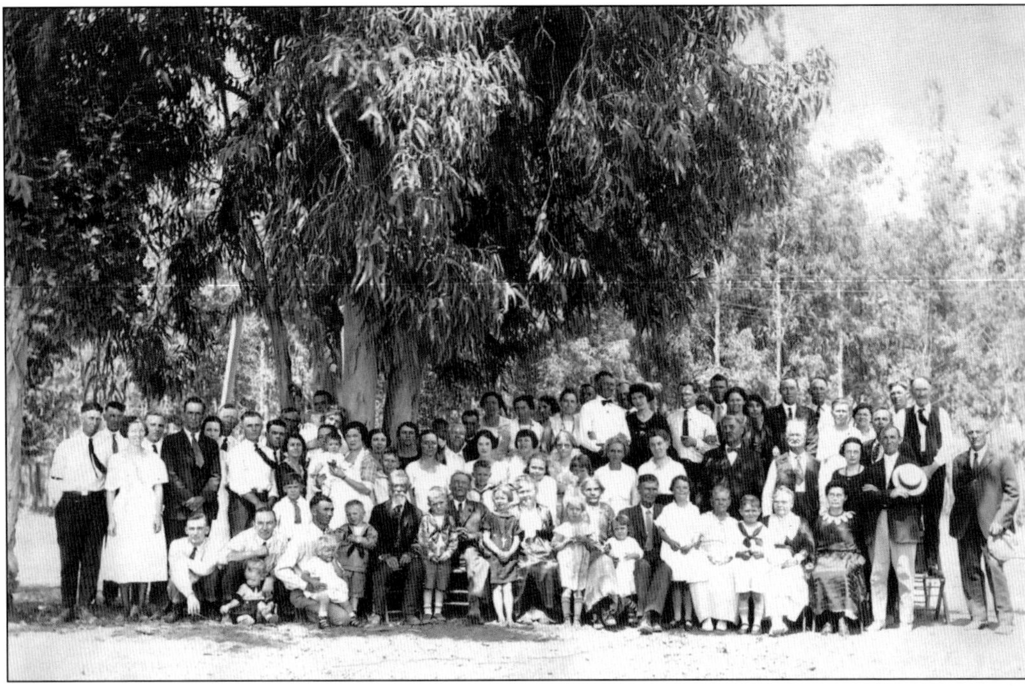

The Pine Family Picnic, 1922. This photograph was taken at the 50th anniversary of John Brown Roberds and Jeannette Henderson (Walkinshaw) Roberds (first row, center) at the McCarty ranch, which is located between Chino and Norco. Jeannette Roberds had five children with her first husband, Thomas Walkinshaw. One of those children was Ella Walkinshaw. At the far right is Edward Hornby Pine. His wife, Ella Walkinshaw Pine, is in the top row directly above Jeannette. (PF.)

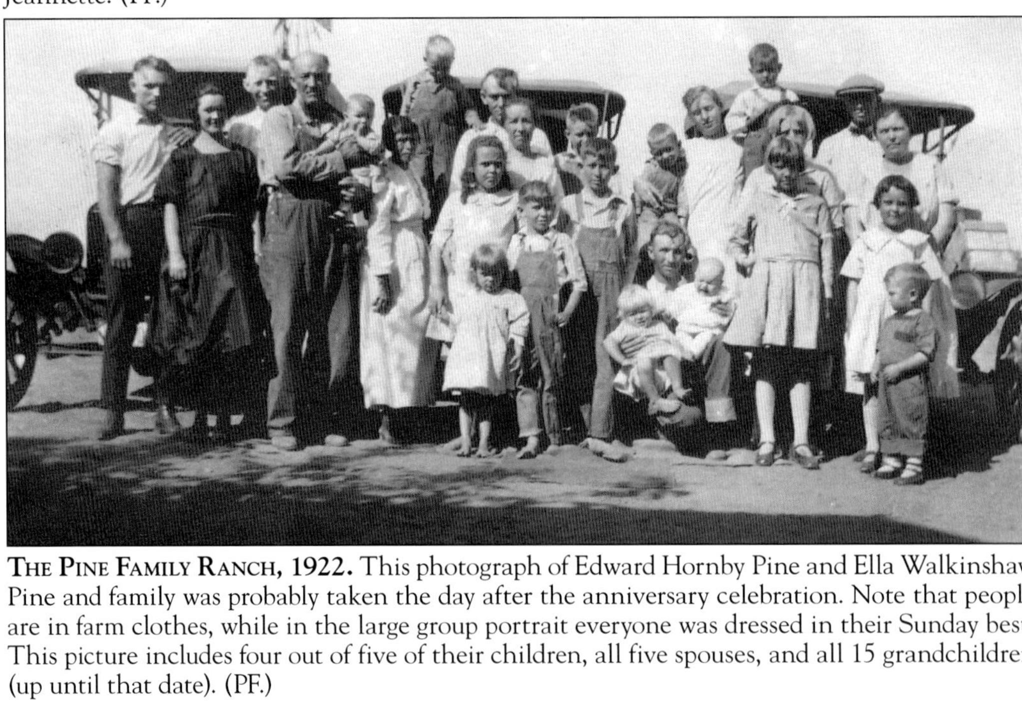

The Pine Family Ranch, 1922. This photograph of Edward Hornby Pine and Ella Walkinshaw Pine and family was probably taken the day after the anniversary celebration. Note that people are in farm clothes, while in the large group portrait everyone was dressed in their Sunday best. This picture includes four out of five of their children, all five spouses, and all 15 grandchildren (up until that date). (PF.)

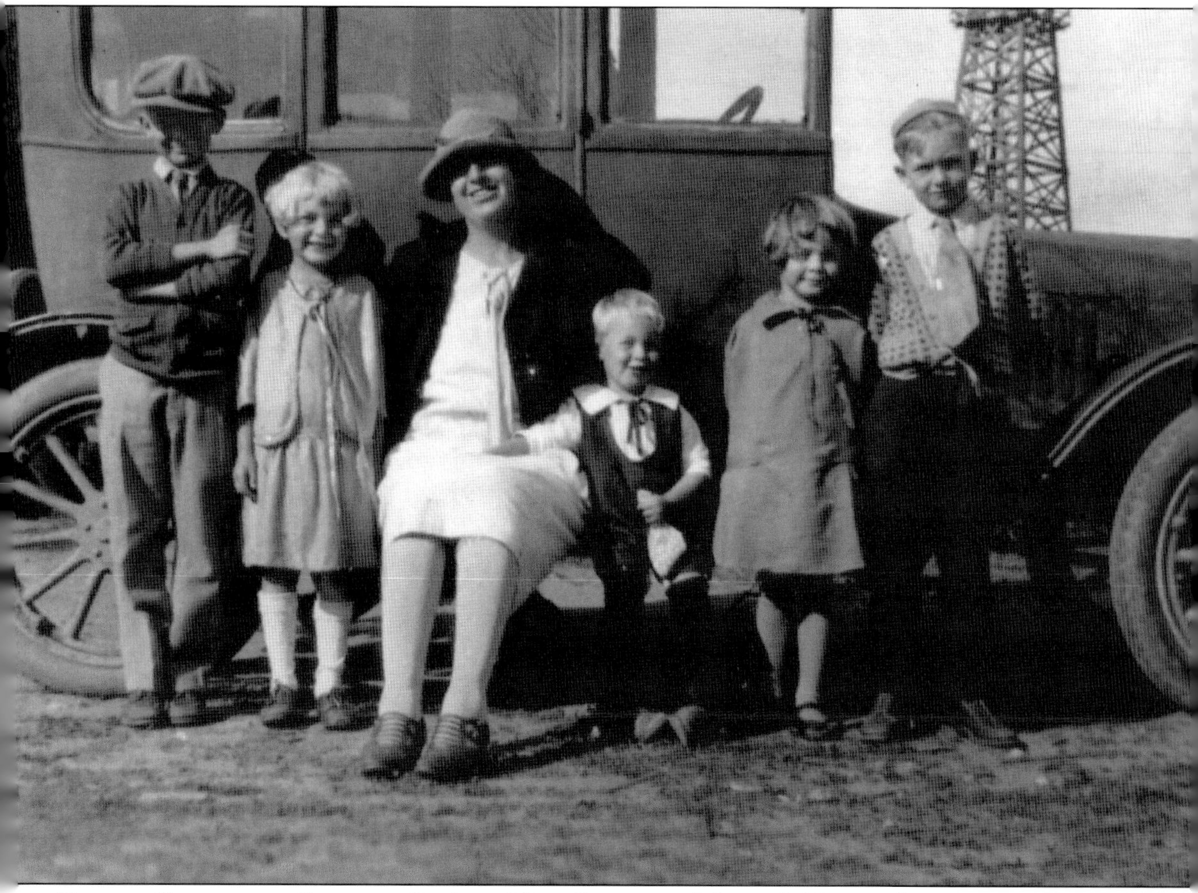

Future Community Leaders. Ruth and Roy Pine raised their children to be active in their community. Members of their family are, from left to right, Frank, Lillian, Ruth, Walter, Margaret, and Edward (Ed) Pine. The son of Edward Hornby Pine, Roy worked his father's ranch until it was lost to the bank during the Depression. He then moved his family to Chino where he sold farm irrigation equipment. Frank, the oldest, flew crop dusters and fire bombers after World War II. He ended his career with TallMantz Aviation, where he flew camera planes for movies and commercials. Edward worked for State Farm Insurance, eventually operating Ed Pine Insurance until retirement. Lillian married Ray Muriset, who worked at the Chino Fire Department until retirement as a fire captain. Margaret married Jim Sanders, a guard at California Institution for Men. After the war, Walter joined the newly formed air force. He retired as a colonel, having earned a Silver Star in Vietnam. Afterward, he worked with Frank, then president at TallMantz, where he flew a B-25 camera plane. (PF.)

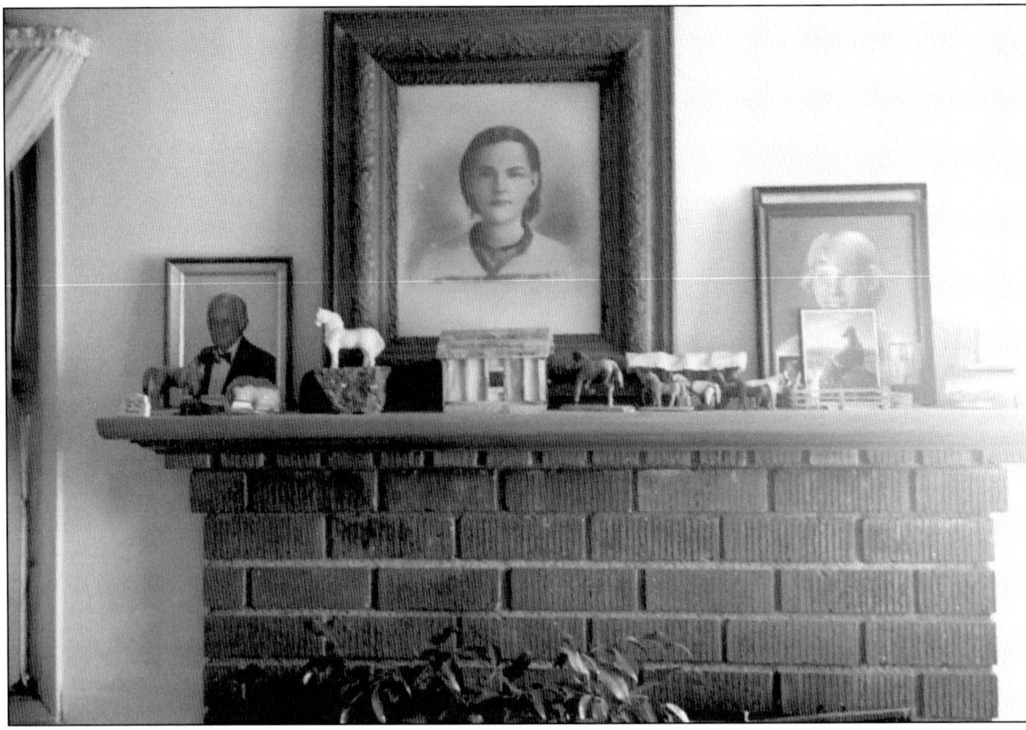

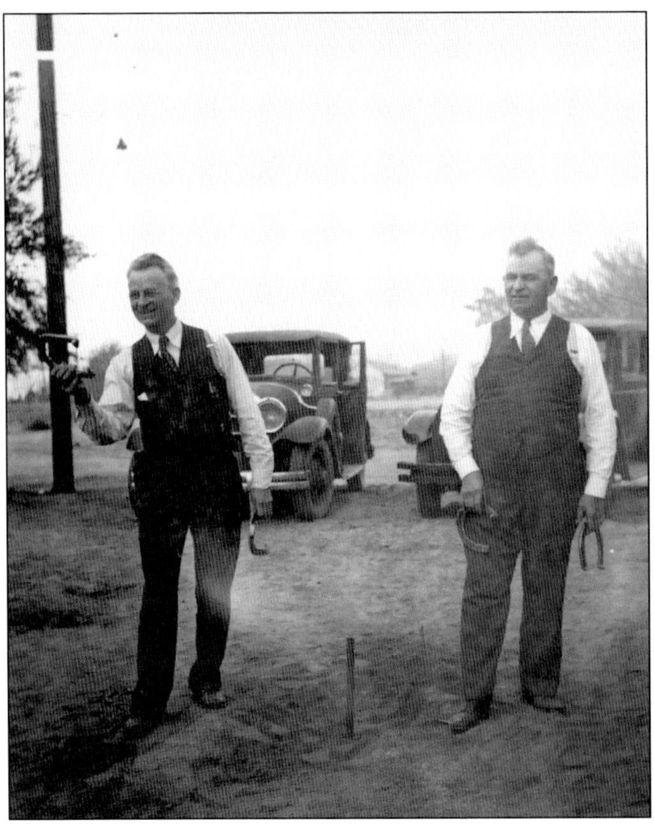

Descendant of a Cherokee Chief. E. C. Daniels's mother was a Cherokee princess, daughter of Chief James Vann. Her beautiful charcoal portrait is displayed here with carvings by grandson John Daniels. When E. C. Daniels was 19, he was an overseer on the Vann Plantation in Georgia. Tired of picking cotton for another's profit, he saddled a horse and rode to California where he settled in Chino and farmed for himself. (VAD.)

A Game of Horseshoes. James Elmer Brown (left) enjoys a game of horseshoes with Alfred Brown in this photograph taken in the early 1930s. Even though pioneer families worked hard in Chino to make a living and life during the Depression was difficult, everyone still took time to get together, relax, and enjoy simple pleasures such as a game of horseshoes. (GB.)

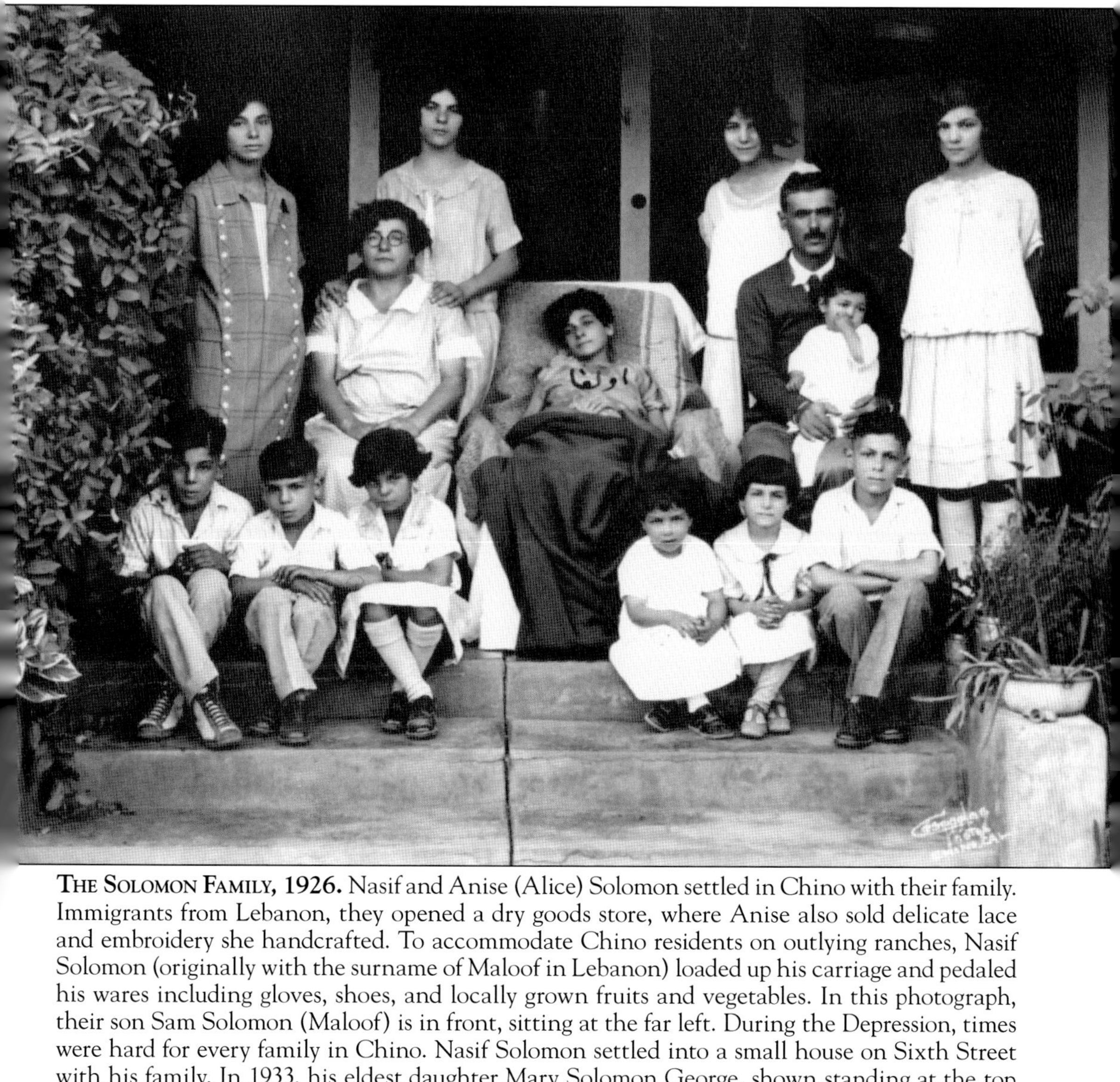

THE SOLOMON FAMILY, 1926. Nasif and Anise (Alice) Solomon settled in Chino with their family. Immigrants from Lebanon, they opened a dry goods store, where Anise also sold delicate lace and embroidery she handcrafted. To accommodate Chino residents on outlying ranches, Nasif Solomon (originally with the surname of Maloof in Lebanon) loaded up his carriage and pedaled his wares including gloves, shoes, and locally grown fruits and vegetables. In this photograph, their son Sam Solomon (Maloof) is in front, sitting at the far left. During the Depression, times were hard for every family in Chino. Nasif Solomon settled into a small house on Sixth Street with his family. In 1933, his eldest daughter Mary Solomon George, shown standing at the top left, tragically lost her husband Nimor George and moved into the house on Sixth Street with her six children. Everyone helped out working various part-time jobs throughout the community and raising a garden along with goats and chickens for milk and eggs. (DG.)

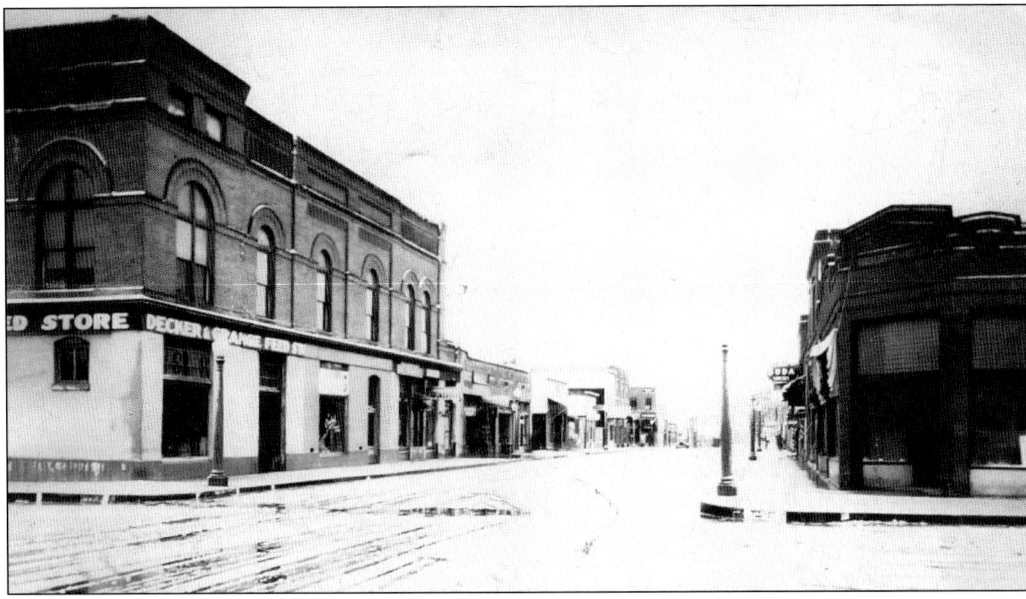

Snow in Chino, 1932. Captured in this January 15, 1932, photograph is proof that there has been snow in Chino. During the months of November through February, the usually hot climate of this community enjoys a reprieve from the desert-like heat with rainy weather and cooler days. Normally, snowfall is only experienced in the nearby mountain ranges, where high elevations allow for sledding and skiing. (CN.)

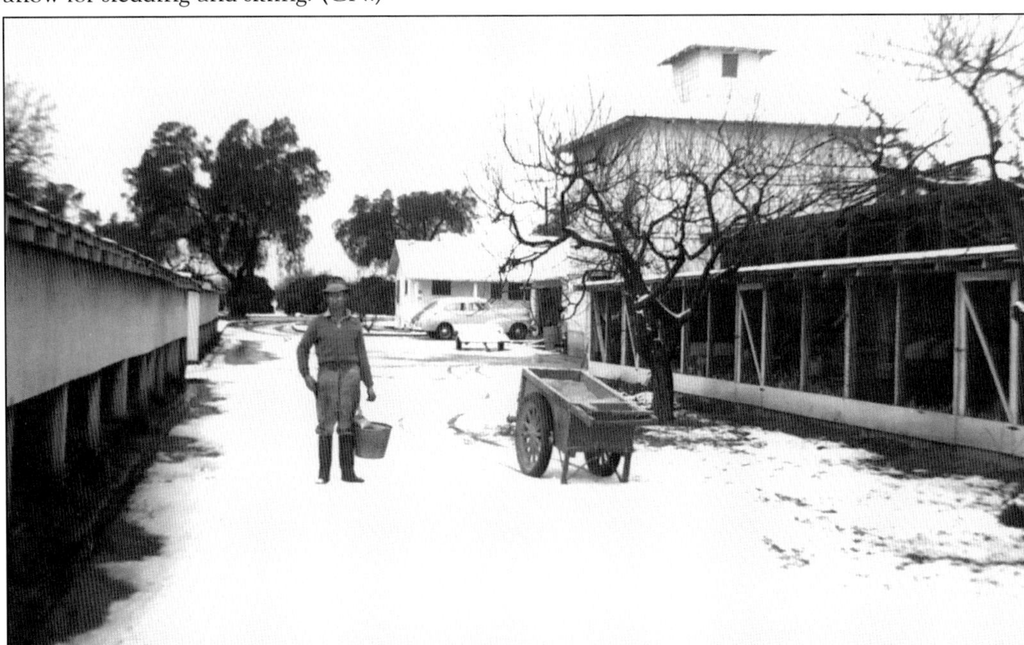

The 1949 Winter Storm. In January 1949, a surprise snowstorm once again blanketed Chino residents in shroud of white. Here in the photograph can be seen poultry farmer Gerald Brown carrying a bucket of eggs at his property on 11565 Central Avenue. The tall granary that he built during World War II can be seen in the background. The granary was constructed because there was a shortage of burlap to sack the grain. (GB.)

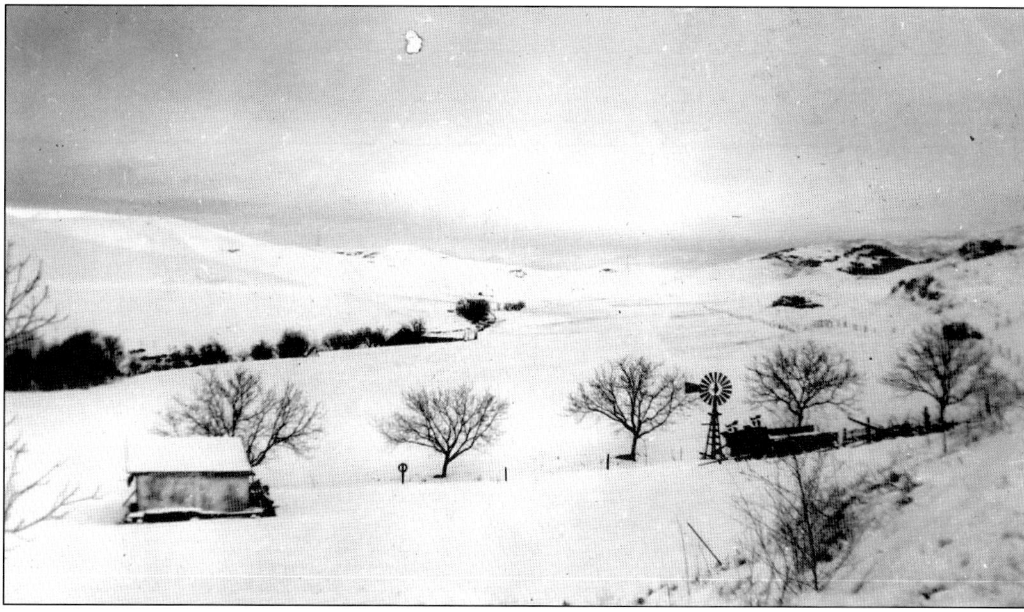

Snowscape Over the Hills. The stark outline of bare-branched trees along with a lonely windmill stand out against the snowy background in this photograph from after the January 1949 storm. These picturesque and low hills in the outlying regions surrounding the city of Chino look like a winter wonderland of snow. (GB.)

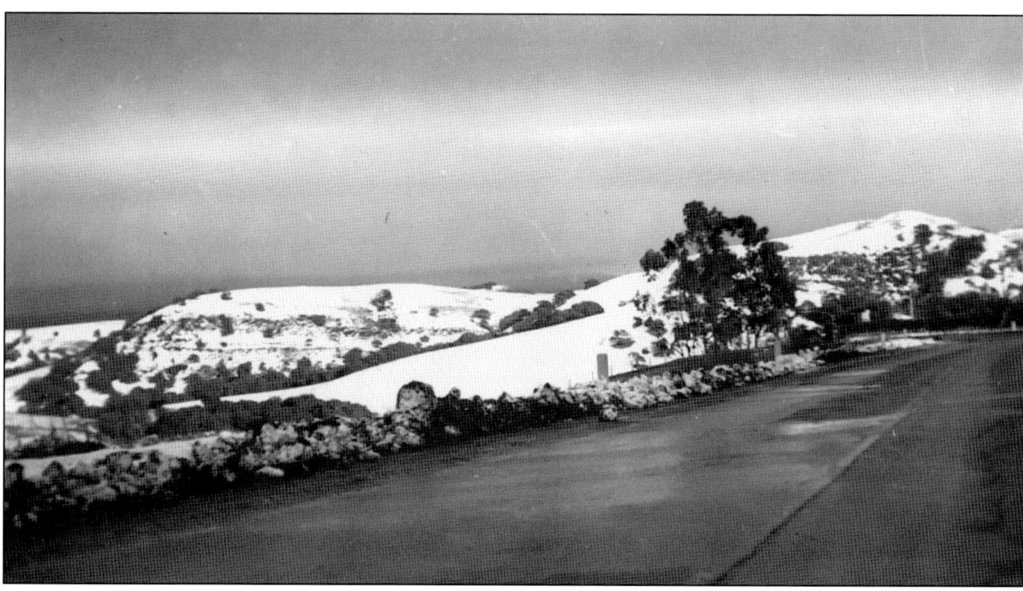

A Beautiful Covering of Snow. This photograph, taken in January 1949, shows that the snow is already beginning to melt. With a low elevation of 750 feet, the city of Chino rarely sees snow on its streets. The rolling hills in this photograph are probably located in the area now known as Chino's neighboring city of Chino Hills. (GB.)

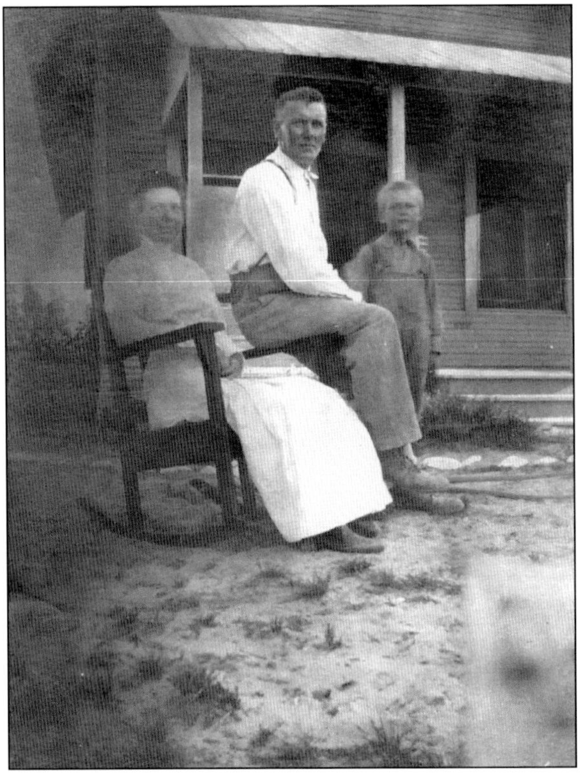

The Henning Ranch. Shown on the Henning ranch at Riverside Drive, between Oaks and Magnolia Avenues, are, from left to right, Eva Henning Walters, Fred Walters, and their oldest son Fred Walters. Because Fred Walters had a job with the railroad driving the train between Ontario and Chino, he did not farm his ranch for a living, as did many of his neighbors. (FW.)

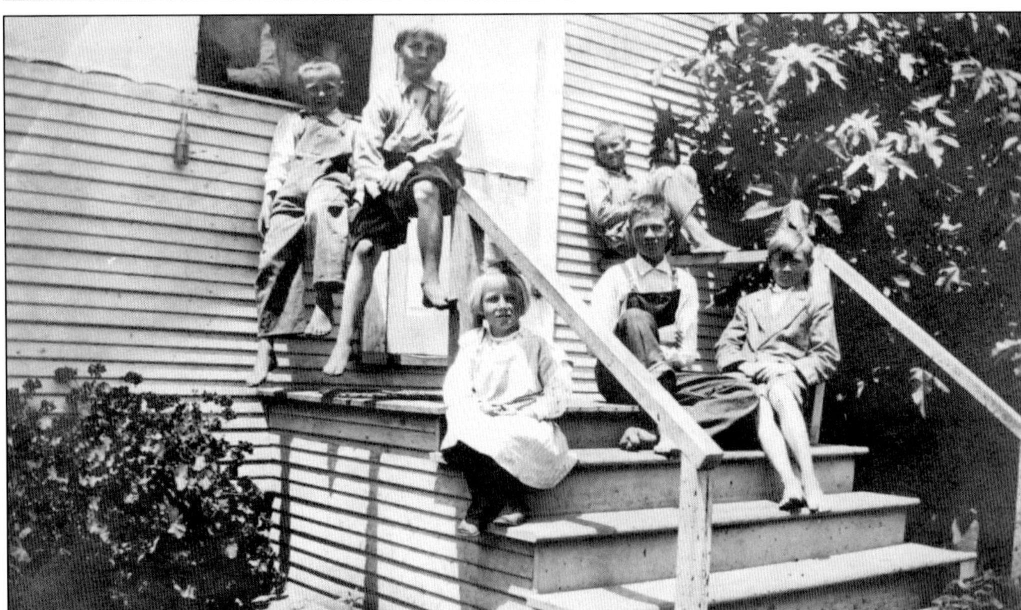

Children at the Ranch. These children are sitting on the back steps at the Henning ranch. Note the boys' bare feet and overalls. On the left banister, second from the left, is George Perry, future owner of George Perry's Furniture in Chino. On the right banister is Russell Walters, George Perry's cousin. Sitting on the steps are, from left to right, Margaret Perry (Arnold), Fred Walters, and Frank Walters. (FW.)

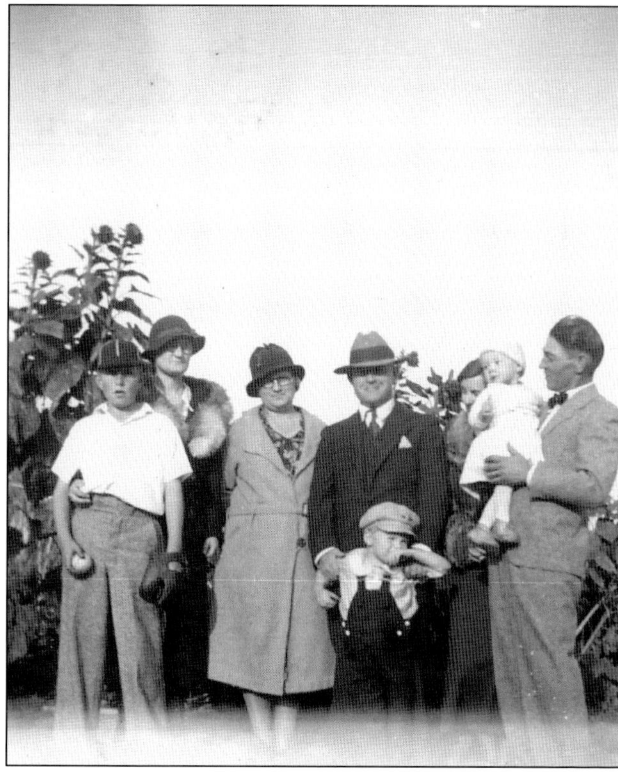

CHRISTMAS DAY GATHERING. On December 25, 1933, the Daniels took this family photograph at their home on 1502 Riverside Drive on the southeast corner of Fifteenth Street and Riverside. Vann Alton Daniels is the infant being held at the far right. Behind the family can be seen the tall stalks of sunflowers, which grew in abundance in Chino before farmers cleared the land and planted orchards, alfalfa, or other crops. (VAD.)

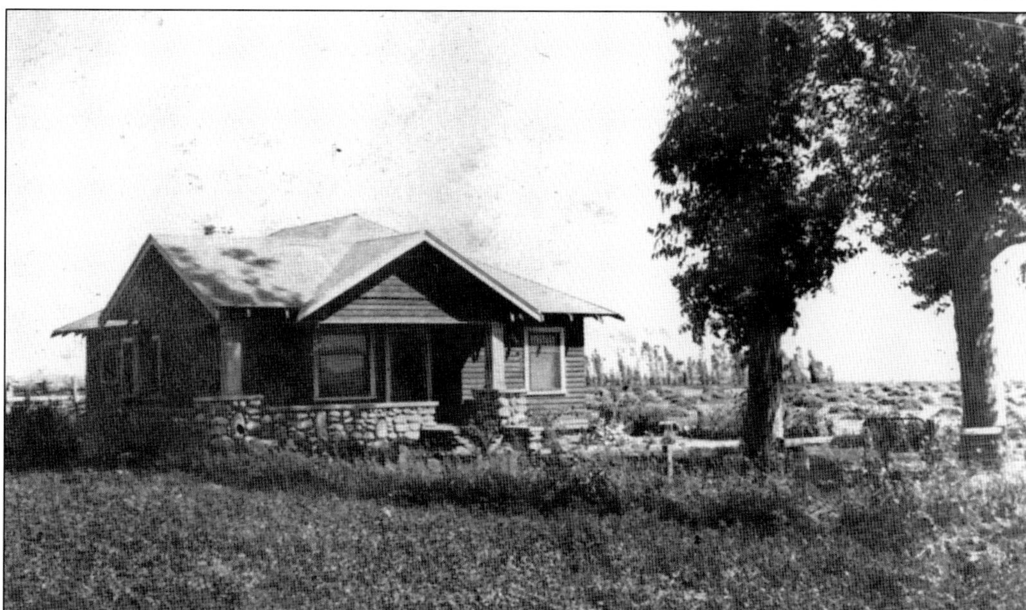

FIRST HOME, C. 1913. This is the home of Alice (Beck) and Alfred Brown on the east side of Euclid Avenue, south of Edison Avenue, and the birthplace of Gerald Brown. Complete with electricity and telephone, it had the modern conveniences of the day. Later, in 1921, the houses were renumbered with four numbers, and residents were given metal numbers for their houses so that the new telephone directory could be published. (GB.)

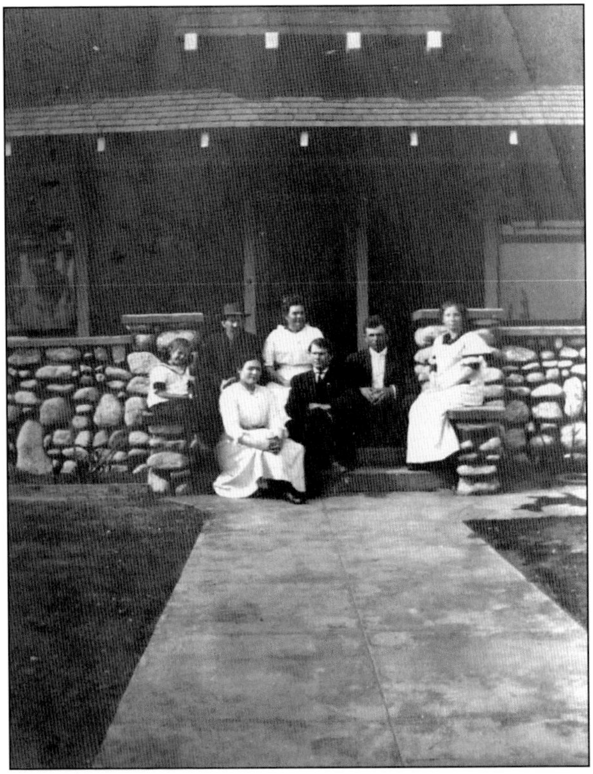

The Riley's House, c. 1912. Alfred and Alice Brown visit the Riley family in their two-story home on Central Avenue and Riverside Drive, just behind the school board's building. Mary Jane (Janey) Riley is seated in the center. Visiting neighbors, family, and friends brought a sense of community to Chino. People helped each other when times were hard and joined one another in celebrations. (GB.)

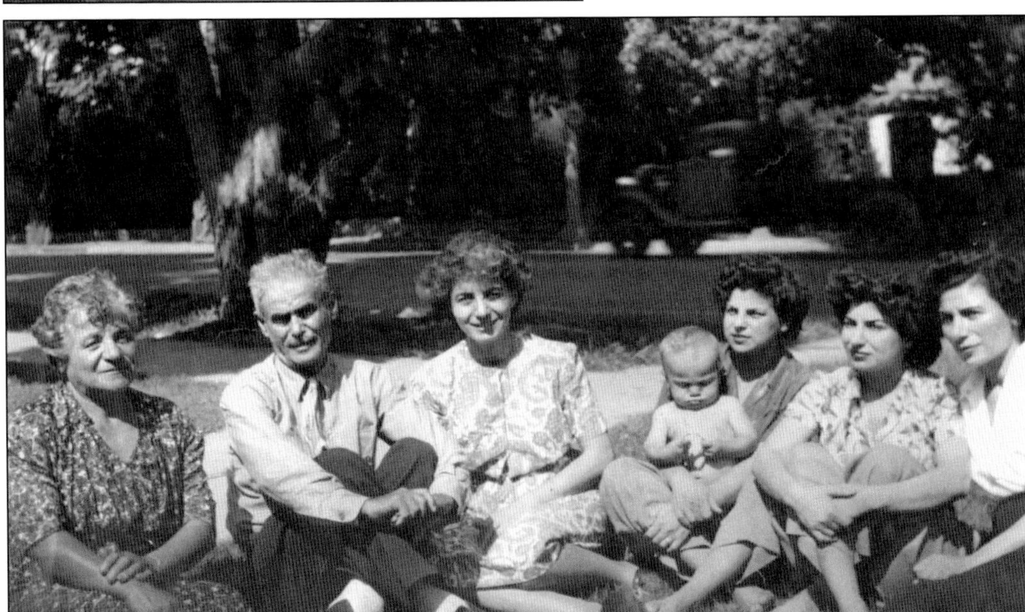

Nasif and Alice Solomon Family. Members of the family are, from left to right, Alice (Anise) Solomon, Nasif Solomon, Rose Solomon, infant (probably Sid Hopkins Jr.), Eva Solomon, Thelma George, and Mary (Solomon) George. When Nasif and Alice came through Ellis Island, his name was originally Slimen Nasif Nadir Maloof. Asked to choose a less common surname, Nasif chose his father's first name, Slimen, which translated into Solomon. (DG.)

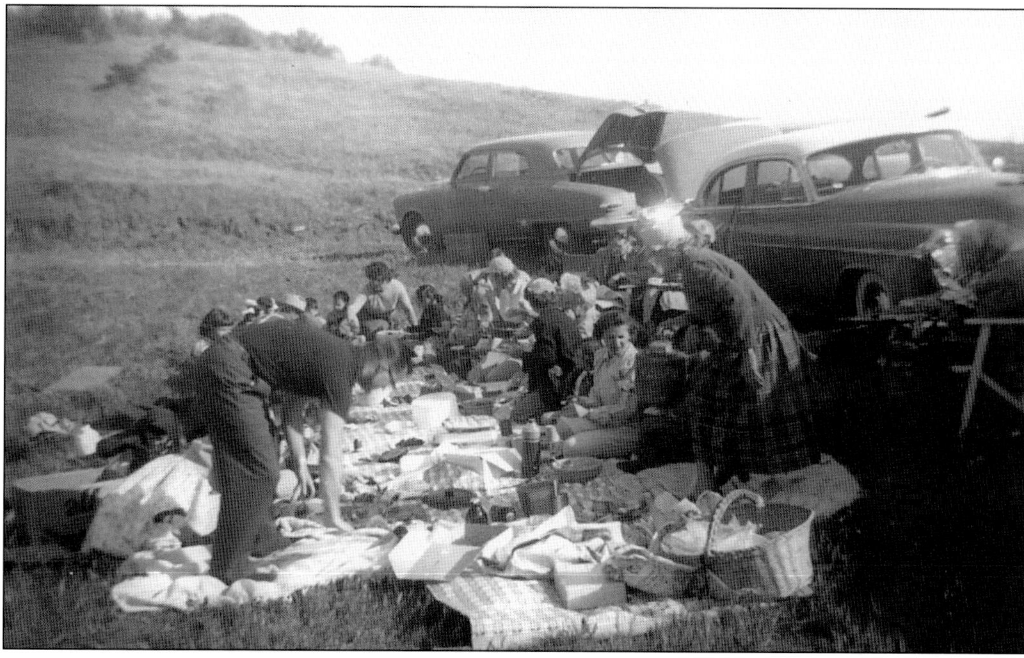

The Brown Family Easter Picnic. During his day, Alfred Brown was known as a local historian of Chino. Starting in 1920, the Brown family gathered for their first annual reunion on Easter Sunday. They usually chose a spot in the rolling hills surrounding Chino, which are known today as Chino Hills. Some years they held their picnics on blankets that were spread over the grass. Other years, they set at picnic tables under the shady canyon oaks of the region. Children hunted Easter eggs in the grass and flew kites in the breeze that gusted over the hills. After Gerald Brown retired from his poultry business in the 1970s, relatives flocked to his home to celebrate Easter Sunday and catch up on family news. (Both, GB.)

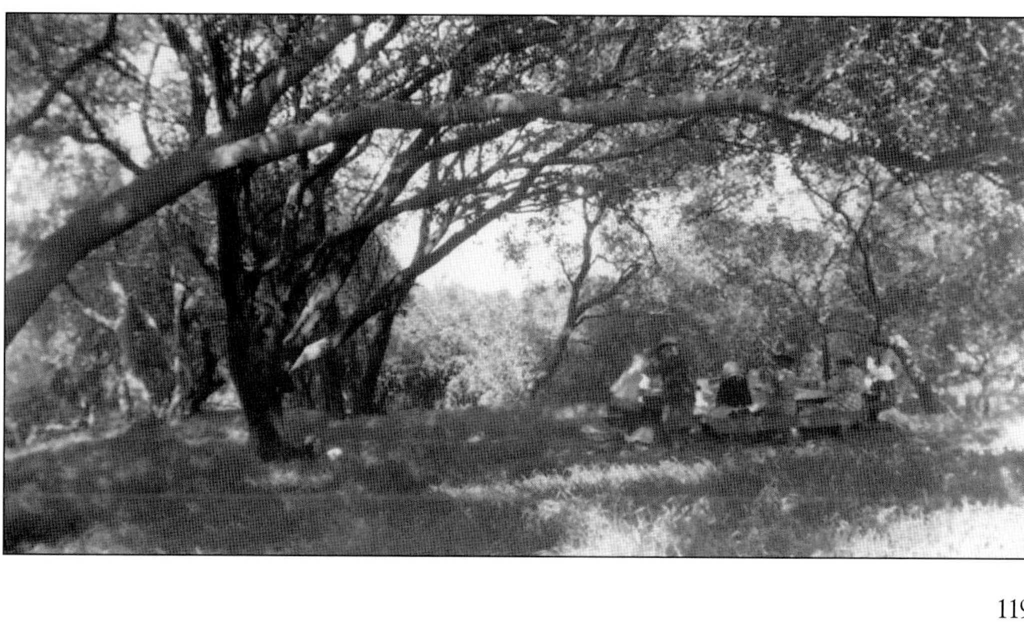

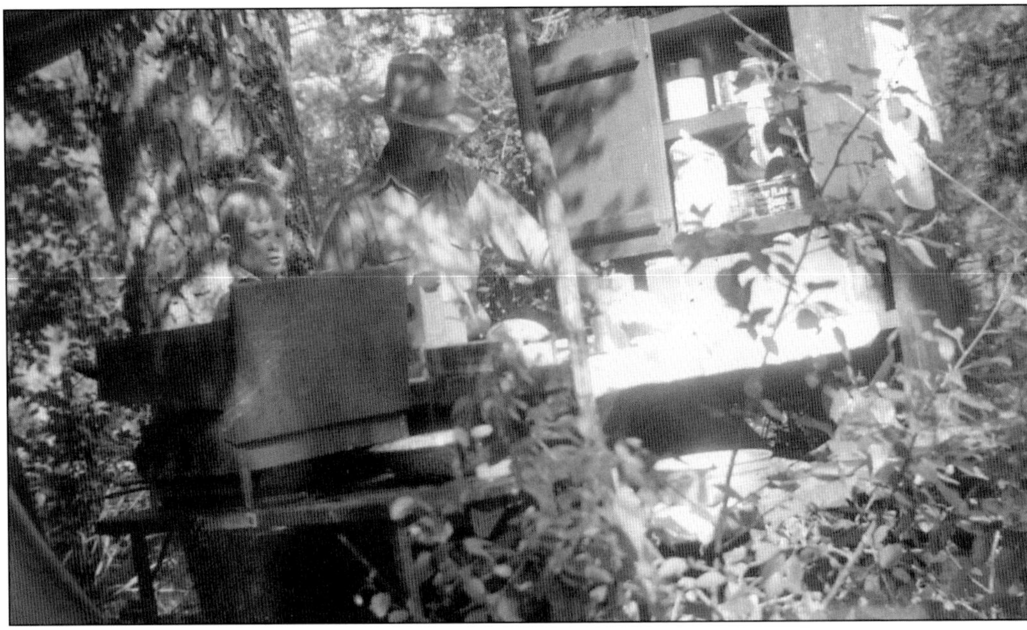

Enjoying the Outdoors. Pioneer families in Chino worked hard to make ends meet, and many were still able to find time for recreation and enjoyable pastimes. In the photograph above, John A. Daniels can be seen camping in the High Sierras. Complete with cookstove and a pantry stocked with supplies, he and his family are enjoying all the comforts of home within the beautiful surroundings of mountain forests. Boating was also a pleasure in pioneer days, as can be witnessed in the photograph below. Ferneena Daniels is enjoying a relaxing afternoon in the early 1910s. Note her sturdy hiking shoes and practical dress, an outfit she frequently wore when enjoying the outdoors near her community. (Both, VAD.)

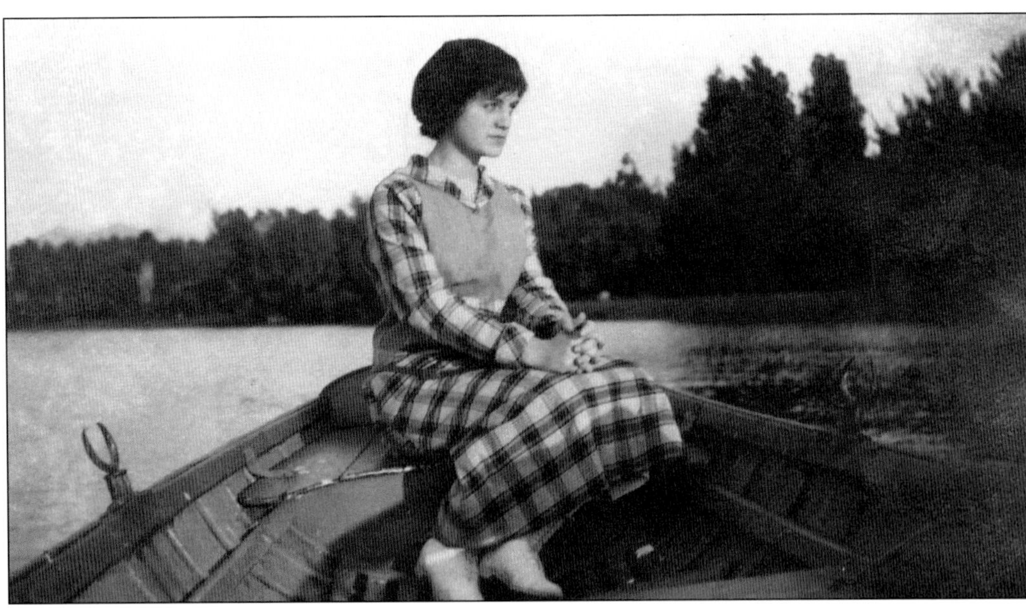

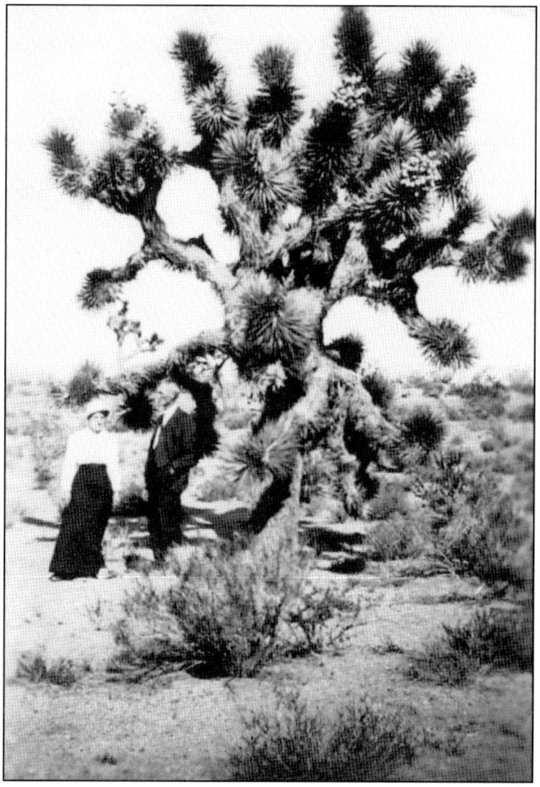

Desert and Mountains. Residents of Chino enjoy the luxury of living close to many regions of natural beauty. Centrally located, Chino is situated close to beautiful mountain ranges, the Pacific Ocean, and the desert. In the photograph at right, E. C. and Mary Daniels stand with amazement next to one of the tall Joshua trees found in the desert region of what is now known as Joshua Tree National Park. In the photograph below, taken on February 12, 1916, Ferneena Daniels enjoys a picnic lunch while hiking atop what is probably Mount Baldy. Just 20 miles from Chino, Mount Baldy rises majestically above the flatland community to an elevation of 8,600 feet. (Both, VAD.)

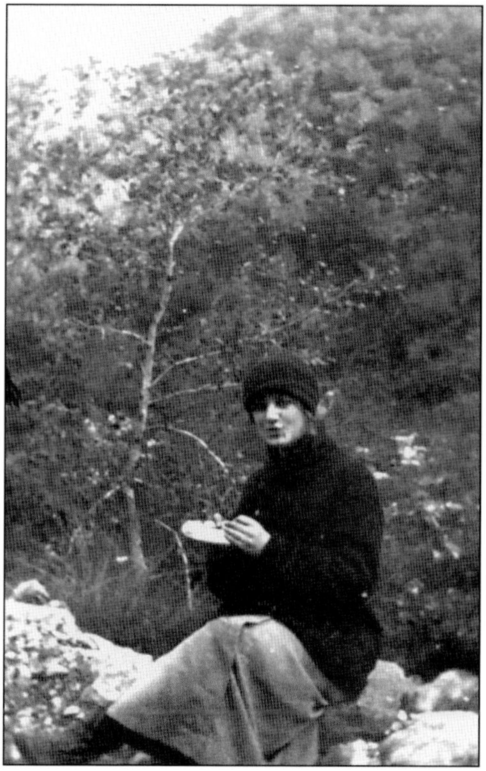

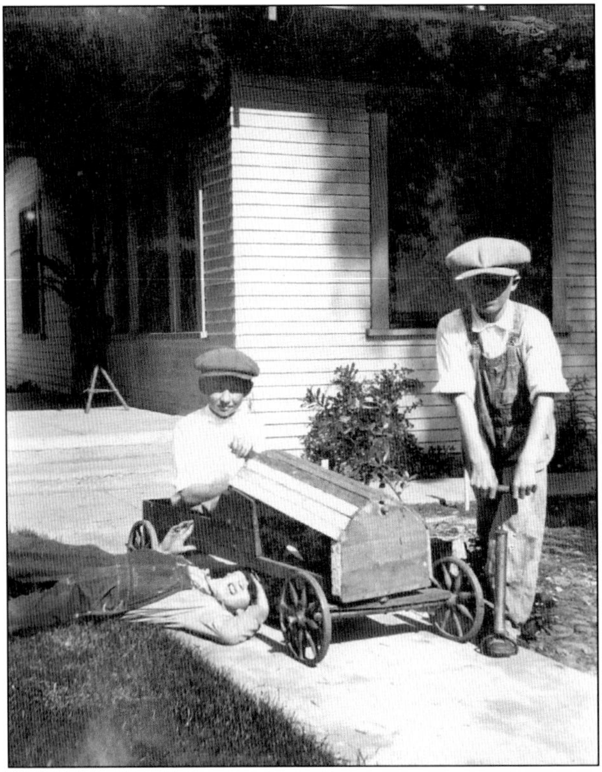

Childhood in Chino. Pictured here are three young boys with a soapbox racer in front of Alfred Brown's house on Tenth and D Streets. Gerald Brown is sitting behind the wheel. In his memoirs, he remembers when his family moved from their ranch into the city of Chino. He loved the concrete sidewalks lining the streets. Having been given a ball-bearing coaster wagon the year before they moved, he was pleased to find miles and miles of sidewalk where he could ride his wagon. When Gerald Brown grew up and settled on his own ranch, however, his children had to ride their wagon on the dirt lane. Melinda and Michael Brown are seen in this 1943 photograph beneath a sign made by their mother, Clara Brown. (Both, GB.)

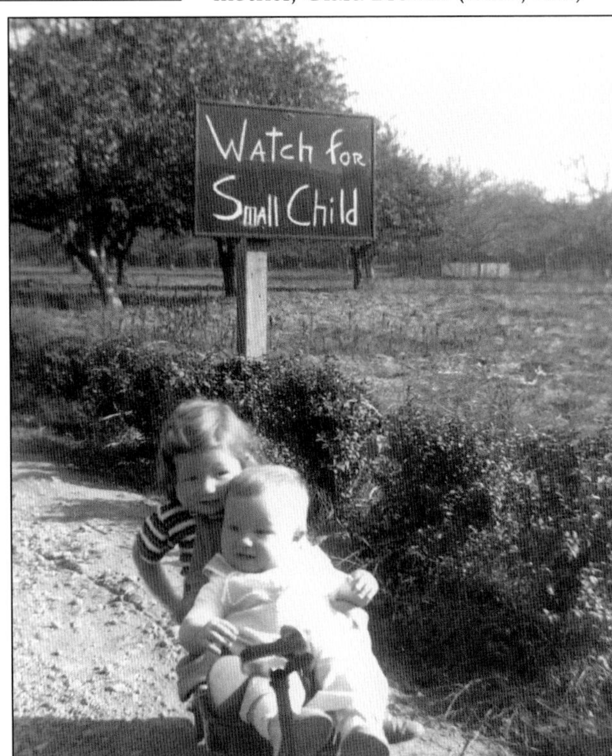

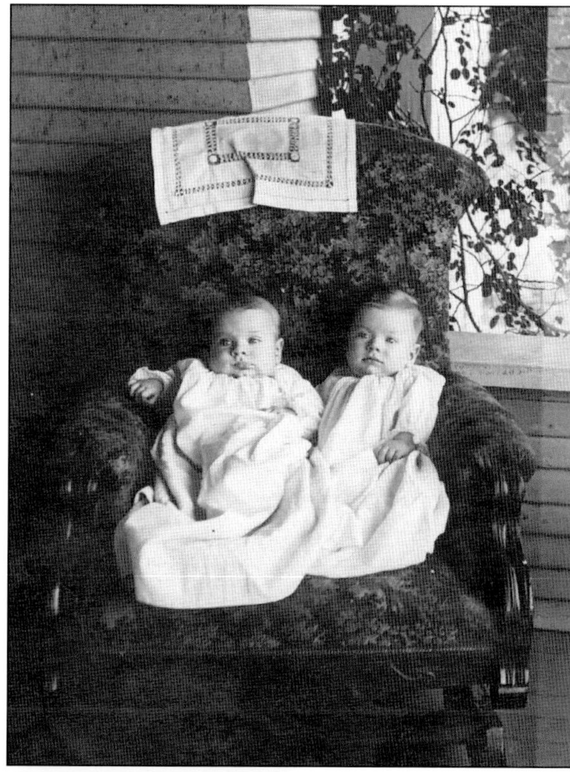

Pretty as a Picture. The photograph at right, taken in 1916, is of twins Evelyn and Everett Walters, born in August 1914. Standing in her pretty spring dress in the photograph below is Georgia Bennett Rudin, daughter of George and Evelyn Walters Bennett. In 1953, the Bennetts moved into town with their daughters Georgia and Marlene. Looking west in the background, behind the tree, Central Avenue can be seen. This is where the Bank of America and the M. K. Smith Chevrolet dealership are currently standing near Riverside Drive. A descendant of one of Chino's pioneer families, Georgia Rudin, now a retired teacher, is active in the city with the Chino Youth Museum, the Chino Historical Society, and other community organizations. (Both, FW.)

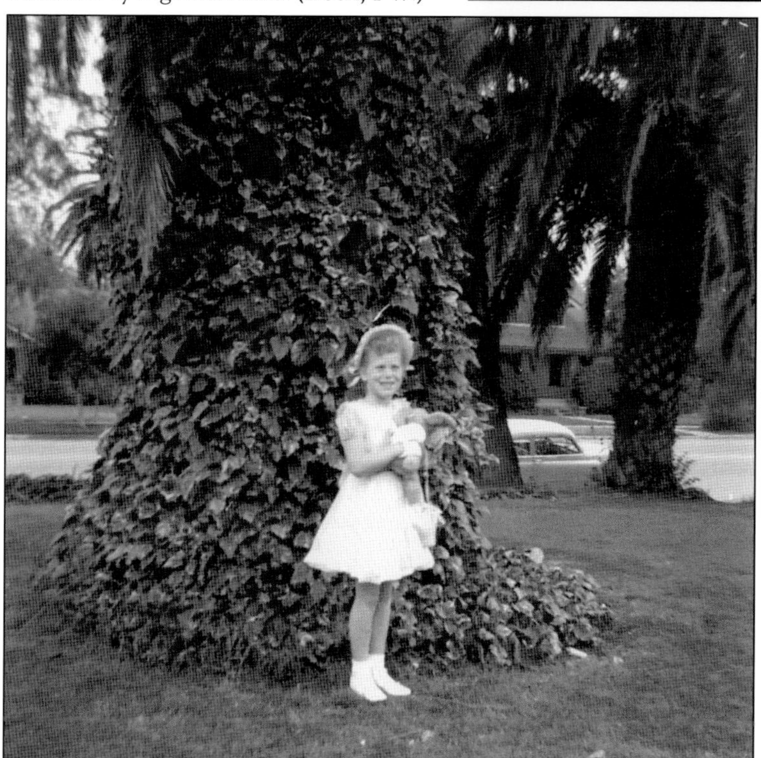

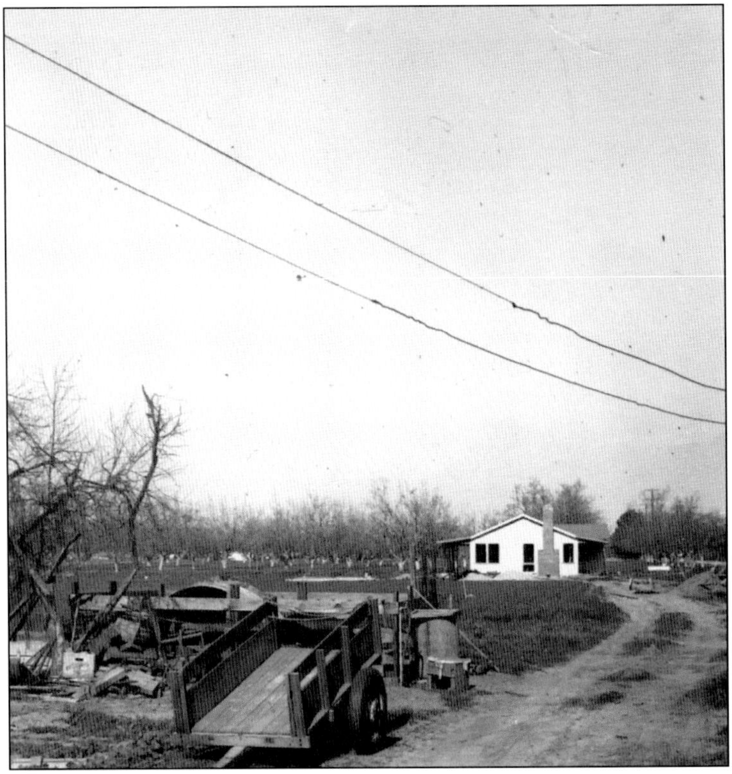

The Bennett Ranch, c. 1946. This photograph was taken looking north on the Bennett Ranch at San Antonio, between Chino Avenue and Schaefer Avenue. Orchards can be seen in the background. The *Chino Champion* noted in a 1926 report by San Bernardino County horticultural commissioner John P. Coy that Chino was the largest producer in the county of peaches, Irish potatoes, tomatoes, sugar beets, figs, corn, sweet potatoes, and beans. (FW.)

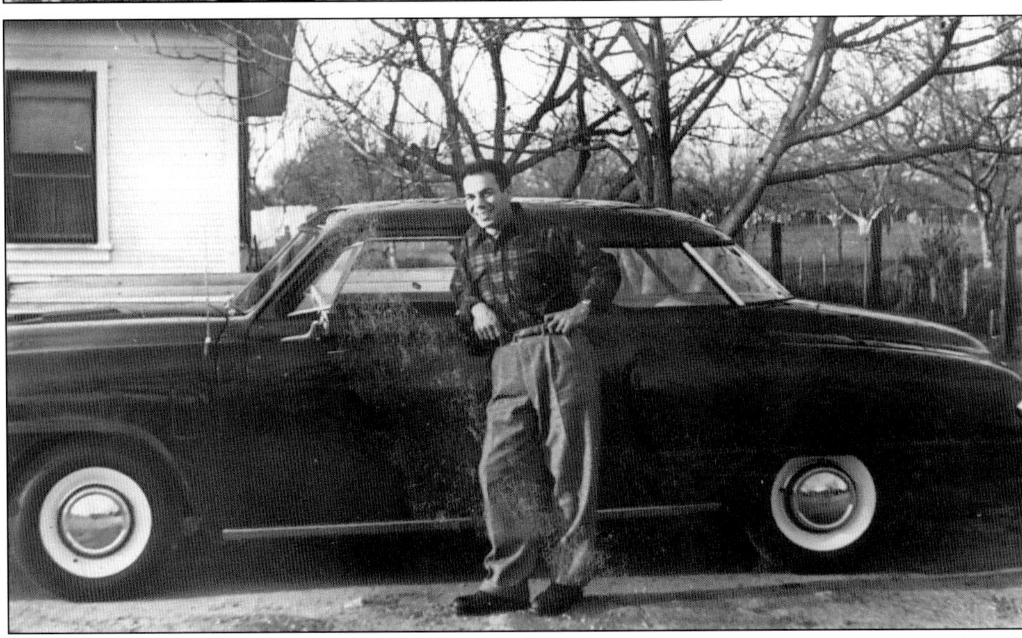

Samuel Solomon Maloof. Born in Chino in 1916, Sam Maloof was the son of Nasif and Anise Solomon. Graduating from Chino High School, he served with the U.S. Armed Forces from 1941 to 1945. When he returned home, he married Alfreda Ward and established a furniture business in Alta Loma, eventually earning numerous awards and honors as a woodworker. Maloof furniture became a favorite of presidents and decorators alike. (DG.)

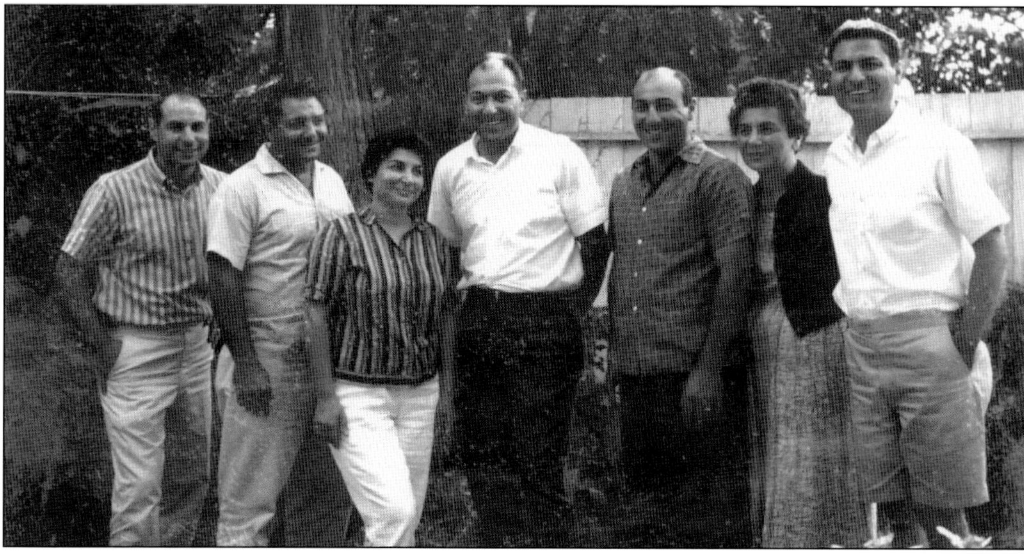

MARY GEORGE AND FAMILY. Mary Solomon George stands with her adult children in this photograph taken in the early 1960s. Shown in the picture with their mother are, from left to right, Tye, Leon, Thelma, Richard, David, Mary, and Robert. After Mary's husband, Nimor George, died, the family moved in with Mary's parents on Sixth Street. Nasif and Alice Solomon helped raise Mary's six children along with their own. (DG.)

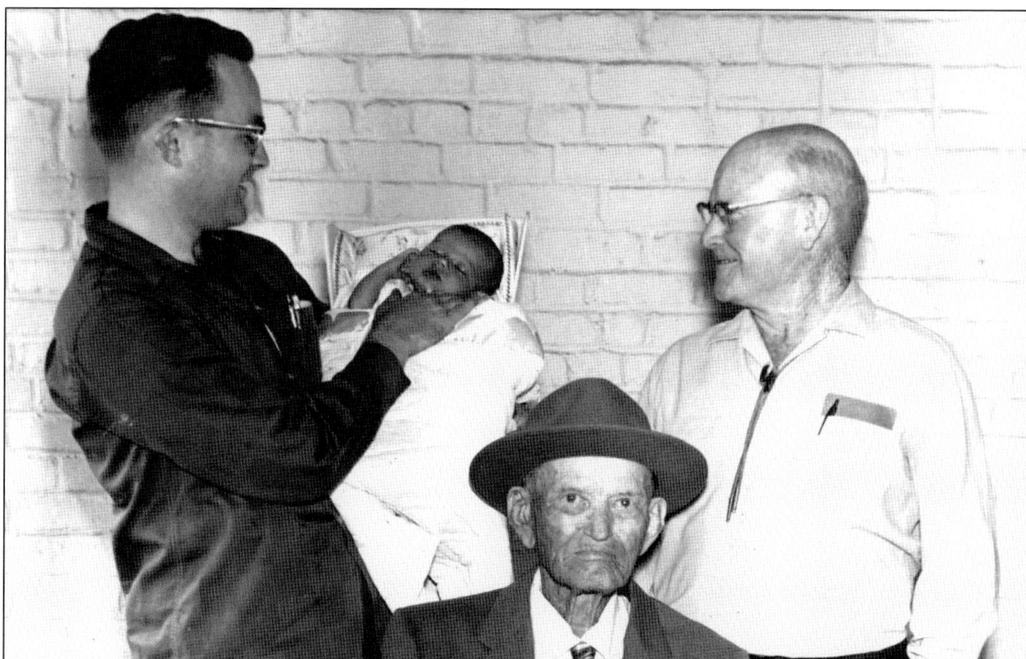

FOUR GENERATIONS OF CHINOIANS. Members of the Daniels family are, from left to right, Vann Alton Daniels, infant John Daniels, Charles Elmo (E. C.) Daniels, and John Ansley (J. A.) Daniels. E. C. Daniels, pictured here at 93 years old, was Chino's first mayor. J. A. Daniels was the first mail carrier hired when the U.S. Postal Service ordered free mail delivery for Chino's business district and most neighborhoods in 1926. (VAD.)

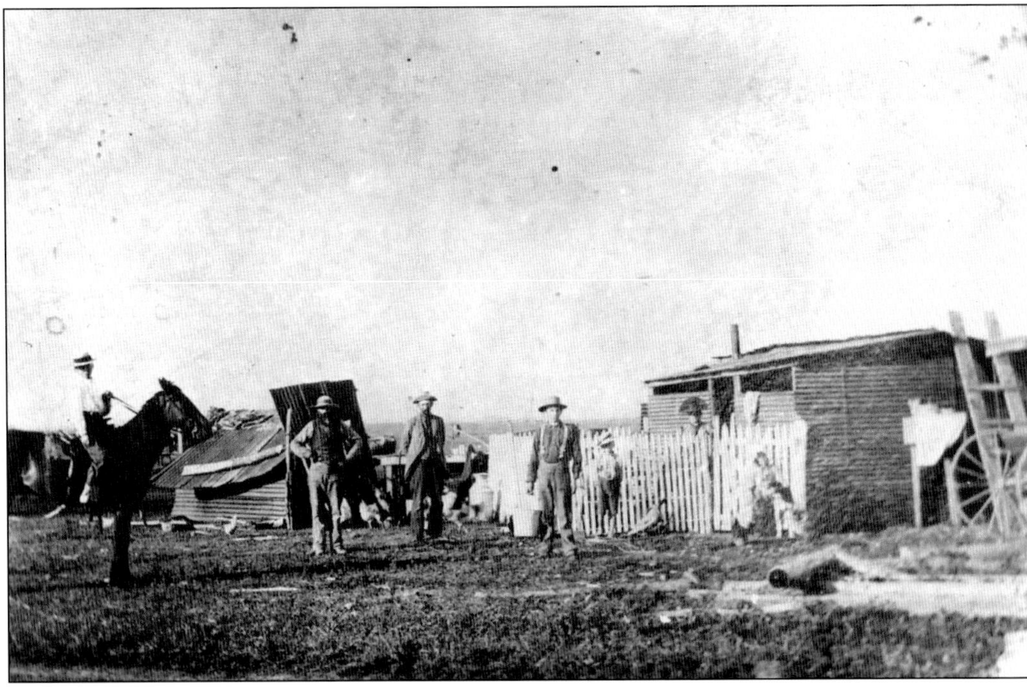

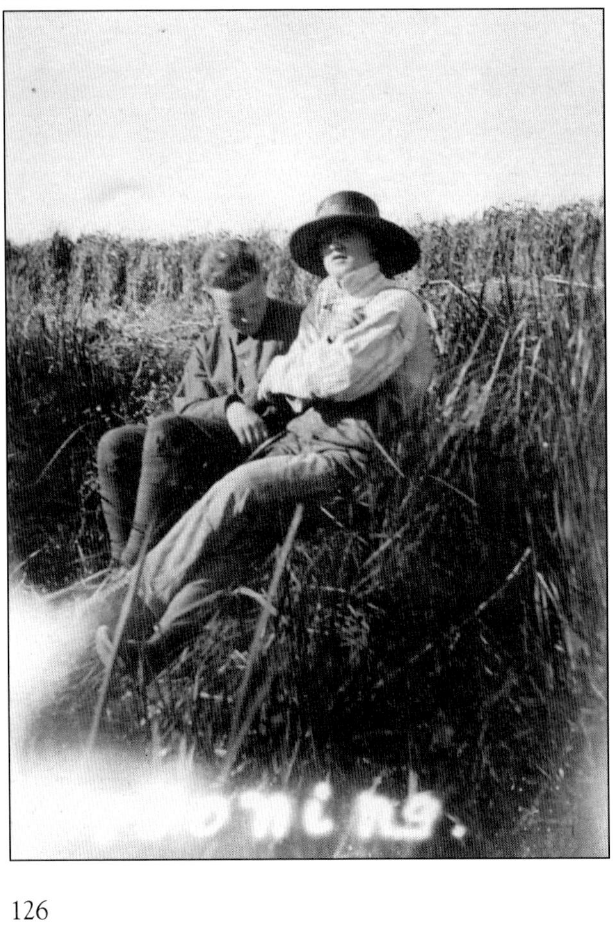

The Brown Family Homestead. This temporary dwelling was the first home in Chino for the Brown family. Pictured on the horse is Elmer Brown. Blind Jack and Mr. Boyd, two men who worked for their keep, are standing in the center. Alfred Brown is holding a milk pail next to Roy, at the fence. Sarah Ann is standing behind the fence. Ruth, far right, is with Leedo, their dog. (GB.)

On the Banks of Chino Creek. John A. and Ferneena Daniels enjoy an outing together on the banks of Chino Creek during World War I. Sporting a large hat for protection against the strong rays of the Southern California sun, Ferneena sits with John among the tall rushes growing along the creek's edge. (VAD.)

Bibliography

Adamson, Jeremy. *The Furniture of Sam Maloof.* Washington, D.C.: The Smithsonian American Art Museum, 2001.

Ayala, Ruben S. *Up From Second Street.* Chino Hills, CA: Ruben S. Ayala Research Center Library, 2005.

Brackett, F. P., et. al. *History of Pomona Valley California with Biographical Sketches.* Los Angeles: Historic Record Company, 1920.

Brown, Michael D. *The History of Chino Prison: The First Fifty Years of the California Institution for Men, 1941 to 1991.* Chino, CA: Vocational Offset Printing Program, California Institution for Men, 1991.

Chino Champion's column, "100 Years of Chino." Chino, CA: Champion Newspapers, 2010.

Chino Valley Independent Fire District, Chino Firemen's Association, Local 3522. *Centennial Celebration Official Program, May 1995.* Lithographics Champion Publications: Chino, CA, 1995.

Rhodes, Edwin. *The Break of Day in Chino.* Chino, CA: P-B Press, 1951.

Watkins, Craig, Chairman of the Chino Rotary Book Project. *Chino Valley: Where Everything Grows.* Chino, CA: Chino Rotary Club, 2005.